Combat Correspondents

Combat
Correspondents

The Baltimore Sun in World War II

Joseph R. L. Sterne

The Maryland Historical Society
Baltimore, MD • 2009

The Maryland Historical Society
201 W. Monument St.
Baltimore, MD 21201
www.mdhs.org

ISBN 978-0-938420-14-9 (paper)

Library of Congress Cataloging-in-Publication Data

Sterne, Joseph R. L. (Joseph Robert Livingston), 1928–
    Combat correspondents : The Baltimore Sun in World War II / by Joseph R.L.
Sterne.
      p. cm.
    Includes index.
    ISBN 978-0-938420-14-9 (alk. paper)
    1. World War, 1939-1945—Press coverage—United States. 2. Sun (Baltimore,
Md. : 1837) 3. War correspondents—United States—History—20th century. 4.
Journalism—Maryland—History—20th century. 5. World War, 1939-1945—
Campaigns—France. 6. World War, 1939-1945—Campaigns—Germany. I. Title.
    D799.U6S74 2009
    070.4'4994054—dc22

                                                                2009021205

This publication has been made possible
with the generous support of

Wright, Constable & Skeen, L.L.P.

The Abell Foundation

Friends of MdHS Press,
H. Thomas Howell, chair

W. Shepherdson Abell

and with the cooperation of

The Baltimore Sun

For my sons Robert, Paul, Edward, Adam, and Lee

Contents

A photo gallery follows page 156.

Foreword

This is a book about journalism, an art form as practiced by *Baltimore Sun* combat correspondents in World War II. How they risked their lives, reacted to blood and horror, shared peril and privation with GIs, filed millions of words under the stress of battle to meet deadlines far away, assessed tactics and strategy, described the mayhem war imposed on civilians and countryside, put themselves and hometown folks into their stories—all this warranted a lot more than wrapping yesterday's fish. They were reporting the "good war," if there ever was one, a war where newspapermen could be unabashed patriots while still reporting the shortcoming of government and the blunders of the military brass. This was a time when correspondents wore uniforms, when censors could block or excise their stories, when they worked with portable typewriters (no spell checks, no send buttons) and jeeped scores of miles to file. Long days, tough days, but also fun days and heady, history-watching days. If the first personal plural appeared often in their copy, it was not the editorial "we" but a comradely "we."

Operating alone or with other reporters and with military units, they enjoyed a personal freedom of movement and decision-making that was, in part, a result of war's chaos. Communication with the home office was a sometimes thing—sometimes welcomed, sometimes frustrating. But this freedom also reflected their own talents and guts and zeal, plus the culture of their newspaper. *The Baltimore Sun* conceived a higher mission for itself in the course of the war. It would be a force in America not only because of the iconoclasm and literary qualities that distinguished it during the between-war years but because it came to realize what its own distinctive worldwide coverage could mean.

One thing it could mean is that aspiring young reporters would bombard *The Sun* with job applications during a golden period that lasted for half a century. I was one. During the 1952 campaign, when I was a cub on *The Dallas Morning News*, I would spend time in the newspaper library reading the 1952 election coverage of *The New York Times*, *The Washington Post* and, by chance, *The Baltimore Sun*. It gradually dawned on me that *The Sun*'s stories were the best of the lot by a wide margin. With fascination I read the reports of Thomas O'Neill and Howard Norton, two correspondents who figure in this book, and Philip Potter, who would distinguish himself in the Korean War. This time they were writing about Adlai Stevenson and Dwight Eisenhower, and when the election was over I was aflame with desire to work for the Baltimore newspaper. It took a lot of pestering and two trips from Texas I could ill-afford, but finally I made it, along with a ten dollar boost in my weekly paycheck.

It was the best of career decisions. *The Sun* gave me opportunities a young newspaperman could only dream of. How lucky I was. The paper was making money. Its owners were willing to spend a lot of it, and reporters, at least those who escaped the city room and monkish wages, suddenly could travel first class, enjoy expense accounts, and work with journalism's big names. My career started on a Sunday afternoon in July 1953 at the police station on Pennsylvania Avenue, part of Baltimore's black ghetto. Driving our own cars, police reporters would race around the segregated city, demand a look-see at police blotters from gruff, reluctant desk sergeants, and call in facts about accidents, fires, and crimes to exacting rewrite men. All the while we yearned to write our own stories—features, city and state government affairs, courts and politics. One of life's epiphanies came when Managing Editor Charles H. (Buck) Dorsey called me in one day in 1957 for the breathtaking news that I was being assigned to London. Thus began fifteen years away from the home office—two years in Britain, sixteen months out of a suitcase in sub-Saharan Africa, Washington Bureau postings in the 1960s, and three years in Germany. Next came a record twenty-five years as editorial page editor of *The Sun*.

As the years rolled by, I stored up memories: small-group chats at 10 Downing Street with Prime Minister Harold Macmillan, Charles de Gaulle's press conference on his way to the French presidency, interviews with African founding fathers as their countries neared independence, the 1960 blowup in the Congo when I found myself in a U.S. Army helicopter hit eight times, Black September in Jordan after a freezing Air Force plane ride from Frankfurt to Amman, Germany's walk on the moon when the West's Chancellor Willy Brandt set foot in East Germany. Home country scenes vividly remembered: the Capitol Rotunda when John F. Kennedy's family knelt before his coffin; Barry Goldwater's hopeless, high jinks 1964 run for the White House; the fight for civil rights at Ole Miss, Resurrection City, and the U.S. Senate; George Wallace mocking the press before an angry blue-collar crowd in Jersey City; Ronald Reagan briefing a small group of editors on NATO plans for nuclear war in Europe (what an eruption that caused!); and a Bill Clinton dinner at the White House with Hillary playing the demure housewife.

Yet, through all those years, I let World War II fade into the background. During that conflict, I was a kid in high school pretending to help the war effort as a junior air raid warden. After the war, it was college and career, a career that led to Baltimore where a most remarkable group of former war correspondents rarely talked about their combat experience. Decades later, one of McCardell's daughters recalled that, when her father came back from the war and discovered that her mother had saved all his wartime dispatches, he was "furious." He took them down to the back garden and burned them.

So these marvelous wartime dispatches collected dust, with old newsprint flaking away and microfilm a challenge to a researcher's eyes and patience. Oblivion was under way. It took the twenty-first-century collapse of newspapers as we knew them to jolt me awake. Overcome with the ephemera of the Internet, I resolved to write a hardcover record that would provide my city, my state, my grandchildren some glimpses of those glory days through the dispatches of great half-forgotten reporters. A retiree no longer haunted by deadlines, I at last had time to get to work.

First stop was a musty attic under the roof of the Central Branch of the Enoch Pratt Free Library in Baltimore. There, in a jumble of dented green file cabinets, perhaps unopened for years, I found small cards that listed reporters' stories from long ago. Second stop was the Special Collections room at the library of the University of Maryland Baltimore County. There I could read *The Sun*, page by page, one by one, from September 1939 to September 1945. No matter how careful I was, each session ended in a landscape of orange-colored edges of deteriorating newspaper pages. What an adventure it proved to be! Great reporters emerged as human beings with all the individuality that creative journalism can evoke.

As Mark S. Watson trenchantly warned of U. S. unpreparedness in 1939, I remembered him as a courtly gentleman who rode the train from Baltimore to Washington immersed in war histories he would review in *The Sunday Sun*. His Pentagon stories combined the insight of his own military experience with Pershing's staff in World War I and the inside information provided by his many friends in the armed services. He won the Pulitzer Prize in 1944 and became the first journalist to receive the Presidential Medal of Freedom. When he died, the Pentagon press room was named for him, a deserved tribute from his newspaper colleagues.

As I read Lee McCardell's deeply felt and deeply personal accounts of war in Europe, the strictly business assistant managing editor of *The Evening Sun* I had seen in office corridors became the most human chronicler one could encounter in a wet, freezing-cold, muddy trench. When, in 1959, we were both covering the Algerian war—he in Algiers, I in Paris—he sent a note to Baltimore commending one of my pieces. I was thrilled. His own dispatches showed that years as a news editor had not ruined him as a writer.

The urbane, meticulous prose of Price Day, a future Pulitzer winner and *Sun* editor-in-chief, made it clear that Baltimore readers were getting the war in historical and cultural context. The history of a small village in the Vosges, his architect's evaluation of an ancient cathedral, his unflinching description of Nazi atrocities—they were all there. Price was my boss for several years, my traveling companion during a trip through the Balkans in 1971, but he never mentioned the war. I did not have the insight to ask him. His graceful editorial columns still have the ability to fascinate.

I read the daredevil accounts of fighting by Holbrook Bradley and no longer wondered why he took a hunk of shrapnel in his leg. He was nonchalant about his bravery but never nonchalant about the Maryland-Virginia "Blue and Gray" Twenty-ninth Division, his main assignment from training in the States till the end of the European campaign. Bradley left the paper after the war. In his 90s he wrote a vivid memoir published in 2007. I never met him until he visited Baltimore in 2008 to promote the book. There he was, the gung-ho young reporter I had first encountered by reading hundreds of his dispatches. I ended up wishing Watson, McCardell, and Day had also written memoirs.

These four great newspapermen followed American troops from Normandy to the Elbe. It is their book. But not entirely. Howard Norton scooped the world on the death of Mussolini when covering the closing phases of the Italian campaign. In the Pacific, he witnessed the Saipan invasion and narrowly escaped death when a Japanese shell hit his subchaser, killing most of its crew. Philip Heisler, later managing editor of *The Evening Sun*, went ashore at Iwo Jima as *The Sun* belatedly increased coverage of the Pacific war. Both were fine newspapermen. Thomas O'Neill was London Bureau chief during the entire war. He watched the Blitz bombing of Britain, explained Britain's political scene as the war progressed, and served as a conduit and connection for reporters on the continent.

For me, the reading and writing and research for this volume have been quite a ride. I thank all these *Sun* reporters for the privilege of getting to know them better through dispatches that sing in voices that authenticate a long-ago era. Their passions, their derring-do, their artistry with words, their willingness to work impossible hours under appalling conditions, their knowledge and judgment of the great issues in conflict—all this is evidence of *The Baltimore Sun* at its best. And its best made it one of the finest newspapers in the United States.

Editorial Note

During World War II, the Baltimore Sunpapers comprised three distinct papers that shared the stories sent back by their combat correspondents. The morning paper had been known to Baltimoreans and most Marylanders simply as *The Sun*, the name chosen by founder Arunah S. Abell in 1837. Its later offshoots were designated *The Evening Sun* and *The Sunday Sun*. However, as the paper gained a national reputation, the national media always referred to it as *The Baltimore Sun* to distinguish it from other newspapers that had named themselves after the chief star in the solar system.

For the purpose of consistency and clarity, this book will refer to the paper as *The Baltimore Sun*, or, in abbreviated form, as *The Sun*. The names *The Evening Sun* or *The Sunday Sun* will be used as appropriate. The term the Baltimore Sunpapers will be used when referring to all three papers as a conglomerate.

This book makes liberal use of the dispatches sent back by the paper's combat correspondents. These are reprinted or placed in context to reflect both the intent of the correspondents who wrote them and the war's compelling narrative. I have made no attempt to standardize grammar or punctuation, except when it is occasionally necessary to clarify meaning. To avoid the use of ellipses, I confess I have often abbreviated the dispatches to eliminate unnecessary detail and repetitiveness, without in any way distorting their meaning. *Sun* correspondents were usually writing at top speed in difficult and often dangerous conditions. Under such circumstances, their prose is amazingly lucid. Many dispatches quoted in this book indicate in parenthesis the date they were published.

Foreign place names have been used in their Americanized spellings in the case of names that have become familiar to readers of World War II literature through their association with major battles, for example St.-Lô is spelled St. Lo, Jülich is spelled Julich. Less familiar names retain their original spelling.

A short bibliography lists only those books that were particularly helpful to the author.

Combat Correspondents

CHAPTER 1

The War Begins

Two days after Nazi tanks and dive bombers smashed into Poland on September 1, 1939, *The Baltimore Sun* published a half-page ad that was at once promotional and modest. It proclaimed that the Sunpapers had "a mighty news staff tirelessly at the service" of their readers in reporting on the war about to engulf the planet. And what was this "mighty news staff?" It was primarily the Associated Press, a news wire service available to every newspaper, large or small, in the land.

So why consider this promotional ad "modest?" Because the newspaper already had two reporters of its own in Europe—one in London and one in Paris—who were filing dispatches from the moment the fighting started. The bosses back in Baltimore had come out of World War I determined to beef up foreign coverage so it would become a must-read in Washington. Long before that war was over, the newspaper was to achieve a splendid record of its own in reporting the global conflict. It had a special connection, including exchange of stories, with Britain's *Manchester Guardian*. And it had a local ownership that drew a lot of psychic income, not least among Baltimore's intellectual and property elite, from possession of a distinguished hometown newspaper.

Few papers outside New York and Chicago had such bragging rights. Before the Second World War was over in 1945, the paper had sent some of it best reporters to the European theater of operations in an initiative not surpassed by any newspaper outside the two great metropolises. Impressed by its European experience, the paper had increased its reporting staff in the Pacific theater as World War II came to an abrupt and welcome end. A postwar compilation of war reporters on the scene of battle gave *The Sun* twenty-two mentions, a number far outstripping such competitors as *The Washington Post, Washington Star, Philadelphia Inquirer, Los Angeles Times,* and *Boston Globe.* The Baltimore dispatches provided vivid and often highly personal hometown descriptions of the war available only to their readers. *The Sun,* for better or worse, sniffily did not syndicate.

These *Sun* correspondents had two great advantages: Their editors left them alone, a tradition that continued until better means of communication and the growth of newsroom bureaucracies in the 1970s put overseas reporters on a tighter leash. And they were blessed with a huge news hole in the paper back home that allowed them to write at prodigious length if they wished.

As the largest conflict in human history began, Paul W. Ward, later a Pulitzer Prize winner for Cold War reporting on the Soviet Union, wrote a portrait of a subway station turned bomb shelter in the Montmartre section of Paris. Arriving there shortly after 3 a.m. during the first week of war, he found *"five thousand men, women and children, plus a large menagerie of pets."*

"There were no signs of panic in this working class crowd," he reported. *"One man promptly seated himself on the edge of the platform and opened a briefcase from which he took bread, butter, some jam, and a bottle of water. Girls wearing pastel pink or blue pajamas under old coats or tattered dressing gowns paused to look in mirrors on platform scales and restore their makeup. A few men stood about in gaudy pajamas looking much more diffident in this predominantly feminine crowd."* [Sept. 9, 1939]

A skeptic throughout his career, Ward presciently wrote that the French *"are enjoying at the moment a false sense of security. This attitude will undoubtedly govern their conduct until the Germans actually start bombing. Most Frenchmen with whom we talked were sure the war was going to last and be terrible but end in a French victory."*

Frank R. Kent Jr., then *The Sun's* man in London, painted a reserved picture of the British. *"The civil population carries on as near normal as possible,"* he wrote. *"The main evidence that the nation is at war is* the fact that cardboard gas mask containers are as much a part of the Londoner's equipment as an umbrella or cane. The Londoner now lugs his mask around in anything from a tissue container to a fishing creel, a camera cover or a haversack." [Sept. 9, 1939]

The next day he somberly reported that "this war was not declared lightly or in a sudden burst of emotion or patriotism. The whole impression gathered is that when the nation finally took the step, it did so deliberately and with full realization of the travail lying ahead." [Sept. 10, 1939]

Soon after the war began, The Sun made a gesture toward frontline reporting by sending Paul Ward with French troops and Frank Kent with British troops as the winter of the "phony war" began. First off was Ward with a front-page story headlined: SUN MAN WITH FRENCH TROOPS IN WAR AREA. Under a dateline, "Somewhere Beyond the Maginot Line on the Saar Front," Ward reported that he and three other journalists were the first Americans to get beyond the Maginot Line and reach German soil behind France's probing patrols.

"We can hear gunfire plainly and although we are only a little way behind the front lines it sounds not more menacing than a distant thunderclap," he wrote. Obviously impressed by French esprit de corps, he forecast that "if the Germans choose to attack they will find the French prepared to receive them as no army in history has ever been prepared before." [Sept. 22, 1939]

Only hindsight would produce the contrary judgment that the overrated French army was hopelessly tentative in attitude and overly dependent on the Maginot Line. It was designed for defensive rather than offensive action. Ward was struck by "the placidity of the front. Except for a brief burst of artillery fire it was as quiet as Vermont. No-man's land is not yet a gush of muddy holes and shell-torn trees."

The Sun's next move was to embed (to use a later term) Frank Kent with the British Expeditionary Force sent to France, where half a year later many Tommies would die in the retreat across France to Dunkirk. Wearing the uniform issued to correspondents in those days, Kent wrote that he and his fellow correspondents "looked slightly self-conscious trying to recognize colleagues last seen in civilian *clothes."* Two days later, there appeared a story in which he reported that French townspeople living only a short distance behind the very quiet front lines were *"going about their business apparently unconcerned."* And four days later, after reporting that the British army is *"rapidly getting set to meet any thrust in this sector,"* he confessed to Baltimore readers *"the war, thus far, has seemed unreal."*

Matching this description was Paul Ward's report on the French army: *"The men in the Maginot Line are having a cushy time at present—dry quarters, comfortable beds, good food, an easy routine and no exposure to gunfire, bombs or mines."*

But then, in dramatic contrast, he described the plight of men assigned to sentry posts on German soil in advance of the Maginot Line: *"Such quarters as they have are carved out of the mud. Rain beats down on them by day and night, and the cuisine is anything but lavish. Their job is to stick out there in front and give the alarm in case the Germans attempt an attack in force. They have little chance of escape, and they deserve to be called suicide squads."* [Oct. 10, 1939]

As it happened, the Germans never launched a frontal attack on the Maginot Line. They went end-around through Holland and Belgium and into northern France when the long *Sitzkrieg* winter ended and the real war began.

In that autumn of 1939, the Nazi nightmare closed in on a pulverized and dismembered Poland, a victim of Germans on the West and Russians on the East. France reneged on its promise to Poland of an offensive thrust within fifteen days of the Nazi attack. Hitler made flamboyant peace gestures largely designed to strengthen the isolationists in America, a situation that produced an Edmund Duffy cartoon in *The Sun* showing Hitler with an outstretched arm dripping blood. It won the *Sun* artist his third Pulitzer Prize. Reporters, finding themselves where almost all was quiet on the Western Front, were reduced to writing flimsy color pieces and thumb suckers. Frank Kent, to his credit, wrote of *"thirty British and American correspondents in search of a war"* [Nov. 11, 1939] and doggedly reported an inconsequential visit to the front by the Duke of Gloucester, a younger brother of King George VI.

Paul Ward, for his part, filed a story contrasting the moods of London and Paris as the war commenced [Nov. 11, 1939]. The British capital, he wrote, was shrouded in a blackout *"as black as the proverbial pitch and the authorities do not permit even a splinter of light to show from any doorway or window. 'Don't panic' was the message flashed on London movie screens. 'Remember, you are British.'"*

Paris, for its part, had become *"merely a badly lighted city"* in which *"everybody is either too fatalistic or too thrifty to board up windows,"* Ward wrote. *"The French at bottom are a tremendously serious people and they take a tremendously serious view of the war."* London, he declared, was *"a gayer place"* even though it was *"much more like a city at war."* His dispatch, as time proved, accurately underscored the resoluteness of the British and the passivity of the French.

During the first part of December, while the phony war dragged along, Kent depicted life among the British Expeditionary Force in northern France. *"A familiar cry is beginning to be heard—nothing is happening out here."* To the average Tommy, who has seen far more mud and digging than action, a six-day visit by King George VI *"acted as a tonic."* [Dec. 12, 1939] The king was seen as *"a slight figure wearing a trench coat and field boots, with a gas mask slung over his shoulder."* In a Gilbert-and-Sullivan remark, the monarch concluded his visit in classic style: *"A jolly good show."* [Dec. 12, 1939]

Nine days later, Prime Minister Neville Chamberlain visited the troops. *"He was without his famous umbrella,"* Kent observed [Dec. 12, 1939]. *The Sun* reporter did not have to add that the umbrella was already seen as a symbol of Chamberlain's appeasement of Hitler before the Nazis finally forced his hand. Asked by a correspondent whether boredom was preferable to bombardment, Chamberlain implied more than he had intended: *"I think I would rather be bored than bombed, but that is a matter of taste."*

Soon after, Ward and Kent went home, Ward to cover the diplomatic side of the global conflict, Kent to join many staffers writing of home-front upheavals that changed American society as profoundly as did the Civil War eighty years earlier. Their places in the European theater of operations, in time, would be taken by four extraordinary reporters, whose extraordinary dispatches will make up the bulk of this book, starting with Chapter 4.

Their names: Mark S. Watson, Lee McCardell, Holbrook Bradley, and Price Day. Each in his writings created a distinctive style and a distinctive personality and a distinctive reaction to the mighty conflict unfolding in real time—when there was no historical hindsight, only the uncertainty and chaos of war.

They stuck to their task through long months away from home, always eager to report the names of Marylanders they met in the trenches and at command posts set up in palaces and mud-splattered tents. They covered the training of the Twenty-ninth "Blue and Gray" Division and other units back in the states and on maneuver in Britain. They were with troops on the long slog up the Italian spine, the horrific landings on the beaches of Normandy, the tensions at airfields as bombers took off and did not always return, the capture of Paris, the desperate Battle of the Bulge and, finally, the collapse of the Nazi regime after the Allies crossed the Rhine. They celebrated their scoops, relished good times, suffered through cold days and nights, rushed copy back to Baltimore, tangled with army censors, and witnessed evidence of Nazi atrocities that still haunt mankind.

Augmenting their work was London Bureau chief Thomas M. O'Neill, who kept his eye on British politics, especially as it affected the course of the war. He described in graphic detail the spectacle of Nazi air raids on London and endured uncomplainingly the dark tribulations and lean rations of a nation fighting for its life.

To the Pacific theater, *The Sun* sent Howard Norton and Philip S. Heisler, the former a future Pulitzer Prize winner and the latter a future managing editor of *The Evening Sun*. Both narrowly escaped death. Norton was aboard a U.S. subchaser during the invasion of Saipan when his ship was hit by a Japanese shell. There was death and blood all around him yet he survived *"with hardly a scratch."* Heisler's closest encounter, aside from his frontline reporting at Iwo Jima, was a terrifying Pacific storm that nearly capsized his escort carrier. As the European war ended, the Sunpapers shifted to the Pacific, assigning a new batch of veteran reporters to cover what loomed as the nightmare of them all: landings on the Japanese homeland. Military experts estimated that casualties could run as high as two million. It would be Saipan, Iwo Jima, and Okinawa writ very large—a tragedy averted only by the ominous advent of the atomic bomb. When Japan surrendered in September 1945, three *Sun* reporters were aboard the U.S.S. *Missouri* to observe the historic scene: Philip Potter, Thomas O'Donnell, and Robert Cochrane.

Several of these reporters stayed on in the Pacific to describe the MacArthur occupation of Japan, the recovery of the Philippines, and the turmoil in China. The Korean War was but five years away, and *The Sun* sent its own staffers there from beginning to end. Gone was the newspaper's emphasis on Europe; its coverage became global during the Cold War era, with as many as ten foreign bureaus operating from time to time. Among their shifting locations: Tokyo, New Delhi, Hong Kong, Beijing, Moscow, Paris, Rome, Bonn, Rio de Janeiro, Mexico City, Johannesburg, Saigon, Seoul, Baghdad, Jerusalem. London was a fixture from 1922 to 2006. World War II had transformed America at home and abroad. And the Baltimore Sunpapers, like other institutions, changed with the times.

CHAPTER 2

Light for All

Two years and three months before World War II erupted, *The Baltimore Sun* celebrated its 100th birthday. The centennial found the paper with its brazen younger sister, *The Evening Sun*, both famous and infamous in the nation—journals with literary merit and influence far beyond their size and city of origin. They had a boisterous penchant for insult, irony and perversity—all in defiance of pecksniffery.

From the days of its founding on May 17, 1837, *The Sun* was not just another newspaper. In its first issue, it defined its purpose as *"to diffuse light where darkness has long prevailed."* Three years later, on May 18, 1840, this sentiment was encapsulated in the masthead motto, "Light for All." *The Sun* was one of the first penny papers in the land, a publication that dedicated itself to news, large circulation, and independence rather than joining the crowd of party broadsheets selling at much higher prices. It was technically innovative, using within its first decade alliances with New Orleans papers, carrier pigeons, and a pony express to alert President James K. Polk's White House to victories in the Mexican War. This was not just a one-day triumph. According to Harold A. Williams, author of the 1987 history of the newspaper, *The Sun* followed up with battle reports, casualty lists, and letters from soldiers in Mexico. He wrote that the newspaper provided a more detailed account *"than any nation's press had ever previously accomplished. It marked the beginnings of the modern war correspondent."*

Yet, one of its luminaries, Gerald W. Johnson, later wrote that *"it is not to be inferred that* The Sun *in 1837 was a good newspaper.*

On the contrary, judged by modern standards, it was almost fabulously bad. But in the realm of the blind, a one-eyed man is king and American journalism of the nineteenth century was a realm of the blind." Since its competitors were also *"fabulously bad,"* The Sun's chief interest had to be obedience to the first rule of publishing: Make enough money to stay in business. This it did by hard work, a small staff, job printing, front-page ads, skimpy size. This was enough for Williams to stake a claim that "The Sun *was becoming one of the nation's foremost newspapers."*

Although the paper's first focus was on local news, a policy it revived under economic pressure as the twenty-first century dawned, it did run a series of letters "From Our Correspondent" in Washington, D.C. within a couple of months of its founding. Written by a postal clerk named James Lawrenson, it proved to be an augury of much that came much later—including a large and respected Washington Bureau.

Despite its Southern sympathies, *The Sun* was savvy enough to keep its head down during the Civil War, thus avoiding suspension of publication and the jailing of its editors—the fate of several competitors. The paper had a correspondent at Harper's Ferry with federal troops during the John Brown raid in 1859. He described the abolitionist leader as *"a monomaniac, possessing a strong will, superior firmness and resources of mind,"* hardly an unsympathetic diatribe. That, however, was the last time *The Sun* sent a man into the field before or during the Civil War, when its city seethed under martial law. General Benjamin Butler's guns on Federal Hill faced the Inner Harbor, the heart of seditious, pro-Confederate Baltimore.

The Sun did make a splash in foreign affairs in 1886 with a series of dispatches on Bismarck Germany's attempt to seize imperial control over Samoa—a Pacific dispute with implications of what was to come in the next century. Secretary of State Thomas F. Bayard declared that the Baltimore newspaper *"contributed materially to the peaceful solution of the complication with Germany, which at one time had threatened to be serious."*

When the nation next went to war—in 1898 against Spain and for Cuban independence—*The Sun* refused to join *"jingo papers"* clamoring for revenge over the still-disputed sinking of the battleship *Maine* in Havana Harbor. None of its reporters rode up San Juan Hill with Theodore Roosevelt's Rough Riders. Nor, during the follow-up conquest of the Philippines, was any correspondent sent across the Pacific. The paper opposed the official U.S. policy of "benevolent assimilation" of the Philippines, asserting this was *"synonymous with the surrender of all their aspirations for independence and self-government."*

Prudence continued to be the paper's watchword after the Civil War. It counted its money and attained a position in Maryland that enabled it to join the security of the successful. When vast acres of Baltimore's downtown burned in 1904, including *The Sun*'s famous Iron Building, the paper's owners and managers and news staff rolled up their sleeves, published heroically on the day after the conflagration, printed on Washington presses, and set their eyes on greater glories.

During most of its nineteenth-century years, the newspaper was very much in the total control of its founder, Arunah S. Abell, an itinerant printer who teamed up with two colleagues to found *The New York Sun, Philadelphia Public Ledger,* and *The Baltimore Sun* in the 1830s. Penny papers all, but Baltimore's paper was the only survivor. Abell was a thorough newspaperman—hard-working, dedicated, a founding father who created a dynasty that lasted exactly 150 years. In his first decade as editor, he beat the combined circulations of Baltimore's six competing dailies. *"To the Public,"* he proclaimed in his first four-page issue: *"Our object will be the common good, without regard to sects, factions or parties."*

This lofty ideal was not always honored. As the Solid South became the post-war segregationist South, the paper's Democratic Party allegiance was fairly firm from the days of Grover Cleveland to the days of Franklin D. Roosevelt. Then it turned against the New Deal, withheld any endorsement in 1936, came out for Wendell Willkie's Republican candidacy in 1940, continued to support the GOP in national elections while turning more liberal in the 1960s, 1970s, 1980s, and 1990s, and finally returned to the Democratic banner as the twenty-first century arrived. The paper had run the full gamut from conservative to liberal, with moderate periods in between.

While some of Abell's progeny, as is the wont of minor royalty, chose to indulge in their good fortune, the family produced worthy successors who allied themselves with smart business associates, brilliant writers, and tough, demanding editors. These were professionals who knew how to underpay reporters by indulging their high jinks and allowing them to booze and feast at the tables of politicians—a practice anathema to upright, uptight newspapermen of later generations. And, to their credit, these increasingly wealthy bosses used a fair amount of their profits to keep the Sunpapers on the cutting edge of newspaper practice and technology from 1910 on. That also was the year the money-making *Evening Sun* was founded. Afternoon papers in those pre-radio, pre-television days ran on a schedule that served factory workers who wanted news when they returned home in mid- to late-afternoon

Thus, the golden years began, and they were to last for eight decades, until outside owners and internet technology proved devastating to many newspapers. When the twentieth century was new, *The Sun* had much to be proud of. Its reputation grew rapidly through the work of one of history's most compelling journalists. Henry Louis Mencken, Baltimore born, bred, and bedazzling, wrote his *Evening Sun* columns with a gusto and a command of language that swept through American letters. As he lambasted the Ku Klux Klan, the women's temperance movement, and, most famously, the anti-evolutionists who blundered through the Scopes trial in Tennessee in the 1920s, he added wonderful new words to the national dialogue of his day. *"Booboisie"* was one of his best, along with *"Bozart,"* his way of describing American Beaux Arts. His nostalgic memoirs of the Baltimore he knew as a young boy and then as a fast-rising newspaperman have never failed to charm.

He was an idol on American campuses coast to coast. Many students tried to copy his inimitable style and wound up undercutting their own. Mencken did not hesitate to mock Methodists, lambaste lynchings on Maryland's Eastern Shore, crucify creationists, and drink to his heart's delight before, during, and after Prohibition. Walter Lippmann, the nation's top foreign affairs commentator, always serious and conscious of the weight of his own words, called Mencken *"the most powerful influence of the whole generation of educated people."* Mencken's prodigious production included three massive works on the American language that were and are respected by academia. He was a key player in two influential magazines: *Smart Set* and *American Mercury*. Quite an achievement for a fellow who never went to college.

Despite his celebrity and his connections to New York's cognoscenti, Mencken always remained loyal to his city and his newspaper. On one occasion he said *"I had more fun doing newspaper reporting than in any other enterprise. It is really the life of kings."* Working for the Sunpapers was like belonging to *"a good club. . . . There was a stately courtesy that is uncommon in the dens of journalists. All hands save the office boys were nurtured by the proprietors, no one was upbraided for dereliction of duty. The worst a culprit encountered was a mild expostulation usually couched in very general terms."* Once, when Mencken himself was such a culprit, having committed an outrage that caused no end of protest, he went to the publisher and declared he was guilty and awaiting sentence. It proved to be a genial conversation.

There were, of course, disputes, differences, and dislikes within the corridors of this *"good club,"* some of a magnitude that led to resignations and stony silences. Various animosities came to light only in Mencken's posthumously published diaries. But Mencken and a few others—Frank R. Kent Sr. (the father of Frank R. Kent Jr.), and Gerald W. Johnson, among them—so added luster to Arunah Abell's creation that *The Sun* began attracting some of the best writers of the day.

One reporter already on the staff as World War I began was Raymond S. Tompkins, who emerged from routine local assignments to become the paper's first real war correspondent. "The Sun *was actuated by a desire to establish a link between the Maryland men in the trenches and home,"* the paper declared when Tompkins' first dispatch from the front appeared. In later wars, many more *Sun* correspondents would be at the scenes of conflict. Yet it was Tompkins who first demonstrated that thrilling eyewitness copy, often with a local touch, was a formula worth pursuing.

Ray Tompkins attached himself to Maryland's storied Twenty-ninth Division as it trained in Alabama and at Fort Meade in Maryland, sailed with the troops to France, then followed them into action as they experienced the horrors and heroics of war. He took pains to send back the names of Marylanders he encountered. He paid special attention to the immense job Johns Hopkins physicians did in organizing the medical services needed for the American Expeditionary Force. He told of the songs doughboys sang, the exploits of dogfight pilots in new-fangled aerial warfare, and the relief that came with the Armistice. What follows are excerpts from some of Tompkins' exceptional stories:

"It is virtually impossible to picture the difference between the 117th Trench Mortar Battery as I saw it last summer and what I have seen in the last two days at the front. They are hardened veterans now and yet they are the same boys. Baltimore's 'first to fight' has been on the front line for more than three months without one single rest. Thirteen of its men, awkward rookies last summer, have been awarded the Croix de Guerre of France for valor in battle." [July 2, 1918]

"Air fighting is the greatest game in the world. They (the fighter pilots) mount into the air every day, little flocks of them, with their machine guns primed, scanning the clouds above and below them for the flying Boche, and when they find him they pounce and fight him to the finish. And they do it with a fervor and a doggedness and a consistency that actually, at this writing, has got the German aviators badly frightened." [July 7, 1918]

"Belleau Wood belongs to American history like San Juan Hill and Santiago Bay and Gettysburg and Yorktown. The night after the final American clean-up I went out with the artillery. This was the world of guns. The noise of them was all about, from far away and close at hand." [July 28, 1918]

"With the American Army at the Front, July 29, 1918. (Delayed 10 days by censors)—Maryland troops are in the front trenches. They have been over the top on patrols close to the German lines. French soldiers are their trench buddies. They went up on a dark night in driving rain. Without a hitch the battalions moved noiselessly as ghosts along screened roads and through black forests to the outermost edge

of the fighting lines. They were as cool as veterans. New steel helmets weighted their heads, gas masks were around their necks, heavy packs were on their backs, full belts of ammunition around their waists, rifles on their shoulders."

"With the American Army, Oct. 5 (Delayed by the Censor)—Columns of fighting Americans are rolling forward day and night. Traffic on country roadways between supply bases and the line resembles busy streets. On main roads army orders prohibit halting for a single moment. The American artillery rolls northward toward the muffled thunder. The made-in-America war engine, built to crush ambitious autocracy forever, is now getting into top speed."

"At the Front, Nov. 12 (Delayed)—In the last hours before the signing of the armistice the Germans quit the hills north of Verdun before the onslaughts of the Seventy-ninth Division. Here, east of the Meuse, the Germans fought desperately until the last minute and their dead are strewn on the mountains that block advance to the Woevre plain. Meade men relieved Blue and Gray men in this sector. For nearly a month, the latter had fought through Boche-infested jungles, and other Marylanders had carried on their advance. Yesterday before the eleventh hour Maryland men had driven the German big guns beyond range of Verdun for the first time in four years."

When Raymond Tomkins' assignment as a war correspondent came to an end, he joined J. Fred Essary, chief of the Washington Bureau, for the Versailles Treaty negotiations in Paris. After a few years in Baltimore on the local staff, he returned to Germany to report on that country's runaway inflation, Hitler's *Bierhalle Putsch*, and other dramatic events.

It was Frank Kent Sr. who gained *The Sun* a controversial world reputation by revealing animosities among the Allies during post–World War I negotiations on the Versailles Treaty. Those were days of tight censorship on all correspondents officially assigned to the European theater. No stories, whether of battle or diplomacy, escaped government vetting or rejection. The Wilson administration, which set up a propaganda machine later admired by Joseph Goebbels, was quite content to let American readers remain in the dark.

Kent, then a veteran reporter and editor, went to Paris in 1918 as guest of the British War Mission. Thus avoiding the harsh restrictions that cosseted journalists caught in the system, he sought out many sources, including fellow newspapermen, who passed along information they wished to write but could not. One was Charles H. Grasty, briefly an owner of *The Sun* and an outstanding correspondent. He probably leaked a lot of behind-the-scenes material to Frank Kent. The result was an international sensation, disclosing controversies during the Versailles negotiations that took some of the glow from President Woodrow Wilson's personal intervention in creating nations and redrawing maps.

Kent's huge scoop appeared on November 28, 1918, under the headline: *"Paris Seethes With International Jealousy and Suspicion."* An italic precede told readers that the story had been written by Kent after he returned to America. *"It was not possible to have got this article to America either by mail or cable,"* the editors stated.

The opening paragraphs of Kent's twenty-one-part exposure were explosive: *"For weeks past, under the surface, Paris has been simply seething with international jealousies, friction and feeling, and between us and our noble allies at this time there is a tension and a strain that does not appear on the top, but is very real nonetheless. . . . The truth is, and everybody in Paris knows it, that in governmental and political circles they do not love us at all over there, neither the English nor the French. Between individuals of different nations and races warm and sincere friendships are possible and there are plenty of Englishmen and Americans and Frenchmen and Americans between whom there are the strongest personal ties. But there is something about races and nations as a whole that makes the friendships that exist between individuals impossible. Paris these days most beautifully illustrates this.*

"In the first place, General Pershing is anything but popular over there with the French and British high commands. The distaste for him dates back to the Spring of 1917, when, after first agreeing to permit American forces to be brigaded with the French and British in platoons, he got cold feet on that proposition and in a memorable conference with Foch and Haig stood up, and, in fact, said the American army was at their disposal to do with what they wanted, but it would have to be used as an army, and there would be no splitting up of it. The French

were furious not only at what Pershing said, but at the way he said it, which was in the most outspoken American language imaginable and not, it is said, entirely free from profanity. Had he been a Frenchman, his friends say, he would probably have had to fight a duel with Foch. But he had his way and subsequent events proved him right . . .

"As to the French, there is believed to be a disposition on their part to reach out for more territory than is just. There is talk of extending France to the Rhine and to the Alps—God's boundary lines as they call them there—and to look to the acquisition of certain German colonial possessions. In other words, the French statesmen are disposed to feel that the situation rather justifies the 'picking of bones' of the enemy, and it is said that Clemenceau, furious, forceful and a fighter with a tremendous personality, despite his great age, is sympathetic with the idea of gaining some material advantage to France beyond the items of 'indemnity and restorations.' Likewise, the French politicians are not averse to England maintaining her sea dominance provided France is permitted to maintain her military machine of several million men. We are expected to sit still, look pleasant, and agree to this programme like a good nation. Some of our representatives over there say emphatically they'll be damned if we do.

"You hear, too, in Paris what will be news in America, of the serious mutiny of the French army in 1917, and of the difficulty of suppressing it. In this direction the advent of America into the war seems to have saved the situation. Neither England nor France has any use for Italy. They tell you that the Italian troops were a bitter disappointment, that they fight all right when things are going their way, but they cannot be depended on when they are not . . . As for the Portuguese, they are said to be the limit."

In the centennial history *The Sunpapers of Baltimore*, a 1937 book written by four authors including Kent, this comment appeared: *"This sort of stuff, in the complacent days between the Armistice and the Peace Conference, naturally made a huge sensation. Today what Mr. Kent wrote is known to everyone as fact, but in November, 1918, it seemed like the worst sort of treason."* He was condemned right and left, including by other newspapers, but his editors stuck by him.

The importance of Kent's scoop became manifest. Prominent foreign journalists signed on as stringers and the paper exchanged material with the highly regarded *Manchester Guardian*. It was recognized as one of the nation's best newspapers. At war's end, the newspaper sought to hold this preeminence while making an ever wider mark (with Mencken's help) in home-front America.

Between the world wars, Kent's conservative column, "The Great Game of Politics," was syndicated throughout the country, a departure from *Sun* tradition. Within the corridors of *The Sun*, fierce if gentlemanly disputes flared on "brain alley," the lair of editorial writers near the newsroom. There was, indeed, a need for calm, and it was offered by Gerald W. Johnson, an enlightened Southern historian with a complicated relationship with Mencken. As far back as the Scopes trial of 1924, the newspaper relied on Johnson to offset Mencken's diatribes against William Jennings Bryan, the three-time presidential candidate who was a lawyer for the anti-Darwin forces. Johnson wrote a quiet, dignified obituary on Bryan, never endorsing his theories, when the Great Commoner died at the end of the sensational trial.

During the New Deal, when the traditionally Democratic *Sun* turned against Franklin D. Roosevelt as he set up federal programs to fight the Depression, Johnson (an FDR admirer) was often kept out of the paper. He opposed publisher Paul Patterson's decision to refrain from endorsing Roosevelt in 1936, later asserting it was a *"ghastly mistake."* Even if an endorsement had been only half-hearted, Johnson argued, it would have made *The Sun* "the most authoritative paper in American journalism." He hung on for years at the paper, finally retiring in 1943 to the economic perils of freelancing. His emergence as a major American author redounded more to the paper's credit than it perhaps deserved.

As the Great Depression smothered the country after the Wall Street crash of 1929, and as war clouds arose in Europe with Adolf Hitler taking over as German chancellor three years later, *The Sun* became more conservative on domestic policy but remained internationalist in its approach and strongly pro-British in its instincts. Editorially, it opposed Republican isolationists and welcomed Wendell Willkie's selection as the 1940 GOP nominee for the presidency. Like FDR,

Willkie favored U. S. efforts to aid standing-alone Britain. Had the Republicans nominated an isolationist, Roosevelt might have been limited in his effort to help England in its gravest hour.

More relevant to *The Sun's* role in World War II, the newspaper had recruited reporters who proved quite able to face the harsh trials that lay ahead. They would go into the trenches, take on air and sea assignments for the assault on Normandy beaches, go ashore at Iwo Jima, and face the myriad other challenges and risks. Never did they forget their duty to their readers. The paper published the names of more than 6,000 Marylanders in uniform during the course of the conflict. One newspaper's account of that terrible struggle is what this book is all about. But first, let us review Mencken's despair at the prospect of another war against Germany after a hiatus of only twenty-two years. He warrants special attention because in those days he was the image if not the reality of *The Baltimore Sun*.

CHAPTER 3

H. L. Mencken's Wars

enry Louis Mencken's infatuation with all things German turned World War I and World War II into personal conflicts that alienated him from his own government, his friends, and even his beloved Sunpapers, the Baltimore publications he had made famous. From his childhood on, he was conscious of his ties to the land of his forebears. He developed a passion for German philosophy, German history, German food, German beer, and that craving for familiar comforts called *Gemütlichkeit*. "*There is German music—and other music,*" he once said.

William Manchester, an *Evening Sun* reporter turned Mencken biographer, wrote that as early as 1912 he *"had so pledged his soul to his dream of Bavarian culture that no war, not even a Hitler, could ever shake him awake."*

Mencken's reaction to both conflicts became a weird continuum, one in which such profound differences with his *Sun* colleagues arose that his column disappeared in mid-stream during both conflicts. He repeated much of what he wrote in 1914 when he found himself attacking and under attack three decades later: Germany was the victim, Germans were much to be preferred over the hated English, American intervention was a blunder history would condemn.

One later biographer, Marion Rodgers, wrote that Mencken *"remained mired in the mind-set of two decades earlier."* Another, Terry Teachout, commented that in 1914 Mencken *"was writing about Germany with an ardor for which the kindest word is naive."*

The crucial difference, of course, was in the top German leadership. The Kaiser, for all his faults, could go quietly into exile after World War I, just a pathetic figure in retrospect. Hitler proved to be vastly more troubling. Mencken could call the Nazi leader a were-wolf, a shabby ass, a buffoon, a quack, a lunatic. But he apparently never called Hitler what he really was: a genocidal mass murderer. He never wrote publicly about the Holocaust. He taunted Jews, including some of his best friends, by suggesting that their *"hysteria"* over the Nazi pogroms would lead only to more anti-Semitism.

For Baltimoreans, Mencken was the intellectual giant who made their city famous across the land and across the seas. He also was the columnist who caused constant chatter and consternation all over town as he mocked the patriotism that accompanies all wars. First came his column, "The Free Lance," a feature from 1911 to 1915 in the brash, new *Evening Sun*. Until the conflict drew near in 1914, he was wont to ruminate with good-natured acerbity on a number of topics, some local. But once the fighting started he defiantly *"whooped it up"* for the Kaiser even as his hometown changed the name of German Street to Redwood Street.

"War is a good thing," wryly wrote this man who hated war. *"It affords a natural, normal and undisguised outlet for that complex of passion and energies which civilization seeks so fatuously to check."* [Aug. 4, 1914] Then, two days later, he brought out the cudgels: For 44 years, the French had menaced Germany with *"melodramatic plans for revanche."* The English were intent on overwhelming Germany even at the risk of creating an *"irreconcilable foe sure to pay them off soon or late."* As for the United States, its newspapers were unanimously pro-Allies even though the *"sole offense"* of the Germans was *"attending strictly to their business."* [Aug. 6, 1914]

As the guns of August roared on, Mencken got more specific. *"I see the German war machine as a means of defense only. Should she (Germany) stand idly by while England prepared so openly to crush her. The one wise thing for Germany to do was to prepare to defend herself. To picture Germans as brigands and swashbucklers is to do a grave injustice to a people whose one genuine desire is for peace, a reasonable security, a chance to do their hard and useful work in the world."* [Aug. 27, 1914]

Day after day, Mencken turned "The Free Lance" into a column that hammered more than it humphed, that repeated more than it surprised, that affirmed his loyalty to Germany and loathing for its foes.

"The Germans so far have kept their heads," he averred. *"Facing forces double their strength and pursued by a campaign of misrepresentation and vituperation unmatched in history they are still proceeding calmly and patiently. But the time may come, and perhaps it is not far away, when self-preservation will demand from them a supreme and wholly ruthless effort."* [Dec. 18, 1914]

Early in the next year, Mencken came to the defense of his fellow German-Americans, who *"have had to face a constant succession of insults and injustices."* Popular hostility toward them in the first war was far greater than in a second, when Japanese-Americans became the hate objects of choice. Mencken complained that everything German had become anathema, that England was controlling the war news from Europe, and that the American newspapers were *"gallantly beating the tom-toms."*

"I speak here," he declared, *"as one whose belief in the German cause, though deep-seated and unbounded, has very little sentiment to it."* (His biographers would agree with the first part of that statement, not with his denial of sentiment for the Germany he romanticized.) [Feb. 16, 1915]

Mencken's defiance reached a peak when he defended the sinking of ocean liners, including the *Lusitania*, by German submarines. Passengers aboard such ships, he said, *"had been warned"* and had no justification for thinking themselves protected *"from the normal hazards of war."* [May 8, 1915]

Such comments drew the outrage Mencken intended, not just from the public but from close colleagues at his newspaper. He mocked their support of the Allied cause. *"Day by day the patriotic nightmares of the estimable Sunpaper grow more gorgeous and horrible,"* he jeered. *"No matter which way its popping eyes roll, it sees a German spy, a German bomb-thrower, a German assassin."*

All this set the stage for the shutting down of the "Free Lance" column on October 23, 1915. *"It is five years since I first bawled at the faithful from this pulpit,"* he wrote. *"This fellow is slowly submerging in a skepticism that leaves him, in the end, almost non-compos."*

A quarter of a century later, in another war, another era, Mencken would again bawl at the faithful in *Sunday Sun* columns that dared to defend, albeit with caveats, a Germany grown monstrous under Nazi diktat. And, once again, with his own country and his newspaper throwing their support to Britain and against Germany, Mencken became so alienated that he gave up writing his column on June 26, 1941, thus repeating his World War I pattern.

In the dread September of 1939, as German forces vanquished a helpless Poland, Mencken soon made it clear that his pro-German inclinations were as strong as ever [Sept. 10, 1939]. He flailed away at a favorite target, President Franklin D. Roosevelt, for his efforts to enact legislation that would enable the United States to send military aid to Britain and France even while proclaiming U. S. neutrality. This, he wrote, was *"preposterous rumble-bumble,"* a position that contained a large kernel of truth.

Had Mencken left it at that he would not have become an embarrassment. Instead, turning his attention to the war as it was then unfolding, he declared *"it is hard to take seriously the doctrine that it was an act of aggression for the Germans to try to get their property back."* (He probably had Danzig and the Danzig Corridor in mind, a territory inhabited by many Germans that had been bequeathed to Poland in the Versailles Treaty.) Ignored was clear evidence, even then hard to discount, that Hitler had staged a border provocation to justify his blitzkrieg.

Two weeks later Mencken was at it again. *"There is no difference between (England and Germany). They will look precisely alike in history. If there is any preponderance of rationality, it manifestly runs in favor of Hitler. After all, no sensible ruler of a great nation could consent to being shut in between two walls of steel* (i.e., France and Poland). *He (Hitler) was bound to make some effort to bust out and he naturally took the softer side first."* [Sept. 24, 1939]

Mencken's provocative writing contrasted with *Sun* editorials that cautiously supported Roosevelt's foreign and defense policies in spite of the newspaper's opposition to the New Deal. It also clashed with the cartoons of Edmund Duffy that appeared atop the Mencken column each Sunday—a delicious juxtaposition. As Hitler sought to consolidate his conquest of Poland and Czechoslovakia with peace feelers, Duffy won the Pulitzer Prize with a cartoon showing the Nazi leader's *"Outstretched Hand"* of peace dripping blood [Oct. 7, 1939].

As the war thundered on, Mencken had nothing to say about the Nazi rape of Denmark and Norway. When France tottered in June of 1940, leaving Britain all alone, the Baltimore curmudgeon made no effort to disguise his sentiments. *"The Hon. Mr. Roosevelt's heroic attempt to rescue England from the law of natural selection has got off to a good start. The plain people, having abandoned the barber shop, the village grocery and the dream book for radio, are now wholly dependent on it for information and ideology and in short order they will be getting a doctor's dose of both. Six successive nights of White House crooning will make them pant for Hitler's poisonous blood."* [May 5, 1940]

Mencken was plagued by prejudices that were repeatedly overtaken by events. It resulted in self-contradiction in his treatment of Axis enemies, the Roosevelt administration, and the England he detested. A Mencken column [May 26, 1940], the day the Dunkirk evacuation began, deserves to be quoted at length:

"If it is in the books that the werewolf Hitler shall wreck England, that wrecking will be achieved, Roosevelt or no Roosevelt. It is hard to imagine Hitler, after devouring the sweating Motherland, setting off at once to tackle this great republic.

"If England is to be saved to rob the mails, hog the high seas and boss the world, we'll pay all the bills. And if England throws up the sponge before rescue, we'll have not only Hitler on our necks but also Mussolini, Stalin and the Japs. Roosevelt, Hull & Company have not been content to do these blood-thirsty fellows foul and constant injuries, hitting them below the belt and behind the back, they also have heaped upon them a long series of gross and intolerable insults.

"If Hitler manages to outfight the poor French and proceeds to give the quaking English a really formidable wallop, nothing we can do can stop him and all we'll accomplish will be to convert him into an open and really dangerous enemy."

Although Mencken's huge reputation had long rested on outrageous prose that focused national attention on *The Baltimore Sun*, his war positions had little if any overt support among his colleagues. Frank R. Kent Sr., a respected conservative columnist, advocated a U.S. declaration of war against Germany—this only two days after the Mencken piece just quoted. The sympathies of the chairman of the board of the Sunpapers, Harry Black, may be gauged by the fact that he remodeled his house on Baltimore's Warrenton Road to resemble his English wife's home in the Cotswolds, that most quintessential region of rural England.

In thundering against Roosevelt's interventionist policies, Mencken may have been an odd man out so far as his *Sun* colleagues were concerned. However, he reflected the strong views of a strong minority of Americans eager to avoid involvement in another European conflict. The America First Committee, headed by the country's favorite hero, Charles A. Lindbergh, had an estimated 800,000 members in 650 chapters, many located in a vast newspaper circulation area dominated by the *Chicago Tribune*. Isolationist members of Congress were potent enough to come within one vote of ending the military draft. They made Roosevelt leery of demanding all he may have wished in aid to beleaguered Britain. It would take the Japanese attack on Pearl Harbor and Hitler's convenient declaration of war against America to get the United States fully involved in World War II. Even on the very day of Pearl Harbor, isolationist Senator Gerald Nye complained that *"we've been maneuvered into this by the president"*—thus encouraging a conspiracy theory that never quite dies.

As the grim summer of 1940 brought more black headlines of German air attacks against England, Mencken continued writing columns that did no credit to him. On July 7, 1940, his loathing of Roosevelt, hatred of England, and loss of faith in democratic societies all meshed to produce the following: *"Nor is it at all certain that democracy will survive the coming fireworks in England. On the contrary, it may blow up before the Hon. Mr. Roosevelt can perfect his pious scheme to save it (England). The present government of England is hard to distinguish from a German concentration camp, and when the time comes to make terms with Hitler it may go the rest of the way. No Englishman of any sense actually believes in democracy. If he gabbles about it, as all English politicians do, it is only as a means of hood-winking the vulgar. England has been governed many years past by a small group of prehensile gentry."*

On July 14, 1940, the Baltimore curmudgeon continued to rage. Excerpts provide the full Mencken flavor at this perilous moment of the war:

"When the history of this revolutionary age is written at last, with its turmoils far behind and its alarms forgotten, a long chapter will have to be devoted to the naïve imbecility of contemporary opinion in America. Nearly all the accepted publicists of the country, whether official or journalistic, appear to view the titanic struggle now going on as if it were a simple conflict between good and bad, right and wrong. On the one side there is a band of innocent Sunday school scholars, engaged in holding a peaceful picnic in a sort of cosmic Druid Hill Park, and on the other side there is a gang of wicked ruffians from across the railroad tracks bent upon chasing the little angels home and stealing their ice cream. . . .

"The Germans, Italians and Russians are scoundrels even when they seek to recover their own undisputed property, and the English are saints even when they massacre French sailors who were saving them from an ignominious death only a month ago. As for the poor French, they were so pure in heart as infants in Limbo so long as they shed their gore freely for England, but became villains of purplish dye the instant they began giving first thought to France.

"Plainly enough, the United States, at the moment, faces grave difficulties. But what has been the American response to this, as exemplified by political pronunciamento and journalistic homily? Has it been an intelligent effort to examine the facts?

"Everyone knows the answer. There has been no such inquiry. Instead, we have been entertained with an inane series of imbecile objurgations. The whole problem has been dismissed by arguing that anyone who doesn't think as we do is an abandoned criminal, with no rights which we are bound to respect. In so far as any effort has been made to search out and remedy the defects of democracy, it has taken the form of making them worse, and nearly all the persons

undertaking the job either have been unconscionable demagogues or their bleating dupes.

"It would be hard to describe the history of the Roosevelt Administration in any other terms. On the domestic front it has robbed all honest and self-respecting people to fatten a horde of knaves and mendicants, and in foreign affairs, save when restrained by Congress, it has carried on in a grossly unintelligent, hypocritical and dishonorable manner. There has hardly been a time when it has given any apparent thought, even the most casual, to the true welfare and security of the United States; from the beginning of the present war it has subordinated every American interest to the interest of England.

"To this end the country has been harassed by constant alarms and mare's nests, and drenched in floods of balderdash. At the extreme we have been asked to believe seriously that Poland, the original agent provocateur, was a noble exemplar and defender of democracy, and at the other end we have been told officially that Hitler and his goons contemplate the bombing of Omaha and Kansas City, and that only the chivalrous British navy keeps them off. And in between, day in and day out, we have been dosed with scores of other grotesque lunacies, all of them directed to the one end of holding up the tottering British Empire, and preserving its hegemony over the entire world, including the high seas and the United States.

"We have clawed and sniped at the totalitarians without hurting them and now face their probable revenge without adequate weapons and not an honest friend in all the world."

These words were written as the Nazis overran France and the British had bombed French ships only to prevent their going over to the Germans. Unfortunately for Mencken, he went on to make an assertion later refuted by wartime events and post-war scholarship. *"There is not the slightest evidence,"* he wrote, *"that the Totalitarian Powers, whether European or Asiatic, have been planning an attack on this country . . . On the contrary, they have been at great pains to treat it with politeness. All the major invasions have been made by England, not Germany, Italy or Japan. In so far as the United States is now or has been at odds with the totalitarians, it is simply and solely because the Roosevelt administration has constantly and deliberately given aid to their enemies in violation not only of international law and the statutes of Congress but also of common honesty and decency."*

Finally, the editorial writers Mencken loved to disparage had had enough. Buried within an editorial [Sept. 3, 1940] supporting the transfer of fifty old destroyers to Britain in exchange for strategic Caribbean islands came this riposte: *"The man who attacks our course on the grounds that Herr Hitler might not like it is a man whose notions of the realities of the world are strangely warped, to say the least."*

A Mencken reply of sorts came six weeks later [Sept. 10, 1940] when he contended that *"the majority of plain Americans . . . are a great deal less eager to sacrifice their legs and limbs for England than the editorial writers of the newspapers appear to think. The issue, to such poor folk, is not one of embracing Hitler on the one hand and fighting for 'religion and morality' on the other but simply one between barging into a bloody quarrel and staying out."*

With the wartime winter setting in, [Dec. 1, 1940] Mencken predicted that England would follow Germany, Spain, Italy, and France in turning *"fascist openly, as it is approaching fascism in fact."* A month later, [Jan. 1, 1941] Mencken dismissed warnings about the dangers implicit in U.S. unpreparedness. Instead, he argued that Britain was seeking *"hegemony"* over continental Europe and Asia. The rest, said Mencken, was *"sound and hooey."*

One week later, the columnist turned his fire on the *"mountebank,"* Winston Churchill. Both Churchill and Roosevelt, he held, had promoted hatred and waged *"raucous war upon common humanity, common decency and common sense."* Not a word about Hitler and Mussolini.

The ongoing debate over war policy placed Mencken in the ranks of the increasingly lonely isolationists. At last, he told publisher Paul Patterson that he would quit writing for the editorial pages of the Sunpapers. In a final column [Feb. 2, 1941) he declared that *"Win or lose, the United States is doomed to suffer some appalling headaches during the next dozen years. If the cause of humanity triumphs we will have the bills to pay, and if Beelzebub gets the better of it we'll have the damages. In either case, half of the human race will hate us very earnestly, and the rest will hold us in a kind of esteem hard to distinguish from contempt."*

After this parting shot, the most famous of *Sun* writers fell silent. He would write nothing more about public affairs—for his newspaper or any other publication—until 1948. He left his battlefield with his wartime opinions a lasting source of discomfort—not least to those who extolled his writing talent, his linguistic achievements, and his charming autobiographies about growing up in Baltimore and breaking into the newspaper business.

CHAPTER 4

Watson's Warnings

If there was a moment when *The Baltimore Sun* launched its distinctive coverage of World War II, it was the morning of November 15, 1939. On that date appeared the first of four dispatches authoritatively warning of America's woeful unpreparedness as it watched Western Europe fall under the fist of Hitler. The author of this devastating analysis was Mark S. Watson, who for many months in many battles was destined to report from North Africa, Sicily, Italy, Britain, France, and, finally, a Germany going down to defeat.

He once wrote of diving into a trench in Sicily to avoid incoming shells, an experience that reminded him of the days when he took similar evasive action in World War I: *"When incoming shells threaten, men flatten themselves hastily in shallow ditches. You do not have to re-practice that maneuver even after twenty-five years. It comes back naturally. You make the ditch in a single, graceful dive, tug your helmet to a new horizontal and hug the earth approximately as close as in 1918, regardless of added poundage in all the wrong places."* [Aug. 12, 1943]

As he traversed Verdun and other old battlefields twenty-seven years after that war, he recalled his service at Chaumont on the staff of General John J. Pershing, then commander of U.S. forces in France. It was there, one can surmise, that Watson developed his understanding of the awful burdens of top officers as they ordered young soldiers into mortal combat. He never forgot the lessons of military lore: the fateful mix of intelligence, luck, timing, and personality in strategic/tactical decisions, the crucial role of logistics and supply, the importance of accurately assessing terrain, and the puissance of the enemy.

After the first war, Watson, as a major, worked as officer-in-charge of *Stars and Stripes*, the doughboy's newspaper, then moved into civilian life as managing editor of *Ladies Home Journal* (quite a switch). He joined *The Sun* in the mid-twenties, taking over editorship of *The Sunday Sun* and a handsome new magazine. During the second war, when he found his real niche as the newspaper's military correspondent, he won the Pulitzer Prize for his 1944 reporting in the European theater of operations. Many years later, in 1963, the citation for his Presidential Medal of Freedom was laudatory: "Soldier in the First World War and correspondent in the Second, he has given the American people informed, wide-ranging and independent coverage of the nation's security and defense." When he died in 1966, aged 78, beribboned brass in dress uniform filled a large Baltimore church in tribute to a reporter who tried responsibly to report on the assessments of the military community. His fellow reporters named the press room at the Pentagon in his honor.

Mark Watson, who was born in Plattsburg, New York, and graduated from Union College, was a self-effacing, courtly gentleman whose intellectual toughness appeared only in his writing. And on that November day in 1939, when the first of his four-part critique appeared, he sternly addressed the *"grotesqueness"* of disarray in the top ranks of the War and Navy Departments, the alarming weakness of America's armed forces and the attempts of isolationists in Congress to thwart rearmament and aid to Britain. He reportedly irritated President Roosevelt while actually helping FDR's efforts to prepare for war.

"The least militaristic citizen cannot ignore the massing of troops and resources by warring powers of Europe and Asia, the engagement of their armies, the heavy losses at sea, including hostilities in the oceans that touch our shores," he wrote. *"However effectively we suppress war spirit in America, we must guard against the possibility that war may be brought to us by men and events which America cannot control. Only that conviction can explain the extraordinary unanimity with which Americans have entered on our vigorous program of rearmament. The military establishments are now engaged in catching up with preparations that would be required for even a defensive war. The theory that we can accomplish* (a defense buildup)

in a few minutes is one in which America has always liked to indulge. But the fact is that a million civilians do not spring to arms overnight. The army itself will not spring to arms effectively for even a serious defensive war until fully a year and a half has passed. It will not because it cannot."

Watson warned the next day that the 1939 state of U.S. readiness was closer to what it was when World War I began in 1914 rather than when it ended four years later. Such specifics were confirmed by scholars long after the second global conflict ended. One said the U.S. armed forces ranked seventeenth in the world, behind Rumania. Another put it this way: "When the Germans struck in the West, the U.S. Army could field fewer than a third the number of divisions Belgium put into the field."

Turning to the navy in two follow-up articles [June 18 and 19, 1939] Watson declared that the United States lacked a two-ocean navy to combat strong foes in both the Atlantic and Pacific. *"It is quite clear that we have a one-ocean navy and even with the additions now contemplated will still have a one-ocean navy."* While the United States was ahead of all nations except Britain in its battle fleet, he warned that the nation was *"perceptively behind Britain and about equal with Japan"* in aircraft carriers. As for submarines, the U.S. had *"fewer than any other sea power."*

Behind Watson's bleak assessment was his frustration over the *"no-building decade"* when the United States adhered to international agreements limiting sea power, even to the point of sinking a battleship nearing completion while Britain and Japan pushed ahead. He deplored the *"very unsatisfactory status"* of tankers, seaplane tenders, ammunition ships, mine layers, mine sweepers, submarine chasers, motor torpedo boats, and supply ships. *"With madness in foreign chancelleries, even the least militaristic can hardly question the wisdom of preparedness—not against logical but against mad possibilities,"* he contended [Dec. 12, 1939]. He thus took a position diametrically opposed to Mencken.

As disaster followed disaster during the ominous springtime of 1940, Watson warned the United States was ill-prepared for *"the new sort of war,"* citing the *"astonishing success"* of German *Blitzkrieg* techniques. Each weapon in Nazi hands was *"perfectly familiar to the personnel using it, each wielded by flawlessly trained battalions, each available to instantaneous use at the will of the high command and each employed with consummate skill at exactly the right place and exactly the right time."* [June 2, 1940] *The Sun's* military correspondent left it to his readers to figure where he got such blunt and unflinching assessments.

"For fully a year in the future, our present small army will remain tragically unprepared for any serious defensive effort against a powerful foe. Our vast hordes of tanks and airplanes will not be delivered for a long time to come." Visiting the First Armored Division at Fort Knox, Kentucky, he said the Germans were *"miles ahead of anything in American experience."*

Based on his World War I experience, Watson made the case for a selective service system, asserting that a draft was the only way to get a half a million men quickly into uniform. *"In World War I we raised twice as many men by the Selective Service Act as were raised throughout the Civil War. It cost us only one-twentieth as much money as the 1861–65 floundering. It saved untold time and it eliminated favoritism as fully as can well be expected."* [June 8, 1940]

When President Roosevelt revealed his plan to exchange fifty old U.S. destroyers in exchange for British bases in the western Atlantic, Watson—unlike Mencken—gave it his support: *"The arrangement with Britain has provided us with such a screen of outlying bases to protect our Eastern Seaboard as no one envisioned a year ago."* [Dec. 4, 1940] He spoke up before the much larger Washington struggle over the Lend-Lease Act that would roil Congress for months.

As the fateful year 1941 began, Watson displayed impatience over the administration's lag in appointing a single war-production czar, a complaint that brought action in three days, and warned that by June there would be more planes coming off the lines than engines to power them. This was the kind of professional detail that gave *The Sun* a distinctive role in war coverage.

Watson approvingly mentioned such U.S. military improvements as the *"unity and autonomy"* acquired by the Army Air Corps, [June

6, 1941] the army's increase in heavy guns, [June 26, 1941] the faster retirement of unfit officers, [June 28, 1941] and the overdue adoption of dive bombing tactics [July 6, 1941]. But he disapprovingly cited the War Department's *"grotesque blunder"* in failing to anticipate a shortage of silk for parachutes.

By September 27, 1941, Watson was ready to credit the U.S. armed forces for their *"immense progress"* in one year, citing the emergence of twenty-seven well-trained infantry divisions, two armored divisions, and two others on the point of being activated. Little did he know that in a dozen weeks Pearl Harbor would be attacked and the United States fully committed to a worldwide struggle against both Japan and Germany.

The Baltimore Sun had already nailed its interventionist colors to the mast earlier in the year. An unusual front-page editorial almost two columns long flatly declared [May 2, 1941] that *"Britain Must Not Stand Alone."* Warning that the United Kingdom *"is being crushed and strangled"* as Nazi submarines prowled the Atlantic sinking a *"devastating"* number of merchant ships, the editorial asserted that the sea line of supplies must be kept open and expanded *"come what may."* Though it left what methods should be used to the government in Washington, the editorial listed patrols, convoys, and the transfer of U.S. warships to the British Navy as possible options.

This passionate appeal had come at a time when an American crowd in Madison Square Garden had cheered denunciations of Britain's *"last desperate plan"* to draw the United States into *"the fiasco of war."* The editorial took a diametrically opposite view. *"The plight of Britain compels the United States to make (the) final decision whether we shall go further in aid of the nation who is our friend or by standing alone on our own soil to face whatever issues the conquering totalitarian powers may present to us."*

Many prestigious British newspapers lauded the Baltimore paper's forthright stand and it was also discussed widely and much appreciated in other informed quarters. Despite the wartime rationing of newsprint that restricted papers to abbreviated editions, both *The Manchester Guardian* and the London *Times* featured the editorial.

James Bone, the London editor of *The Guardian*, wrote on May 5: "The eloquent and arresting leading article in *The Sun* is a characteristic example of the urgency with which informed American opinion is now viewing the state of war. Americans are realizing even more acutely than some people in this country the gravity of the coming months.

"But," Bone continued, "and this is the most encouraging thing, they are not dismayed. Even if Hitler were to overrun Egypt and gain the Suez Canal it would not be the end, and they are prepared to stand by us to the end." *The Guardian* quoted with added emphasis *The Sun*'s declaration that the line of supplies must be kept open and expanded come what may.

The Star, London's liberal evening paper, carried an editorial with the heading *"America Speaks."* The writer underscored the message, saying: "The giant realizes at last that his strength cannot save him if freedom's enemy ever gets within his guard. The issue, the decision and soul of a great people are all summed up in these words of *The Sun* editorial: 'There is no escaping fate.'"

The deep impression made by *The Baltimore Sun*'s editorial stand can be gauged by the fact that, over the weekend, various other British newspapers published excerpts.

In retrospect, it was a trip by *Sun* publisher Paul Patterson to Blitz-battered London that solidified the newspaper's decision to fully fund major coverage of the war. He urged other publishers to visit the British capital and do likewise. A wealthy, well-traveled executive, a man who protected Mencken even while shutting down the curmudgeon's column, an Anglophile who valued his British friends and his paper's connections with *The Manchester Guardian*, Patterson revealed his affection for Britain to his Baltimore readers.

Describing his arrival at London's posh Savoy Hotel, Patterson wrote: *"The approach to the hotel is startling. The brilliantly lighted entrance is gone. Porters help travelers from cars, fumbling about for luggage and guiding arrivals through blackened revolving doors. Inside is a familiar scene, with the familiar faces of the staff who give a warm greeting and guide the guest to well-remembered quarters."* [July 31, 1941]

Of the British he encountered, Patterson wrote that *"there is a note of gayety in their occasional references to their experiences. There is no pretending it was not grim, deadly grim, but there is also grim satisfaction in having seen it through and being just as grimly confident of weathering it successfully once again. Bundles for Britain,"* he advised, *"should include chocolates, not soap, cigarettes, or tea. Razor blades are prized packages."* Two days later he described a government-arranged midnight visit to a central fire-fighting headquarters where brigades *"rated as front-line troops."*

On October 13, 1941, in a dispatch from the London Bureau of *The Sun*, the publisher's son, Maclean Patterson, wrote that all segments of British opinion were clamoring for an invasion of Europe, with the loudest demands coming from the working class. British officials were obviously eager for *Sun* coverage—and they secured it. There would be the appointment of Thomas M. O'Neill, as the wartime chief of the London Bureau, and the all-important assignment of the Watson-McCardell-Bradley-Day team to the war on the continent. For the rest of the profitable golden years of newspapering, an era that closed at the end of the century, *The Sun*'s own staffers would report the world.

With the Japanese attack at Pearl Harbor on December 7, 1941, Watson predictably waded in by grimly analyzing the U.S. position after devastating losses to the nation's Pacific fleet [Dec. 10, 1941]. *"It would be folly to deny that we have been hurt by Japan's first series of blows,"* he wrote. *"Even on December 6 our military task was a hard one, and before we finish we will be hurt again. Even a year ago it was recognized that our own fleet was not strong enough to lose a single one of its components. Several of these components are gone now and that is why the Pacific problem calls for new calculations. One of the greatest needs in the Pacific is the immediate whittling down of Japanese air power. It is air power which has contributed most impressively in every Japanese success so far, and it is air superiority which Americans and its allies must gain for themselves before there can be any substantial hope of turning the tide of war. Fortunately, one defeat does not end a war. It is the last battle, not the first or second or third, as was evidenced in 1914–18."*

After the U.S suffered multiple defeats in January, Watson was guardedly encouraged by a U.S. counter-attack in the Battle of Macassar Strait and on the Marshall and Gilbert Islands. But he turned a clear eye toward the prospect that Japan would seize Singapore, [Feb. 7, 1942] warning that the effect on the whole Far East situation would be tragic. It would mean the release of large Japanese land, air, and sea forces to be diverted to the Burmese front while potentially cutting off oil supplies from the Dutch East Indies. He asked, too, how long General Douglas MacArthur's defense of the Philippines could last [Feb. 19, 1942]. *"The prospect in Bataan, never bright, is now dark indeed."* Watson would not sugarcoat the news. He said setbacks in the Philippines were *"a further grim reminder that putting General MacArthur in the high command in Australia did not win the war for us."* [April 4, 1942] Taking even more pointed aim at MacArthur, he said the fall of American forces in Corregidor was rooted in the *"very large destruction of the general's air fleet hours after Pearl Harbor had been struck."* [May 6, 1942]

Historians have long criticized MacArthur's failure to disperse his aircraft—a blunder matched only by his decision to march to the Yalu River in Korea, thus bringing the Chinese into that war.

The paper's military expert described the first period after Pearl Harbor as one of *"almost unbroken disaster."* However, he took heart in the impressive re-gathering of American strength, a process culminating in the battles of the Coral Sea, at Midway, and in the Aleutians.

Still reporting from Washington before his assignment across the Atlantic, Watson continued to follow the course of war in North Africa—his first destination. His admiration for the military genius of German General Erwin Rommel, the nemesis of the British Eighth Army, was unstinting. He credited Rommel with showing that air power was *"a principal rather than an auxiliary force in driving British armies."* [June 24, 1942] Anticipating what lay ahead, Watson warned *"it is Rommel or his successors whom our own growing tank force will have to meet on some terrain of the future. For desert warfare, he is the best teacher the war has produced."*

On Sunday, July 7, 1942, *The Sun* began featuring front-page dispatches from "special correspondents" (or stringers) in its news pages. Heretofore, the newspaper had based its war coverage chiefly on reports of the Associated Press, *The New York Times*, *New York Herald Tribune*, and *Chicago Tribune*. Submissions from the paper's London Bureau were few and far between—mostly pickups from *The Manchester Guardian*. Only later, after American troops were committed to battle, did *The Sun* send its reporters into the fields and the trenches, the air and the sea.

CHAPTER 5

Lone Pine
Tragedy

Before Lee McCardell joined Mark Watson in Europe, he took on two major stateside assignments: First, reporting on the immense buildup of West Coast industry after the United States plunged into war. Second, gauging the extent of post–Pearl Harbor jitters that led federal and state authorities to strip 110,000 Japanese-Americans of their homes and occupations and send them to bleak concentration camps.

If it was the intent of Baltimore editors to give priority to the first mission, they underestimated the compassion and humanity McCardell brought to his work. He dutifully described an acres-long aircraft plant that outshone a Barnum and Bailey circus. He observed the massive entry of women into jobs heretofore reserved to men.

But it was the plight of Japanese-Americans, at the time widely feared as a potential fifth column, that drew McCardell's attention long before most Americans realized these fellow citizens were being treated shamefully—and unconstitutionally. Even President Roosevelt and California Governor Earl Warren (later Chief Justice of the United States) blotted their records by giving in to the hysteria. McCardell reported [March 16, 1942] how Californians were pressing the federal government to round up Japanese-Americans and *"get 'em out,"* a mindset fostered by the San Francisco office of the FBI. That bureau alleged its agents had found firearms, signal flags, shortwave radio transmitters, and ammunition in their raids on Japanese homes and establishments. *"We've grabbed so much stuff,"* the local FBI chief told McCardell, *"that we haven't attempted to list all of it."* Such scare talk was aimed at Japanese residents who, in the opinion of white Californians, were both *"notoriously law-abiding"* and *"clannish."*

Long before there was any thought of reparations for the economic damage inflicted on the Japanese community, McCardell quoted a Japanese-American citizen named Mike Masaoka, [March 18, 1942] as saying that produce markets in San Francisco, with revenues of $5 million to $6 million year, had to be *"sold out"* for only $5,000 or $6,000 apiece. *"Anything to get away,"* Masaoka told the Baltimore reporter. *"We've been boycotted. Our savings have been completed (sic). They're meager."* McCardell next reported from Los Angeles that a *"floodtide of liquidation"* had engulfed Little Tokyo—the vortex of all Japanese commerce and culture in southern California [April 2, 1942]. Businessmen went broke and sold out at fire-sale prices under the impact of an 8 p.m. deadline to sell their produce each day at harvest time.

More and more Japanese-Americans were being ordered to railroad stations to begin their journeys into remote areas. Their destinations were not death camps of the Nazi variety, but they were places of imposed exile and idleness under strange and harsh conditions.

In a dispatch datelined Lone Pine, California, [March 28, 1942] McCardell told of a mountain scene where thousands of Japanese residents, many of them U.S. citizens, were being sent as part of a massive relocation campaign: *"The grass up here, such as it is, shows no tinge of green. The flowers that bloom in the spring in the lower valleys rarely bloom at all up here. Within a week the farmers in the Salinas Valley will be harvesting the first of their lettuce crop. They are thinning their sugar beets now. But there are no lettuce fields here in the Owens Valley, no sugar beet plants, only dull brownish-gray flats tufted with sagebrush and stretching away to the bare feet of the High Sierras. The mountains to the west show signs of reluctant life. You see fences for the first time in 200 miles around coarse pasture land. The wind, whistling down the valley, tosses the leafless branches of locust and poplar trees along the road."*

In this kind of bleak environment, thousands of Japanese forced from their homes and businesses were settled in Manzanar, a ghost town suddenly sprung to life. *"When complete, the new Manzanar will be a town of CCC barracks, one-story wooden buildings with tar-papered gabled roofs, barn doors and sliding windows. Patrolling the entire area is a provost guard of U.S. infantry. You have to have a pass to enter. American-born Japanese admitted to the camp as evacuees might obtain permission to leave but if they did they could not return. Once an alien Japanese passes in through that line of soldiers, he stays there."*

Baltimore Sun readers were thus given a taste of the McCardell copy that would vividly describe the European war in the next three years—years in which he would be away from his wife and three daughters, years when his stories would reflect the chill of wet, muddy trenches, the hilarity of military SNAFUS, the threat of instant death or injury to anyone, including reporters, on the front lines. He was one of four American newsmen who observed the Normandy beaches from the air on D-Day. He was the first, or surely one of the first, American reporters to enter re-occupied Paris. He defied censors, grieved for doughboys, listed the names of Maryland soldiers wherever he went, wrote his children a letter published on *"Black Christmas"* during the Battle of the Bulge and, after the German surrender, traveled 4,000 miles throughout Europe seeking information about missing Americans for anxious folks back home.

McCardell was covering General George Patton's Third Army during the depths of winter 1944–1945, when a BBC commentator broadcast the following: *"Lee McCardell is terrific—first into Metz, first in St. Avid, first into Saurlauten and one learned (not from him) that he was first into Paris and the only reporter to get into Fort Driant, and, all the same way, inquiring quietly after Marylanders and appearing not to notice the war."* D-Day was not McCardell's introduction to the mud and blood of warfare. His first battle was one of the longest and fiercest in the entire war—the yard-by-yard winter campaign to break through the German chokepoint at Monte Cassino on the road to Rome. Somehow he found the time to write an unpublished piece, "How to be a War Correspondent" that one of his grandchildren discovered decades later (2007) in the proverbial box in the attic. *"I suppose every war correspondent has to go through his first battle,"* he wrote to his homefolks. *"I went through mine on February 2, 1944, at Cassino in Italy. Because it was my first battle, anything I wrote about it was bound to be more or less personal, and I put the writing off for four days. I had been living at the front with the men who fought the battle. It was their battle, not mine.*

"I had been trained and seasoned for this as much as many of the men who did the fighting. But as a spectator I felt slightly indecent writing about my personal reactions. I had walked across the battlefield before all the wounded had been carried back, before the dead had been picked up. Who was I to write about another's Armageddon? It looked and sounded to me like the end of the world. I was fascinated. Toward the end, when the Germans began air bursts over the face of my hill, I was scared silly. Now (the artillery) opened up with a roll of thunder, the shells slamming and crashing into the town of Cassino which lay ahead, below us. Clouds of dust and gray smoke rose from the town, and a west wind blowing gently around the foot of Mount Cassino carried a haze across the valley like a streaming scarf. The famous old Benedictine Monastery of Mount Cassino remained silent, serene and majestic as God during the bombardment. I wondered if any Benedictine brothers were still up there. If they were I wondered what they were doing. Praying for the souls in the town below that was being methodically blasted from under their eyes?"

McCardell witnessed a U.S. tank being hit by German fire. *"Terrified but inquisitive, I crawled to the edge of the terrace on my belly and looked over. Jesus Christ have mercy on the poor guys inside— burning up alive if any had survived the hit. We probably knew that crew if they were members of the battalion we had followed the last few days."*

What is striking about this letter is its resemblance in tone to the stories he wrote for the newspaper during his three years in Europe. Of all *The Sun's* correspondents, McCardell was the most intimate. Intimate with his readers in conveying the emotions he felt. Intimate with the soldiers he followed into battle as he watched their tangle with death. Intimate and straightforward with his family back in the States, as this letter demonstrates. Journalistic distance was not for him.

A month later, after he had followed American boys in their drive to capture Cherbourg and then had been assigned temporarily to the Army Air Force, he wrote to a friend in Baltimore that he was glad to be back with the infantry. *"I'll always be a foot soldier, earthbound, and with mud in my ears. It is good to get where soldiers march and gun trucks roll."*

Following the war, this gifted newspaperman was appointed city editor and later assistant managing editor of *The Evening Sun*, an elevation that must have brought him more income but denied his readers the joy of reading his copy. But not always. He served as chief of the London and the Rome Bureaus of *The Sun*, the latter assignment giving him an opportunity to cover the Algerian revolt in 1958. Somehow, and typically, he made it through the French lines to cover the Arab side of the war. This coup stirred memories of the 1948 Democratic National Convention, when he vaulted police lines to cover a walkout by Dixiecrats whom he followed to Birmingham, Alabama, for their rump convention. He received honorable mention for the Pulitzer Prize in 1933 for his coverage of the Bonus March on Washington.

Lee McCardell was born in Frederick, Maryland, in 1901 and remained interested and loyal to his hometown. His first story stateside after the European war was a feature on Frederick. Having grown up in the shadow of Braddock Heights, he wrote a well-received biography of *"ill-starred"* General Edward Braddock, the British officer who ignored the advice of young George Washington and fell, mortally wounded, in a French and Indian ambush. Lee McCardell died in Baltimore in 1963. Accolades poured in not only from his colleagues but from *Sun* readers. Allan H. Burns Jr., of Cockeysville, wrote that McCardell had used his name in a story about the liberation of a Nazi concentration camp where he was a prisoner. The newspaper quickly notified his parents. *"Eighteen years have passed since that day,"* he wrote. Describing McCardell as *"one of the world's great reporters,"* Burns said *"his passing leaves The Sun a desk which can never be filled and it leaves me the memory of a kindness which I shall never forget."*

In a reminiscence [Oct. 6, 1957] of the Cassino campaign, McCardell set parameters for himself that are quite applicable to eyewitness accounts in this book: *"Every man who goes to war fights his own battle. He sees only what takes place around him."* *Sun* reporters brought the war up closest to their readers when they described *"what takes place around* (them)."

CHAPTER 6

Watson and McCardell Overseas

As a brand-new American army exchanged broomsticks for rifles during a massive, urgent training effort coast to coast, Mark Watson and Lee McCardell journeyed to Britain in February 1943 for assignments that ended only when Nazi Germany toppled almost three blood-soaked years later.

Early March of 1943 found McCardell "Somewhere in Scotland" [March 4, 1943] there to watch American recruits turned into elite Rangers. *"Here amid the haunting beauty of the Highlands, at a cold, wet mountain camp where British commando troops are trained, a battalion of American Rangers commanded by Major Randolph Millholland of Cumberland, Md., is following an agenda reserved for hard-hitting assault troops.*

"They wade mountain streams swollen by runoff from snow-powdered summits surrounding the camp. They scale hundred-foot rock cliffs. They wriggle on their bellies and backs under barbed wire and through quagmires while crack-shot British instructors pour machine-gun fire over their heads and under their feet. The Rangers dash from cover to cover on treacherous hillsides and over rugged battle courses. Wringing wet and covered with Highland peat-moss mud, the trainees finished their ten-hour demonstration reasonably fresh and grinning, proud of their endurance."

War in the trenches was still ahead of them. So McCardell and Watson focused on the Allied air war then gathering momentum against Germany. Watching Flying Fortresses taking off from an unidentified British airfield, McCardell wrote: *"There is tension when the Forts fly away, while they are on the wing out of sight, and when they come swooping home from across the Channel. Some of them come back badly shot up. Some never come back."* [Feb. 7, 1943] Watson put it this way: *"It is awesome to stand in the open air by night and hear the roll of motors in steady waves as a succession of invisible British night bombers rolls overhead on the way to Nazi Germany. The beauty of the night is in strange contrast with the sternness of the task in which unseen armadas are bent."* [July 1, 1943]

Sun publisher Paul Patterson, who accompanied Watson to London, noticed among the British [June 30, 1943] *"a serenity, a confidence born of a feeling that the situation is fully under control"*—this in contrast to his remark that London was "quivering" during the Blitz two years earlier. He urged other publishers to visit Britain. But Watson, despite his feeling that the tide of war had turned, elected to emphasize *"certain undeniable facts: No early victory is anticipated by military chiefs here. It is time that one fact be fully understood. British and American planes have knocked out many Nazi fighter planes but, contrary to the common delusion, we are not yet destroying as many a month as Nazi factories are producing a month."* Only after the war did Allied intelligence discover that German aircraft production actually increased to the very end of the war, despite massive American-British strategic bombing. What really undercut the potency of the Luftwaffe as well as the Japanese air forces was a diminishing supply of well-trained pilots. Each flier lost to the Axis powers was irreplaceable.

By the end of the following month [July 24, 1943] Watson was reporting from Allied headquarters in North Africa, a location where green U.S. troops fighting under a confused command structure had suffered setbacks at Kasserine Pass and in other battles against hardened German veterans who had mastered desert fighting. Only sheer Allied manpower succeeded in throwing enemy forces out of Tunisia.

On July 10, 1943 came the invasion of Sicily, where Watson was to witness actual fighting for the first time since World War I. The Allied amphibious landings were hotly contested but ultimately successful. Watson described a visit to Licata, a small Sicilian port that had been the easiest of all the enemy landing sites encountered by Allied invading forces. *"The Castle of San Angelo, from whose tower the first Ameri-*

can attack party had unfurled its flag (two weeks earlier), *has resumed its calm medieval demeanor. The town's walled road leading down to the sea, along which had so recently trooped the first columns of quite unreluctant Italian prisoners, was again deserted, drowsing in bright sunlight."* [July 25, 1943]

Even before the Italians ousted Mussolini only to suffer German occupation, Watson discerned the Italians' aversion to the war being fought on their own territory. *"We have seen Allied warships steam up against Italy's shores without shaming so much as a single Italian motor boat into a single desperate effort to launch one torpedo for defense of the land,"* he wrote [July 27, 1943]. *"The Italian army, which lost its best division in Africa and, apparently, its heart as well, has made only a feeble defense of Sicily. It is most unlikely that the presumptive oozing away of Italian zeal will spread to German troops."*

Citing the battle for Sicily as an example of using air power *"on the basis of equality,"* the military correspondent was cautious. Air power's *"origins are too recent"* and its operations *"too experimental. Extremely important military figures"* are unconvinced that *"any war can be won, or nearly won, by air power alone"*—this despite the contrary belief of *"numerous leading aviators."* Thus, he cited a debate in the high command that remained unsettled when World War II came to an end. *"Never in all history has any single weapon served as the one indispensable weapon. If we become committed too fully on air power alone, the alert enemy will seize the opportunity to hit us on land and sea by new techniques."*

Thursday, August 12, 1943, became a banner day in increasing staff coverage of World War II. A five-column headline spread across the front page above the fold unveiled the paper's first eyewitness dispatch from an actual battlefield. Watson began his landmark story quietly by describing history's grip on the picturesque Sicilian landscape. By his second paragraph, however, the war took over in harrowing detail. *"One flies past the ruins of medieval castles—some of them ruined more thoroughly by last month's shells than by the normal deterioration of a thousand previous Julys."*

Soon he described what he saw in Sicily: its beauty, its village traditions, its scarred battlefields blighted by the rancid aftereffects of war.

"The air is no longer drenched with geranium blooms, but now with all the stenches of a war theater, where battle has lately raged and where sanitary squads have not yet had time to clear away and bury all the tragic residue of conflict. The blinding heat does not help greatly by day and even the night's faint breezes are found as one remembers them along the Aisne and Marne and Meuse."

Before the Second World War was over, Mark Watson would again be sniffing the breezes of the Aisne, the Marne, and the Meuse. At age fifty-five, he was the "old man" of *The Sun*'s war team, providing constant analysis, diving into ditches, and indulging his memories for his readers back home.

Continuing his narrative of his day in Sicilian battle, Watson was in full flow: *"We wished to be upon a nearby hill before daylight to watch a considerable attack by coordinated forces scheduled at dawn. I awoke to the sound of gunfire. The explosions stopped for a time. Wham, wham, wham, wham—down smacks another enemy salvo. Now comes another salvo so close that a few pebbles come over us in a light shower.*

"At length a faint light touched the horizon and we scrambled to our feet. What we hoped to see would be starting soon. Before leaving division headquarters the previous evening we had been informed that the progress of American troops had been held here by a new German defensive line. The aim in this day's particular enterprise was to plaster every known enemy position with a torrent of steel and heavy explosives. To blind the enemy, the chief reliance would be on smoke clouds. Then, in perfect timing, would come heavy bombardment by our planes and artillery, and by long-range destruction from our naval support. Then our infantry was to move out on an exact schedule for a difficult job of mountain fighting. Few in America can know how immensely difficult has been the task, how tedious and perilous. We lunge ahead by blood, sweat and tears and with an uncommonly high percentage of blood in the total. No collapse ever comes save as we earn it.

"Today's plan is for hammering away on a front of several miles to force a crack of a few hundred yards. From a lofty aerie a vast panorama is visible. Below and beyond us we see at last a few tiny figures creeping forward and know that certain elements of our infantry are

advancing. Then, suddenly we are caught off guard. What movement by us, if any, the enemy had detected we could not know, but we all hear a much louder scream just overhead and then a mighty blast in mid-air a few rods away. Every man dropped flat. Several took to prepared foxholes.

"I chose a clump of stunted cork trees, into which I dove with two companions. Twice we started back to our old position only to be driven below again. From nearby foxholes, we all moved back to the crest to see what had happened. It was not a pleasant sight. A hasty call went out for medical troops. Our small incident on the hill was just routine."

Watson's eyewitness account of battle, one that would be followed by many, many more *Sun* exclusives, illustrated for the careful reader two key elements of ground war: One was the ever-present uncertainty that the most exacting plans could be carried out, an uncertainty spelling life and death for tens of thousands of soldiers. The other was that frontline newsmen always risked being drawn directly into the line of fire or of incoming shells no matter how high and protected are the *"aeries"* from which they watch the tide of battle.

Another danger for reporters lay in the public relations units of all military commands. The task of the PR officers was to make their leaders look good, to cover up mistakes and setbacks that threaten all military operations, to use deception and obfuscation and censorship to mislead the press. In a controversial war (Vietnam and Iraq) tension between the armed forces and the press is palpable and predictable. But even when the public is fervently behind the national cause, as was the case in World War II, reporters had every reason to be wary. Sometimes correspondents were duped, even the militarily savvy like Mark Watson.

Thus, in an atmosphere of relief after Nazi troops were finally expelled from Sicily, Watson praised *"the smoothness and precision"* and the *"excellent planning, excellent timing and excellent performance"* of Allied forces [Sept. 2, 1943]. Historians with later access to memoirs, letters, and official histories judged otherwise, especially regarding the Anglo-American failure to cut off the escape of enemy armies at Messina, just across the water from Italy itself. This blunder—partly the result of a race between U.S and British forces to get to Messina first—gave the Germans an unwelcome opportunity to fight on and on in the mountains of Italy.

The first task of the Italian campaign required Allied amphibious landings near the foot of the long mountainous peninsula. For the Americans, their fiercely opposed attack at Salerno initially threatened disaster and even being thrown back into the sea. It was a hard-earned experience that proved valuable on the beaches of Normandy nine months later.

Watson's reporting, like the dispatches of other correspondents for single newspapers, had to yield pride of place at first to wire service coverage. His first story [Sept. 13, 1943] put a positive slant to the battle situation: *"Extremely heavy bombarment by our air and naval forces and excellent work by our anti-tank artillery today put an abrupt end to the enemy counter-thrusts against our narrow beach-head south of Salerno.*

"It does not appear we yet have reoccupied certain areas from which enemy tanks ejected us yesterday but the bombardment has battered the enemy so hard that the areas may be considered neutralized temporarily. American airmen struck heavily deep in enemy territory as well as at nearby positions. The air aid gave welcome relief to infantry men who have been fighting for five days now."

With some relief, he reported a day later that *"the situation is more cheerful"* though U.S. progress away from the landing beaches was not nearly so fast (as in Sicily). *"That is due to our meeting with extremely quarrelsome Nazi divisions at the outset."*

Watson's next task was to explain why Salerno was so difficult. *"The enemy has the advantage of interior lines so he can not only move troops from one front to another more easily and quickly than we but can do so without our knowledge."* [Sept. 17, 1943] Although American air domination has been a problem for the Germans, *"our own Fifth Army is still pinned to a painfully narrow beach area where the main transport routes are frequently under enemy artillery fire. He also has the advantage of existing supply dumps. We on the other hand, must transport all supplies by sea and over beaches where we are far from secure from enemy bombing."*

Watson minced no words about the prowess of the Nazi military machine once the Allied campaign began in Italy with the amphibious invasion at Salerno. Described as *"The Sun* Military Correspondent Representing the Combined American Press,"* Watson warned that *"German troops facing the British and American forces, far from being beaten, remain very tough and eager for a fight without the aid of its former ally."* Two days later he wrote that the battle at Salerno showed *"Nazi troops remain the best trained and fiercest fighters anyone wishes to meet, with professional leadership extraordinarily adept at defense and delaying actions, interspersed with bold counter-assaults when least expected."* This analysis, written in the heat of war, proved to be right on the mark, not only for the duration of the war but in military judgments issued for decades afterward. He recalled finding the German *"a resourceful defensive fighter in 1918 even when defeat was imminent."*

Watson, ever eager for eyewitness, described the Salerno battle scene that he watched aboard a transport carrying troops to the beachhead: [Sept. 18, 1943] *"Two bombs exploded harmlessly at a distance. The third whistled so close astern that we instinctively ducked and braced ourselves. The shock never came, for that single well-ticketed bomb failed to explode. It was an impressive demonstration of many things, including luck, destiny or providential protection, depending on your brand of theology."*

In describing an enemy night aerial attack he witnessed, Watson said it had outshone in *"spectacular splendor"* anything he had seen in World War I. As enemy planes drew near, *"whole night heavens are illuminated by streams of tracer bullets, explosive shells bursting in profusion, the brilliant but short-lived burst of enemy bombs striking the surface of earth or water and very often the long continued blaze of parachute flares which the enemy drops in order to illuminate the area where his second wave of planes will seek to bomb.*

"To this stupendous spectacle, all the boom and roar and rattle of all the weapons, at a distance or near at hand, as the enemy formation departs or approaches one's own situation, you acquire some faint idea of the manner in which even a modest enemy air raid overwhelms eye and ear alike."

After Salerno, Watson went on to witness the capture of Naples, asserting it had come with *"surprising suddenness and completeness."* [Oct. 4, 1943] He then produced a vivid and sometimes rollicking account of what he saw as his jeep approached and entered the strategic metropolis. Excerpts follow:

"I was fascinated by the extraordinary spectacle of our advancing tanks and troops and carriers roaring down the main road to Naples, lurching over bomb craters and around hills of debris from houses in total ruin. Old men, women and middle-aged persons, children, dogs and donkeys surged over the rubble-strewn sidewalks in such numbers that we repeatedly slowed the jeep to avoid striking them. This certainly was the most extraordinary approach to a nearby battle in my experience. The closer we came to Naples' City Hall, the prettier and better dressed and higher spirited the girls became and, from time to time, I heard from the driver a slightly suppressed whistle and an eloquent murmur of 'Oh, did you see that one?'

"We rolled through Torre Annunziata where we had been held up only the day before by persistent German fire. We passed a little garden wall from the top of which we had previously stared over into German sniper positions while our infantry patrols crawled up a ravine to catch the snipers from the flank. Not yet had we heard anything that sounded like sound opposition. Not yet had we seen a single enemy plane. Our earlier doubts and the high command's caution were now gone. We were on our way into Naples in a matter of minutes. The highway was lined with exuberant people. Some of the prettiest girls I ever expect to see came running with flowers and bouquets, some with great armfuls of daisies."

This happy scene abruptly ended as Watson arrived at a waterfront devoid of people but brimful of havoc. *"Not a single pier examined was intact. Warehouses were blasted to ruin. Ships were sunk or capsized. Lofty buildings of the whole maritime district were in ruins. This might have been as completely a dead city as Pompeii itself.*

"We drove perhaps a block and came upon a pitiful procession of an old woman and a little boy being carried to a dressing station for treatment of wounds received from bombs just fallen. Two other victims were motionless and apparently dead.

"As we were leaving the center of Naples, we saw the tall figure of General Mark W. Clark, making his entry which his troops had fought hard to present to him. It was pleasant to see that sort of entry without ceremony and outriders. Behind him rolled the first large contingent of our assault troops. All of them looked tough and cheerful and confident. They should. Naples was won and the first big prize of the Italian campaign is ours."

Such words carry a sorry burden for readers who know what lay in the future for these tough, cheerful, confident soldiers: Defeat at the Rapido River; mud, snow, cold, and death on the slopes of Mount Cassino; chaos at the Anzio beaches. The triumphant capture of Rome, alas, brought no closure. The Italian campaign stretched on and on until the end of the war.

Little did the American Fifth Army know what it was getting into when Mark Watson reported in the October 16, 1943 issue of *The Sun* that *"our long-expected crossing of the Volturno River was at last underway."* It started at 1 a.m. on what Watson described as an *"extraordinarily luminous night"* with a full moon and winds with bite whipping up heavy seas in the Bay of Naples.

"Almost in unison, batteries of light and heavy artillery turned loose, and the air was filled with a tumult echoing and rebounding from the hills. Considerable elements of our infantry had made a crossing by multiple means. Some made the crossing in the most primitive fashion of all. They forded the stream holding their rifles well above the current and making the fastest time possible to get out of this cold mountain water.

"By the time daylight permitted us to see what was going on at the river itself, it also permitted German observers the same privilege. Not all of the evidence of gunfire is that the enemy is using his batteries most skillfully against us. It is an extraordinary thing to see one of our artillery observers soaring about in his little plane directly over the target, watching where our shells fall and sending back corrections for their ensuing salvos. The bridgehead usually must be widened considerably before tanks can be risked."

Two days later a Watson report [Oct. 18, 1943] filled with optimism asserted that *"the battle of the Volturno is now assumed a victory."* A bridgehead across the river had been firmly established. *"In so strong a defensive position as this Volturno, (the enemy) might have held us longer. We are very fortunate that he did not. Things now look promising for further advances all along the front."*

Watson concluded his report, however, with prescient words of caution. *"We must count on running into the enemy in considerable force not many miles to the north. He clearly is not going to stand long enough in one place to risk envelopment and capture of large units of his army. He presumably aims to hold as long as possible and then fall back to the next defense line, destroying as he goes. Even in defeat, the Jerry is permanently a tough fellow."*

While Watson was reporting the beginning of the long, hard crawl up the mountainous spine of Italy, Tom O'Neill wrote a story [Oct. 22, 1943] about a typical air raid on London. *"An air raid is largely sound. First the far-away ululation of the sirens as the raiders cross the coast, a howl that grows steadily closer until the moment when the city is enveloped by the wail.*

"Then, all together, the off-beat drone of the bombers in the black, the clatter of feet as fire watchers race up the stairs to the roof, the shattering bark of the nearest anti-aircraft guns and the soft roll of the others in the distance.

"If the raiders get through the curtain of fire raised against them, the climax comes in a mighty 'krhrummmm,' which is a high-explosive bomb fulfilling its deadly mission.

"Searchlight fingers probe the darkness, shells burst in Roman candle splendor, flares hover with a ghostly glow, and a myriad of miniature crosses of red flash for an instant like fireflies. A searchlight catches a plane. The German twists and dives in search of darkness. As he escapes beyond the range of the searchlights, fighters are in hot pursuit. He must be a faster Nazi than anyone believes if he is ever to get back to Germany."

In wry contrast, O'Neill noted how raid-wise Londoners took this bombing in stride. Crowds surged through Piccadilly Circus. Diners rushed from restaurants to sidewalks to watch the show. Bus lines and taxis ran as usual, as did underground trains. Then quiet. Rain began to fall. Finally, the steady blast of the signal meant the raiders had passed.

"In the morning, the authorities announce the score: Bombers over London, fewer than a dozen; bombers downed, two; civilian casualties, 'a number.' Everybody agrees it wasn't much."

Back in Italy, Watson filed a report [Oct. 25, 1943] on an interview with Marshal Pietro Badoglio, the former army chief who became prime minister with the fall of Mussolini. Badoglio told Watson and reporters from the London *Times* and *New York Times* that Mussolini had committed his country to war without the consent or even knowledge of his military chiefs. *"It was an appalling record of cold-blooded decision to buy power with Italian blood,"* Watson commented. The new prime minister vowed to leave office once hostilities ceased. He and his interlocutors had no means to know that Italy would be embroiled in war under German occupation to within a week of the Nazi government's collapse.

Meanwhile, from a U.S. bomber station in England, Lee McCardell put a light touch on a story about well-decorated U.S. bombers flying over Nazi-held Europe. "Ein Pfennig *for the thoughts of a Luftwaffe pilot who, barreling into a Flying Fortress formation, has time to notice the airborne art display on the nose of almost every bomber. He sees women and more women, apparently happy and content in various stages of undress—if he has time to look."*

McCardell reported that gunners aboard planes flying from the base he was visiting had shot down almost two hundred German fighters in the last few months. *"But such missions can be deadly for the bombers as well. Reason enough to give soldier-artists an opportunity to develop their skills."*

CHAPTER 7

McCardell Reports
The Air War

Of all *Baltimore Sun* war correspondents, Lee McCardell was by far the most explicit in telling readers what his job was like. They learned over the course of the conflict how worrisome it was for a reporter to watch airmen take off on flights from which they might never come back, how dangerous it was to be on front-line patrols, how irksome were the politicians and media big shots who treated quick visits as photo-ops or showoff-ops, how senseless or annoying were censors and press officers, and how gratifying it was to witness Allied triumphs or the bravery of soldiers, or to savor his own scoops and escapades. He did so with élan, never querulous, often generous with his innermost thoughts, connecting with readers as only candor can. An early example of the McCardell approach appeared on November 11, 1943, when he was stationed in England covering the air war.

"*Bizarre characteristics of this war don't tell the real story, particularly when a communiqué says: 'From this operation sixty bombers and two fighters are missing.' When people back home occasionally complain that war news is sugar-coated and slanted by censorship, it sometimes occurs to correspondents that we ourselves are not altogether blameless, that the conventional reportorial technique in which we have been trained may not be adapted to adequate war correspondence.*

"*No exercise of that technique can faithfully portray the drawn-out, continuous strain to which bomber crews and fighter pilots are subjected. This nervous anxiety is all the more pronounced because flyers feel it most when on the ground between missions at bomber bases,* relatively removed and safe from ordinary hazards of war. Awed by the speed and vastness of the air offensive and handicapped by lack of an adequate communications system in a country properly geared to fight the war first and talk about it later, we rush from airfield to airfield hurriedly seeking the kind of information reporters always have been trained to seek—names, pictures, addresses, incidents, factual detail.

"Our notes assembled, we are faced with the competitive task of transmitting, then fast work at high speed to get our copy through the hands of over-worked press censors who, while sensitive to our difficulties, often fail to understand that a time differential of five hours in our favor does not prevent early editions from going to bed early.

"It is true we can't write all we hear and know and see. We cannot answer the questions uppermost in the minds of many back home. The army believes that, except in special cases, there are considerations of policy and security which make quick detailed answers inadvisable. Thus a correspondent fully aware of the terrible suspense he has helped to create can only pass along the cold words of a communiqué. It is also true that we are forbidden to describe—usually for good reasons—certain unpleasant aspects of bombing missions.

"To allay unnecessary worry at home, correspondents are often willing parties to voluntary editing of their own copy, which does name names and addresses. In this seeming conspiracy of silence a reporter is more likely to be motivated by the quality of mercy than by a desire to sugarcoat the news. Worst of all, it is impossible to be briefly personal and objective, to tell your story fully, because war is a matter of individual life and death and not merely a list of names, general facts and mass figures. We are aware of this.

"The kids who fly these ships are more than names and faces to us. They're guys with whom we have lived and talked and come to like and even love as friends. They're the heroes. We're just the worshippers. But even for us it's a rather weird business, this going to bed at night wondering who'll be here tomorrow night. We're always hopeful that others who don't come back have landed safely somewhere. Sometimes we know they haven't or that the chances are against them. Someone saw their ship blow up in mid-air or counted the men *parachuting to the ground—and found them one short. Even then we tell ourselves they might have counted wrong."*

A Baltimorean who clipped the newspaper and read the above story could, with profit, have given a second look at several McCardell articles that had appeared earlier—articles that reflected some of what the reporter had been writing about.

On May 23, 1943, *"after ten days of the most intensive aerial bombardment of Nazi territory,"* McCardell reported that bomber crews, including many Marylanders, *"are settling down to the grim business of blasting the daylights out of the enemy. The boys from this field who ride the bombers—and many of them are still boys in their early twenties—are doing the job of supermen with less sentiment and better aim, more confidence and a colder determination than understandably enough marked earlier missions. They still go to battle gaily these May mornings. They wave to each other lightheartedly as thundering motors gather speed and lift the ships into the hazy sky."* McCardell mentioned a raid on Wilhelmshaven by a plane named "Maryland My Maryland." *"The pilot and co-pilot were, respectively, Lieutenant Ferdinand Onnen, of 2924 Calvert Street, and Lieutenant Woodrow Wilson, of 504 Harwood Avenue."* (Note the precise local touch.)

"What it meant to be a bombardier on one of these Flying Fortresses was described by Lieutenant Stanley Silverstein of 2906 Allendale Road, a former Forest Park High School ice hockey star: 'German fighters were waiting for us when we reached our rendezvous. If there was one, there were a hundred single or twin-engine jobs. They came in on us from all angles between 11 and 12 o'clock (an attack almost head on and slightly to the left). *My left gun went out of action when the ejector sheared off and my right gun hung fire. There I was in the nose and could not shoot. Twenty millimeter shells knocked out two of our engines. Oil was streaming behind us. It's a wonder we didn't catch fire. Shrapnel also knocked out our radio, cut oxygen tanks and wounded one man on his left side.'"*

As usual, McCardell tracked down Baltimoreans on war duty in Britain. Lieutenant Charles Lane told him of an early mission when enemy flak wounded the pilot of his plane and the squadron commander was injured. *"From his post in the ship's nose, Lane held the stick while the injured major climbed into the unconscious pilot's seat. Lane flew the plane home that day, the major landing her."*

McCardell also wrote of two Maryland airmen who were on dangerous secret missions to photograph targets in Germany. *"The Nazis were puzzled by the ability of the British to obtain quickly photographs of target areas and bomb damage in localities where Nazi airmen had not seen reconnaissance planes."* [Sept. 2, 1943]

What happens when an American or British airman is forced to abandon his plane in the English Channel? In an exacting report [Oct. 10, 1943] McCardell said he has *"an even chance, or better, of being fished out alive. Each pilot is equipped with a parachute, a self-inflating 'Mae West' life belt, an inflatable yellow dinghy, food, water, a collapsible pole with a red signal flag, stoppers to plug leaks, a bailer and paddles to fit on the hands like gloves. If a downed airman is able to send a radio SOS signal giving his coordinates, the British Air-Sea Rescue Service sends out a plane to find him. The search can go on for a long time.*

"It is no easy task to find a little yellow dinghy in a gray expanse of water, even under ideal conditions of bright sunshine and calm sea," McCardell wrote after listing the above inventory. But, he said, *"in July 1943, the service had rescued within fifty hours more than one hundred Allied airmen—plus the occasional German navigator who is 'mighty glad to see his enemies.'"*

The human touch McCardell brought to his coverage came through in a dispatch [Oct. 10, 1943] describing the early morning scene at an Allied bomber base: *"For combat crews, somebody stumbles into their cold, blacked-out Nissen hut with the news that a briefing will be held in an hour's time. They crawl out of their sacks, breakfast and go to a briefing room where Colonel Nye is waiting to show them where they are going. Out in the dispersal area the engines are roaring. The bombers are being warmed up. The crews go out and get aboard. They taxi around the perimeter track to the runway. The waspish Marauders, whose tricycle landing gear keeps them in an airborne position even before they have left the ground, make a graceful getaway. Each spits out a little brown trail of exhaust as it folds up its wheels and climbs at breakneck rush to battle level."*

The correspondent covering the air war had a much different assignment from one covering land battles. He could not be an eyewitness to actual encounters or describe the terrain and weather conditions in which they were fought. He had to depend on interviewing skills that required real empathy with airmen coming back from harrowing missions. Obviously, the "complete correspondent" had to fulfill both assignments. Lee McCardell did so.

CHAPTER 8

Watson and McCardell at Cassino

Foot by foot, yard by yard, the first protracted campaign of the war covered by *Sun* reporters evokes the names of two Italian towns—Cassino and Anzio—on the road from Naples to Rome. Cassino was a choke point that defied capture for more than five months as German troops dug in to a rugged mountain dominated by a thirteenth-century monastery. Anzio was a little seaside resort that Allied amphibious forces seized in the hope it would lead to a breakthrough at Cassino.

Both tactics resulted in bitter battles, some of them disheartening setbacks that lasted far longer than Allied commanders anticipated. The struggle for Cassino turned into a winter horror with soldiers on both sides gripped by mud, ice, snow, unrelenting cold, soaked clothing, trench foot, and supply lines scarcely more than pack-mule trails. Anzio unfolded as a remarkably easy landing that turned into a nightmare as enemy troops from surrounding heights threatened a small, exposed beachhead long doomed to a defensive crouch. Watson, McCardell, and Price Day drew successive assignments to the Cassino-Anzio operation, which started in January and lasted until Rome fell one day before D-Day in Normandy on June 6, 1944.

With weather very much on his mind, McCardell had celebrated his mid-January transfer from wartime London to the *"Promised Land"* of Algiers by exulting over *"warm and white sunshine,"* market place stalls *"heaped with oranges and shell eggs"* and white bread that at first tasted like angel food cake [Jan. 15 and 16, 1944]. Such luxuries would remain unimaginable in Britain for the duration—and its medium-term aftermath.

The reporter's respite was fleeting. Ten days later, he was in Italy, hitchhiking a ride to U.S. Air Force headquarters. On the way he observed *"countless supply depots, billets, camps, trucks, parks, mobile repair shops, ammunition dumps, antiaircraft batteries, radio transmitters, trailers, army gasoline trucks, water trucks, trailer trucks, tractors, ambulances"*—in other words, the long logistics tail of a large military offensive. At the end of the day he found himself assigned to an old Italian hotel where all cots were taken. He laid his sleeping bag on the floor of the hotel's kitchen *"between a cold, fireless stove and a waterless sink."* [Jan. 25, 1944]

McCardell welcomed the news that the Allied landing at Anzio had encountered little resistance but cautioned his Baltimore readers that *"if the Germans run true to form—and the Germans are always true to type—they will counterattack the beachhead."* How right he was. It would take months, not the anticipated few weeks, before Allied forces broke out and raced to Rome.

Datelined *"With the Allied Fifth Army before Cassino,"* McCardell's first frontline dispatch [Feb. 6, 1944] took up from where Mark Watson had left off: *"It rained today, and the cold wind whipped down over the snow-capped mountains into the upper valley of the Rapido River. The marshy floor of that valley, already flooded by the river, was a two-mile morass of black mud as tired, drenched infantrymen of the American army waded across for another attack on Cassino."* It turned out to be a distant objective; the Rapido would become the scene of one of the worst defeats in the war, and a river defying permanent crossing for months.

The *Sun* correspondent described one of the obstacles facing American infantrymen as they attempted to follow tanks (where tanks could operate) in the mountain passes corrugating the Cassino chokepoint. Foot soldiers encountered *"a new type German device, called shoe mines, wooden boxes painted brown, green and yellow that cannot be located by ordinary magnetic mine detectors."* McCardell wrote that the shoe mines *"carry a light charge sufficient to blow off the foot of a doughboy who steps on one."*

His story went on to describe what GIs discovered when they could overrun German pillboxes equipped with food, ammunition, firewood, and armor thick enough to withstand anything other than a direct hit. *"The gunports of these pillboxes look out toward the American lines over deep ditches and broad belts of barbed wire, minefields and flooded marshes. Every tree and bush in their lines of fire had been cut down. By daylight, and by flares at night, their defenders had complete observation across the Rapido Valley. For weeks American artillery had been hammering that barracks area. Today it is almost an absolutely level stretch of wreckage but its pillboxes are still intact."*

Having offered this gloomy description of battle conditions, McCardell followed up the next day [Feb. 7, 1944] with an eyewitness account of American battles against entrenched German opposition: *"With time out for frequent retreats into foxholes and dugouts during an air raid and occasional artillery concentrations, we crossed the upper valley of the Rapido to the barracks. Only when you have crossed this stark muddy valley, pitted with shell holes and dugouts, littered with military equipment and bodies not yet gathered up, do you realize what the American doughboy has done in his effort to capture Cassino.*

"The foxholes hug the edges of fields and irrigation ditches, wherever scanty thorn bushes and a few low hedges promise to screen the occupant from the aim of machine-gun sites on the towering rocky hillsides beyond. Then come the minefields, now white-taped with narrow paths marked 'Safe Lane.' It isn't safe to drive a vehicle over the ground. Rations, water cans and ammunition must be carried across by hand or on pack mules—after dark when there is less danger of enemy observers spotting movement. Beyond the minefields come the marshes and the barbed wire and, finally, the hidden pillboxes. Walking toward all of these, you wonder how any human being could have survived their fire.

"When at last you climb the hill to the pillboxes and look back across the death valley, you know beyond a shadow of a doubt that the supermen are the ones who came across first, not those who manned the guns to shoot them down. The face of that hill, worked on for weeks by American artillery, looks like it had suffered a major earthquake. And once again the war had tossed up a strange assortment

of debris—discarded German military equipment, smashed medical chests, Singer sewing machines, a 'Snow White' record album."

Two days later [Feb. 9, 1944], McCardell reported a lowering of immediate Allied objectives. He asserted that *"the battle for Cassino to open the road to Rome has now become a battle for Mount Cassino, a 1,500-foot peak on which stands the famous old yellowed stone Benedictine monastery."* American forces had been told not to fire on the ancient building, a stance later rescinded because of suspicions that the Germans had established an observation post there. (The abbot later denied it.)

On February 11, the correspondent reported the Allies had been put on the defensive after advancing within a thousand yards of the monastery. Stalemate was confirmed. This led four days later to one of the most controversial Allied actions of the entire war. U.S. bombers blasted the thirteenth-century monastery to rubble—rubble that made it easier for Germans to defend and allowed them, indeed, to establish the type of observation site the Allies dreaded. It was a *"terrifying spectacle,"* McCardell reported in the next day's edition of his newspaper, one in which *"red bursts of the bombs created fountains of black smoke"* as in a Hollywood production.

A subsequent McCardell dispatch [March 3, 1944] ended on a note of frustration. *"When will we take Cassino—when will we clear it?"* he asked. *"Nobody here will venture a guess. Tomorrow? It's not likely. Day after? We might. Next week? Maybe? The Germans will undoubtedly put up a stubborn rear-guard fight as they withdraw up the Liri Valley to their next line of mountain defenses."* Had anyone told McCardell his suggested timetables would prove overly optimistic, he no doubt would have been even more disheartened.

"It seemed incredible that anyone could survive the terrific concentrations of artillery our batteries poured into the ruins of Cassino, which now bears a closer resemblance to a public dump than to a town," he wrote. *"That portion of Cassino which lay at our feet was a complete shambles of masonry. We've seen a good many ruins but those of Cassino are the worst."* The bloody month ended as it began—in deadlock. McCardell observed that *"newspaper correspondents here exhausted their vocabularies in an effort to pay adequate*

tribute to soldiers waging arduous mountain warfare for which they were neither trained, conditioned nor equipped."

All in all, it took four offensives, one each in January, February, March, and May, with terrible casualties to exhausted armies on both sides, before Allied forces broke through the Nazis' Gustav Line. After linking up with troops at Anzio, the Allies at last could resume their drive on Rome.

From Washington, Mark Watson had ever so subtly suggested the drive northward from Naples did not make *"good sense,"* a judgment subsequently supported by military historians who held that the capture of Naples would have been enough. *"The Italian campaign to date has effectively cleared the Mediterranean for our traffic to the Middle East, which was not the case before,"* he wrote [Feb. 13, 1944]. *"It has driven Italy from the war, given us remnants of the Italian fleet for our use and many harbor installations—notably the indispensable port of Naples. It has established for us a series of impregnable air bases in easy range of occupied France and Yugoslavia and in reasonable range of Germany."*

Significantly absent from Watson's list was any mention of the Cassino offensive, which he had personally seen prior to passing the baton to McCardell. *"Great land victories, which smash enemy armies, are likely to need space greater than Italian soil offers,"* he contended. *"The Italian campaign cannot do too much itself. Our real strength must be and should be conserved for other and more important fronts."* He obviously had the coming invasion of northern Europe in mind.

Watson, with his understanding of the hard decisions the high command had to make, said it was important for civilian Americans to understand that in war gambles have to be taken. *"Generals who do not risk their men and themselves do not win battles. If we maintain our grip on Anzio and enable our main forces to break through the lines at Cassino our original hope will be fulfilled and the risk of* (the Anzio) *landing fully justified."*

Watson's was a remarkable and subtle analysis issued in the heat and fog of war. While warning against *"Monday morning quarter-backing,"* he did a little himself. Distancing himself from then-current

Italian strategies, he defended the right of military authorities to take on such gambles.

For McCardell, his concern was not overall strategy but life or death tactics at Cassino and Anzio. In a story [March 6, 1944] he told of an infantry battalion dug in on one of the seemingly endless steep hills that creased murderous terrain. With Private John Lattimore, of Philadelphia, as driver, the jeep *"bounded us over and splashed us through the roughest, muddiest, wickedest stretch of road we have met in Italy. He (Lattimore) swam his jeep, pitching and tossing, through water two feet deep. He rode the muddy crests of ruts three feet high. He clung to the steering wheel like a man beset with 17 Japanese wrestlers. With a grinding crash, the jeep bellied up on a rock. We waded the rest of the way to a double-wall tent sandbagged and dug into the brow of the next hill."* One of the seven occupants told him: *"'When the weather's clear we may be under enemy observation but we think we're fairly safe. We've got a little defilade and they're not likely to hit us unless they drop one right on top of us.'"*

One of McCardell's next reports [March 15, 1944] found him at the Anzio beachhead, having got there by plane because Allied forces had fatefully failed thus far to link up with units trying to get through the Cassino mountains. He described the Italian farmland below his plane: *"Little white farmhouses and village clusters of red tiled roof dot the campagna. In its green fields herds of cattle, sheep and goats gaze serenely, indifferent to the shells that arc above them and burst in black and white smoke puffs further on.*

"We landed within what is left of Anzio's stone breakwater. Sunken hulks, shattered buildings, shellfire and swarms of soldiers—all were earmarks of war, but there was a slightly nostalgic atmosphere about the place, something of the same feeling you have in arriving at Ocean City, Maryland, out of season. Even in the ruins of war, walking along waterfront streets, strewn underfoot with picture postcards from bombed out souvenir shops, you missed the summer vacationists who normally should be part of this scene."

Turning later to the war at the borders of the beachhead, McCardell described a scene in which *"light, rippling ack-ack strings interlacing beads of light fire across the night sky (and) larger crashing guns spray the darkness with white shell bursts."* Noting how correspondents scrambled to cellar safety during a German air raid, he wrote: *"Don't get the idea we're brave. We're not. We're badly frightened and close to panic when a close barrage blows open latched shutters and jars. Creeping out by morning light, we thank God for having seen us through another night."*

McCardell held that the Italian campaign had taught the Americans *"an outstanding lesson"*—war will not be won by air power alone. *"At Cassino our tactical air force has enjoyed a free hand, bombing at will, when weather permitted, without the slightest hindrance by enemy planes or flak. But Cassino still holds, an obvious monument to the fact that the finest bombers in the world, manned by the best-trained troops, cannot blast the Germans out of steel pillboxes, concrete bunkers or self-propelled guns fired from concealed positions. The job calls for infantry, assault troops armed with hand grenades, bazookas, light weapons suitable for close combat and reserves who can be thrown into the battle fresh, and quickly."*

This assessment proved true enough as McCardell ended his Italian campaign coverage in April and joined Watson in London. D-Day had become a matter of weeks, not months. However, both of these reporters could not forget a campaign whose veterans later complained it had become "the forgotten war."

Watson concurred in McCardell's observation that there was no substitute for infantry forces defending or holding ground. He compared the house-to-house battle for the small town of Cassino with the German-Soviet struggle for the large city of Stalingrad. Then, turning to his memories of a generation earlier, he wrote that Cassino was a *"small-scale counterpart of the Verdun operation in the First World War."*

As to why the Germans fought so hard to stop the Allies before Rome, Watson presumably tapped his Pentagon sources. One reason was the German fear that Allied control of the whole Italian peninsula would threaten the Nazi hold on France and Yugoslavia. Another was Hitler's need to warn other wavering Axis partners that they would suffer the fate of the Italians if they attempted to defect. These two correspondents now were ready to focus on the coming invasion of France.

Coverage of the next phases of the war—the puncture of the Nazi defense line at Cassino, the breakout from the Anzio beachhead, the capture of Rome, the invasion of southern France, the battles in the Vosges mountains and Alsace, the drive into Germany, the Nazi surrender at Rheims—all these would engage a third *Baltimore Sun* reporter on the front line in Europe. His name was Price Day, one of the most graceful and widely cultured writers in *Sun* history. He was born in Plainview, Texas, in 1907, the great-grandson and grandson of early trail drivers north out of Texas. When he was ten years old, his family moved to Chicago where he spent his teenage years. Then it was on to Princeton (Class of 1929), where he majored in architecture and edited the university's humor magazine. His writing skills gave him access during the 1930s to some of the nation's leading magazines: *The New Yorker, The Saturday Evening Post, Collier's*, and other top publications. Fiction, poetry, whimsy, reporting, art, and architecture, criticism—all rolled out from his typewriter with seeming ease.

He got into newspapering at age 36, first in Fort Lauderdale, Florida, and then at the Baltimore Sunpapers, an institution that in those days inspired lifetime loyalties among its staffers. A future editor-in-chief, Day was one of them. After sixteen months as a rewrite man, Day got one of the big breaks in his career when his bosses tapped him as a war correspondent in Europe. After the war, he covered the Nuremberg trials of Nazi war criminals and the Potsdam Conference of the victorious allies. He then won the Pulitzer Prize for international reporting—a series on India where he became the last newspaperman to interview Mahatma Gandhi before his assassination. Price's wider role was to chronicle the dissolution of the British Empire, a story that took him to South Africa, Burma, Malaya, Australia, and New Zealand.

In 1952, Day switched to editorial writing and in due course, seven years later, took control of the editorial pages of both papers. As an editor, he was soft-spoken, letting his staffers know he trusted them. Always fascinated by national and international affairs rather than local matters, he assigned one of his best men, Edgar L. Jones, to deal with potholes, bus routes, and City Hall. At the time of Day's passing on December 15, 1978, at the age of 71, Jones wrote that as editor-in-chief, Day *"asserted from the outset the primacy of human rights in all their ramifications."* His column, "The Spillway," was leavened by his light touch, humor, and wide-ranging remembrances of Texas, Chicago, Florida, and the never-ending foibles of American politics.

CHAPTER 9

Price Day Reports
the Fall of Rome

Years later, mining his memories of World War II, Price Day wrote that *"for a whole lot of people the early summer of 1944 was the most terrible and vivid of their lives, then or later. . . . That early summer"* was the first time he witnessed a battlefield torn by blood and steel, the first time he saw a wounded man not in a hospital but carried on a stretcher, the first time he was out with a forward patrol and warned not to step wide of a narrow path for fear of mines. It was also the first time in nearly a century that once-mighty Rome would fall.

Day had taken over the Italian Campaign assignment in late April 1944 from McCardell who had taken it over from Watson. The latter two had covered Allied soldiers stymied by a combination of fierce German resistance and terrible terrain at Cassino and a meager beachhead at Anzio. Both of these colleagues were now in London awaiting D-Day.

For Day and other military correspondents, a late posting to Italy had given them the opportunity to write of the Cassino-Anzio stalemate turning into breakthrough. *"For us there was never anything like it,"* he related. *"From May 11 to June 6, it was the only story in the world. Then just before noon on June 6 somebody in the foreign press club in Rome said the radio had reported a landing in Normandy. All of a sudden, as good as unemployed, we went to the bar and had a vermouth."*

Day was entitled to his vermouth. Italy's domination of war news ended with the Normandy invasion. The fighting north of Rome to Italy's Alpine border, which lasted another eleven months, became a secondary story to the battle for Germany itself. Day stayed with it for six weeks. The moment the United States sent its Seventh Army from Italy into southern France on August 15, 1944, Day went with it, leaving Italy bereft of *Sun* coverage until Howard Norton's arrival in the last weeks of war. Although Day was destined to cover the fight against the Nazis right to the end, all this was in his future.

Cassino in springtime gave him his first witness of battle, the horrible winter a thing of the past. His first story [April 27, 1944] set the scene: *"From this mountain village of gray rubble and thin brown mud you look down on one of the most bitterly contested patches of the earth's surface. The town of Cassino lies obscured by rain and mist, and the ruined Benedictine abbey on the height above the town is visible only as a black mass. The lessons of these two points on Highway No. 6, the road through the mountains to Rome, are plain. Here it was made apparent that airpower used in support of ground troops has definite limitations, and that in mountain fighting against strongly held enemy positions infantry today, as 5,000 years ago, still holds the key to victory. And infantry for such jobs as that at Cassino must be employed in great strength. For the doughboys who fought their way toward and into Cassino, the town will be remembered as a monument to the men who died along the tortuous roads leading to this truly vital position."*

On May 2, 1944, he got a first look at the Garigliano River stalemate site near Cassino. *"Mosquitoes aren't the only things which start into activity after dark,"* he reported. *"The roads come alive, too, and artillery starts its loud barking. Men, ammunition, and equipment hurry through the moonlight. On the roads across the valley, enemy vehicles start to move. It is no secret that Jerry has this road zeroed in and can hit it, or something very close to it, almost at will. You don't need a map to tell you that you are approaching the front. You know in the progressive tightening of discipline and control among the troops. One sure sign informs you that this is the front, not the rear. The tents and camouflage nets, which a few thousand yards back stood above the ground, have been set progressively deeper so that their tops now lie flush with the earth. A few hundred yards ahead there will be no tents.*

"Ignorant of noises of war, other than those of bomb and anti-aircraft fire, you try to hear and remember the sounds of shells in the air.

You never thought you'd feel relieved to get within range of German 280s but on the way out you relax as you know that only 280s and not howitzers and viciously efficient 88s can reach you. Meanwhile you keep a sharp eye on the contours of the mountains and the positions of the dipping moon. This wouldn't be a good place to go too far in the wrong direction."

Illustrating the primitive methods of communication available to World War II correspondents, a National Archives photograph shows Price in May 1944 in the Garigliano Valley, affixing message capsules to the legs of two carrier pigeons. The pigeons could reportedly fly about sixty miles an hour in relaying his dispatches from the front.

A follow-up Day story [May 6, 1944] found the correspondent at the Anzio beachhead. *"Whatever initial strategic errors may have been committed, the men of the beachhead can be proud of the job they've done in the bitter weeks since the operation was checked by the enemy. They have transformed what might have been an intolerable situation into a sturdy and aggressive, if still narrow, threat to the German flank. They have fought and worked day and night in the rain, cold, mud, dust and heat. Many have died. Many more have been wounded. They have fought always under the eyes of the enemy, threatened every moment by hostile aircraft and shells. If courage, intelligence, hard fighting and heavy labor have any value, the beachhead cannot be considered a failure. In every forward slope they have dug their foxholes. For every vehicle they have found shelter. With shovels and sweat they have put every hospital tent deep into the earth. What they did not have they made, even to washing machines constructed from barrels and wagon wheels. They have filled with sand great wine casks and built abutments to protect precious material from shell and bomb damage."*

Note the deft criticism of *"initial strategic errors"* and the mention of *"failure"* in Day's real-time writing. The amphibious Anzio operation has not held up well to military judgment over the decades. Originally conceived to relieve the pressure on troops blocked at Cassino, the Cassino forces instead had to break through the Nazi defense line to relieve Anzio.

A poignant moment in his coverage of the Italian campaign came when Day returned to Anzio for a meeting with his younger brother, already a veteran after two years' service. *"He looked healthy. He looked all right to me,"* Day wrote [May 11, 1944]. *"The paint on his helmet is worn off at the edges, showing steel. The sweatband is stained black. There is a small hole through the top made by an anti-personnel fragment but he wasn't wearing his helmet at the time. He wore issue dungarees, their original green faded almost white. Around his neck, besides his dog tags, there's a Soviet coin hanging on a thin gold Italian chain. He found the coin on a dead German in the desert."*

Day remarked that in seeing his brother he felt *"a thousand times luckier than hundreds of thousands of people in the States who sort out the slow mails and read and reread short letters that say so little when you want to know so much."* But noting how he and his brother were at a loss for words at their Anzio meeting, he wanted folks at home to know what wartime reunions can be like.

On May 11, the jumping-off date of the offensive that cracked open the enemy Gustav Defense Line across the Italian peninsula, Price Day was near the front. Here, in part, are his words [May 14, 1944]:

"Infantrymen waiting in the lines, feeling and thinking things only they have a right to report.

"Jeeps full of helmeted men rushing through the gray early light, dust whitening their clothes and hands and eyebrows like drifted snow.

"Bursts of two nearby enemy shells and the appearance through heavy smoke of a soldier running slowly and awkwardly.

"The tension in the command post when news of a unit known to be in serious trouble failed minute after long minute to come in."

Linking up later with French colonial troops driving toward an Italian town named Spigno, the correspondent knew he could not keep up with soldiers *"scrambling like gazelles up the side of a steep, cloud-capped mountain."* [May 16, 1944]

"To reach Spigno, it was necessary for me to leave my jeep in the valley and clamber up a stony trail too rough for a pack train. Supplies of K-ration and ammunition are going up on men's backs. No water is moving up yet; the men in Spigno are drinking well water

made safe with halazone tablets. Most of them slept without blankets last night and will again tonight. The hard stones on the trail are worn smooth by thousands of feet over many years. In contrast, bright new razor-sharp splinters of shrapnel lie among the stones. From Spigno you can see a mountain rising five hundred yards higher in the sky and you can see men at the top. They can look down on you and they're not Germans and the feeling is strange and very good. The climb is hot but without looking very carefully you don't swerve a single foot from the trail. When the Italians see your uniform they grin and wave and buon giorno. *Some of them weep. They are glad to be getting rid of the Germans, whom they hate, and they have high hopes for their lot under the Allies. One hopes they will feel the same a month from now."*

Two days later, Marylanders could read of a French move toward the town of Esperia. *"The usual debris of war, which is oddly without nationality once it is no longer useful, lines the route. One passes dead Germans with the omnipresent dust drifted deep around them; great tanks tumbled like toys off the roadbed to lie upside down in fields of wild mustard; bloated horses and mules with their legs sticking stiffly out; shell holes and more shell holes. Up on the road there is a French cemetery where, with an escort of honor, two soldiers, their uncasketed bodies wrapped in clean brilliant Tricolor are carried to freshly dug graves. Ahead are French women driving ambulances to evacuate the wounded. Often they go within a half mile of the front to evacuate the wounded. One girl was very beautiful, like a daisy growing in a dump. I remembered her sweet, strained face all the rest of the day."*

On May 19, 1944, *The Sun* at last could publish a report that Allied forces—in this case Polish forces—had captured the Monte Cassino monastery. *"The red and white flag of Poland flies tonight above the ruins of the Benedictine monastery,"* Day reported. *"I am neither on Monte Cassino nor in Cassino, but at a Polish headquarters near Highway 6. This Polish unit saw the hardest fighting and suffered the heaviest losses of the first phase of the current drive, and in the last 30 hours it has canceled two earlier defeats with a spectacular if costly victory. Despite terrible losses, the Polish force is tired but jubilant. The feel of victory is in the air."*

Two days later Day reported from the Minturno Bridge a few miles north of Cassino. There he got a glimpse of the Ausente Valley, which he described as *"an alley of smoke and death."* And another two days later he saw more *"rubbled villages strewn with ruined tanks and dead animals and men."* Yet Italians were getting back to normal. At a house that ten days ago was an advanced aid station, *"an Italian boy of about 11 is selling kumquats. Farmers are at work again. They stopped only when the armies fought through as other farmers stopped in the Third Century B.C. when Hannibal's polyglot army of Spaniards, Libyans, Carthaginians and Senegalese passed through here in his vain attempt to reach Rome from the south after his victory at Cannae."*

On May 24, 1944, Allied troops within the Anzio perimeter also had reason to be jubilant. Four months and one day after an easy landing turned into a desperate fight for survival, they cheered the news that the Gustav Line had been pierced and Cassino-based units were coming to relieve them. Two days later [May 26, 1944] Price Day reported the first meeting between GIs at Anzio and GIs coming north from Cassino. They met, he wrote, *"at a small drainage ditch called Macchia Sirena Sinistra, seven eighths of a mile west-northwest of the village of Borgo Gappa"*—a description chock full of the writer's whimsy.

"The first men of the two Fifth Army forces to shake hands were Capt. Ben Sousa of Honolulu, coming from the beachhead, and Lieut. Francis H. Buckley of Philadelphia, advancing on foot across a culvert. 'I'm damn glad you got here,' said Sousa. 'I'm damn glad I did,' said Buckley." Day found the beachhead itself deserted, littered with great piles of cardboard ration cartons. He described it as a *"level and deathly coastal plain—surely the most dug-in area of its size on earth."* Knocked-out American tanks, two fire-blackened German Tiger tanks, trenches and *"holes where too many men lived for too long"* were part of the scene. *"You smell the odor of death."*

In the next report, the correspondent was up on hills long held by the Germans that looked down on Anzio. *"You now know that you weren't wrong in feeling that every time you drove along a road in a jeep raising a small cloud of dust the enemy could spot you and shoot at you if he chose."* A drive along the road inland provides many grim reminders of other quick actions.

In two subsequent dispatches [May 24 and 26, 1944] Day described some of the tough warfare he experienced in the accelerating drive toward Rome. At a town called Velletri, he wrote, *"the area is three feet deep in lush, wide-bladed grass. The infantrymen do not charge. They kneel or lie, fire, run forward awkwardly, hunched over, for a few yards and fall again."* His second story dealt with the German Fourth Parachute Division, where, in the same kind of tall grass, *"they stood exposed in a hopeless battle with no arms but machine pistols."*

On the first day of June, a Price Day dispatch led the paper with a report from the southern suburbs of Rome. *"Desperately, with every resource he can lay his hands on, the enemy is defending his last fortifications south of the suburbs of Rome. Like two heavyweights in the center of the ring, the two armies are fighting with all their strength. So far, our troops have not broken through.*

"That Rome will fall is certain. In this sense perhaps the battle may be strategically considered a victory. It is not a victory of the only kind that means anything to combat troops—the end of fighting. The advance of the Fifth and Eighth armies in the past 20 days has been well planned and executed; but at every point where the enemy has decided to hold he has taken a heavy toll in Allied lives.

"The enemy has been badly beaten since the night of May 11. His casualties have totaled more than three divisions. He has lost much equipment. But the largest single batch of prisoners has been approximately 600. He has not been trapped."

With these acute comments, Day touched on a controversy of long and intense dimensions. Many historians have contended that General Mark Clark, commander of the Fifth Army, disobeyed plans to encircle German forces and, instead, turned westward in a drive to get his army—and himself—to Rome ahead of the British Eighth Army. Clark's protectors evidently saw the danger to his reputation, because they explained to Day (and to Mark Watson in London) that the terrain was such that a trap could not be sprung. It is an enduring dispute, akin to similar arguments that the Allies failed to capture thousands of German troops at Messina in Sicily, at Falaise in Normandy, and as the Nazi Bulge collapsed in the Ardennes Forest.

As the Battle for Rome reached its climax, Day reported [June 4,

1944] Allied forces had broken through enemy defenses and were streaming down Highway 6 toward the Eternal City.

Then came a long-sought though slightly premature headline in the June 5, 1944 edition of *The Sun*. "*ROME TAKEN BY FIFTH ARMY*," read the big black headline. The dateline, "*On Highway 6 before Rome*," gave the game away. Day was reporting on skirmishes on the city's southern outposts, still miles from Rome's historic center.

"*A three-minutes walk up a small rise and there is a city limits sign—Roma*," Day related. "*No one has walked it yet, and we have been here since 7:20 this morning. It is now 11.*

"*Tanks have gone in. Just behind the sign is the blackened hulk of the lead tank we saw knocked out by a German 88 firing point-blank down the road. All traffic has stopped while the infantry is called up. There are many snipers. The crack of rifles and the squirt of German machine pistols sound every few minutes. Now and then a whining bullet clips the top of the hedge surrounding the house in the lee of which we sit typing. We did not choose to be here. It was the roses that fooled us. As we came up the road in the dewy dawn, Italians lined along the road with great masses of rambler roses. From the cheers of the Italians we felt certain everything in front was clear.*

"*Immediately after the episode of the roses the chatter of machine guns made us leave the jeep and flop into a ditch. An 88 shell passing low and straight down the road sent us near a house and we lay flatter than ever before. We stayed there until the shell landed on a hillock 15 yards away, splattering us with dirt. The concussion blew my helmet off.*

"*To the left we can see patrols crouching low as they climb a hillock to clean out snipers. One man carrying a bazooka has a bunch of roses on his helmet cover. We (a group of reporters) saw a German camouflaged armored car with a man in the turret still manning a machine gun. He ran away through a field of wheat. The air overhead is also full of the multiple whistle of our artillery laying a barrage on the enemy ahead.*

"*A squadron of Canadian-Americans with carbines comes back from a trip over the hillock. They think they got the sniper. Their special combat fatigues are stained with dirt and sweat. They all wear five- or six-day beards. They look tired. Some of them have not been out of the lines since D-Day at Anzio."*

Ironically, the epic event of the entire Italian campaign—the liberation of Rome—came on June 5, 1944, just in time for stateside newspapers on June 6 to run the first breathless reports of the Allied landings on the French coast. *"ALLIES INVADING FRANCE, TROOPS LAND IN NORMANDY"* trumpeted *The Baltimore Sun*. And where was Price Day's Italy story? At the bottom of the page under a modest two-column headline. It did not lack in excitement, just the news prominence General Clark had longed for.

"Weary soldiers of the victorious Fifth Army are slogging through and around Rome toward the front, but for the people of this lovely city, today is a day of festival," Day's report began. *"Streets all night seemed full with streams of citizens of the capital where the word 'citizen' came into being.*

"Tens of thousands of flags fly in the brilliant sunshine. They are of almost any kind except Nazi. Some in windows wave the British Union Jack. A great American flag is draped over the balcony near Pincia Gardens. From the flagpole at Corso del Populo flies another American flag. It is home-made and has only 20 stars, and the background of the stars is green instead of blue but the intention is right or at least expedient.

"Many young Italians carry German rifles but their intentions, at least today, seem peaceful. This sight, with the appearance of few prisoners of war, the sound of our artillery firing beyond the city limits and the report that the Germans are holding on the Abruzzi Hills is almost the only sign that Rome is still the scene of possible trouble." The entry into Rome was punctuated by small firefights, wild rumors, and a relieved citizenry. At 7 o'clock the stage seemed to be set for a triumphant and all-but-bloodless entry into the first great capital to be taken by the Allies.

With several other foreign correspondents who had reached the center of Rome, Day found himself at the Vatican in the papal receiving room where Pope Pius XII urged reporters in drab, dirty uniforms to *"let the guiding purpose of your writing be peace."* *"War may be and should be only a means to peace,"* continued the pontiff, whose conduct during the struggle would be of lasting controversy. *"Write in favor of a peace that will be stamped with the approval of every well-meaning individual and by all peoples, a peace that will ensure to one and all those conditions that are necessary for them to live in a manner befitting the dignity of their human nature."*

After the audience, Day was struck by the contrast between Vatican quiet and streets outside *"streaming with the vehicles of war."* *"It was like awakening from a calm and peaceful dream."* Actually the war was over for Rome but not for Italy northward to the Alps. A political objective had been achieved but the military reality of Italy remained. Hard fighting would go on until Germany collapsed. Two days later his report found him once again with Allied troops—this time moving so quickly northward that maps had to be dropped from aircraft to advancing troops.

Combat, at least for a while, was far different from the yard-by-yard, mile-by-mile battles of Cassino and Anzio. Now, seventy-five miles north of the Italian capital, Day covered the fast retreat of the German Fourteenth Army to its last strong defense line in northern Italy.

"German cavalry is still encountered but its resistance is not organized. A typical frontline scene is a well-paved road through increasingly high rolling hills. A reconnaissance outfit sits on the road. In a wheat field a reaper drawn by two white oxen levels the yellow grain. Ahead are Germans—but they are well ahead.

"When our troops enter the little stone villages of this district—a few are damaged slightly but not destroyed—villagers greet them with wine and what food they have. Almost without exception they are pleased to see American, French and British troops and do everything in their power to assist them."

Day provided a shocking story [July 3, 1944] of violence in the little hill town of Guardistallo. Here are excerpts:

"On Thursday morning, Germans soldiers massacred more than fifty Italian civilians. In addition, they killed at least ten and perhaps 15 local Partisans. Armed with machine guns and machine pistols, the Germans went from house to house, forced or shot open doors and murdered the helpless and unarmed people within. These are the

facts. Among those killed were four women, two boys of 14, two youths of 17 and 18 and an old man of 75.

"It is certain that Partisans, many wearing red bandannas and stars, were especially active in Guardistallo. At 6 o'clock, June 29, six German soldiers were found dead. At 7, fifteen German troops ambushed a group of Partisans in the hills west of town, killing from ten to fifteen. The Germans—with some SS troops among them—then went on along a group of houses on the outskirts of town ruthlessly murdering civilian inhabitants.

"The bodies were left where they fell until American troops entered the town after hard fighting. Then, wrapped in sheets, the dead Partisans were placed in family sepulchers in the small village cemetery with its characteristic high walls and tall dark cypresses. The dead were buried today. I did not see the bodies but I talked to four Americans who had seen them and whose veracity is beyond question."

Day stayed with the Fifth Army in Italy until he was assigned to cover the Allied invasion of southern France in mid-August 1944. He then followed the Seventh Army as it drove northward through France and played a significant role in the campaign that finally crushed the Nazi war machine.

CHAPTER 10

To the Beaches
with Holbrook Bradley

Where was Holbrook Bradley?

On June 6, 1944, came the news that millions of people had awaited with dread, impatience and hope—emotions that quickly turned to prayers. American, British, and Canadian troops had landed on the northern coast of France (exact location undisclosed) to begin their historic campaign to crush the Hitler Reich.

News wire services swung into action; so did three *Baltimore Sun* correspondents. Lee McCardell was one of the first four U.S. reporters to fly over once-placid Normandy beaches thundering with war. Thomas O'Neill was covering the announcements of General Dwight D. Eisenhower and Prime Minister Winston Churchill. Mark Watson offered his analysis of the epic invasion, the greatest amphibious operation in history.

But where was Holbrook Bradley? The youngest (at age 28) of the *Sun* correspondents sent to Europe, he had not been heard from. A derring-do reporter, he had drawn the most coveted assignment imaginable—the Twenty-ninth Division landing at Omaha Beach. Yet, no Bradley bylines appeared on June 6, June 7, June 8, June 9, June 10, June 11—all dates of desperate fighting.

Finally on June 12, careful readers of *The Sun* caught a glimmer of the censorship and communications obstacles that had delayed Bradley's copy. His first dispatch had been written June 1, five days before D-Day, a time of absolute secrecy when invasion troops and correspondents were locked down in embarkation camps near the English coast.

"Aboard An LST, June 1 (By Cable—Delayed)" read the dateline.

"This is it," were the first three words in a dispatch that did not appear for eleven days. *"This is the moment for which the men and officers of this outfit* (unidentified) *have sweated and strained, hoped and prayed, during three years of training, much of which has been drab, monotonous routine."* Of this Bradley well knew, for he had watched the Twenty-ninth train stateside for a year and a half and for two years in England—a process that turned civilians into soldiers.

The Twenty-ninth Infantry Division, the so-called Blue and Gray Division signifying its split Civil War ancestry, had three infantry regiments: the 115th, the 116th, and the 175th. The 175th (the "Dandy Fifth" if you traced its origins to the War for Independence) had a greater percentage of Baltimore men than any other unit in the armed forces. It was at the top of Bradley's must-cover list and, as such, he had to spend an uncomfortable D-Day and D-Night on a bobbing, lurching landing craft before going ashore on D-Day Plus One. The 116th (Virginia "Stonewallers" tracing their Civil War origins to General Jackson himself) took the heaviest casualties of any Allied regiment in World War II. Its troops, primarily Virginians, were in the first wave that fought on to Omaha Beach. The 115th was in the second wave which hit the beach on D-Afternoon. Its personnel came primarily from all parts of Maryland except Baltimore City. As the war went on and reserves came on as replacements, the geographical orientation diluted. But the three regiments of the Blue and Gray, to their lasting divisional glory, were destined to fight clear across France into defeated Germany.

Holbrook Bradley went with them, an experience that he later described as "the high point of my life." Born in 1916, he was one of the few persons on the roster of *Baltimore Sun* war correspondents who did not stay with the paper. After the war and a short-lived return to local reporting, he switched to *Life* magazine for a couple of years before starting a career as a press officer for the Pentagon and later the State Department. From the beginning, his status with *The Sun* was somewhat awkward. His wife was the only daughter of publisher Paul Patterson, which was at least one reason why he got his newspaper job after he graduated from Yale with a degree in archaeology. Like other young reporters, he was assigned to the police beat and saved a little money (actually trolley tokens) by walking from one police station to another. Bradley took to a career in writing as though it had been planned all along. He got a big break by convincing his city editor that the paper should have a maritime beat, an assignment that gave him access to many merchant seamen who had survived sinkings by German U-boats prowling the Atlantic.

Next came coverage of the Twenty-ninth Division during its early training in Virginia and Tennessee. This led to the plum assignment of all—joining the division when it went to England, fought its way ashore in Normandy, and drove onward into Germany itself. If there was any grousing in the newsroom about Bradley's swift rise, it could not have survived his splendid reporting. He seemed to glory in taking chances, and, sure enough, he got a Purple Heart in a Normandy battle. Asked during a breakfast in Baltimore in November 2008 why he was so reckless, he noted that his marriage had broken up shortly before he sailed to Europe and he felt free to confront any danger that came along. His copy reflected a zest for front-line action. Decades later, when he was in his 90s, Bradley wrote a lively memoir about his wartime experiences: "My underlying goal has been to recreate—as factually as possible, given dimming memories—what we in the Twenty-ninth Infantry Division went through. This compelling tale should help those who remember World War II, or later generations living through current wars, understand what it was like for a youthful journalist reporting the horror and glory that young men went through in a war fought for a purpose they, and much of the world, firmly believed in."

His book was a loving look-back on the Twenty-ninth as it trained for and fought for the liberation of Europe. "*As we moved in concert during battle, we often developed a comradery I'd seldom if ever known before I joined the Twenty-ninth,*" he wrote in real-time copy for *The Sun*. As D-Day neared—"*This is it*"—troops assembled in vast staging areas in the south of England, where they were issued combat field packs and ammunition. As one, then three, then six days went by, tension increased. For the troops, "*the final period of confinement in camp was first boring, then nerve-wracking. It was only when trucks rolled down to harbor side did the troops see huge massing of invasion craft; LSTs waited in trim lines for the arriving troops.*"

When the set-sail signal came, Bradley focused on these boys and young men bound to make history. *"Weighed down with packs, bedding rolls, gas masks, ammunition belts, shovels, canteens, rifles and pistols, lines of olive-drab helmeted men packed transport ships waiting to cross the English Channel. The men knew by now that this was the real thing. There was an atmosphere of tense anticipation. As the sun set over the harbor (on June 5), the doughboys looked seaward. Looked toward the distant shore on which they were about to begin an attack on an enemy they had been waiting to meet."*

Bradley would witness the division's fateful D-Day attacks on Omaha Beach, the bloodiest of the day's encounters on the northern French coast, *"G-2 information (intelligence) gave us a rough idea of the terrain on which we ourselves would be landing, the time of our attack, and the opposition which the enemy had in the area. Details of underwater and beach obstructions to be crossed were explained in the diagrams, and pictures testified to the completeness with which the plans had been laid."*

The Sun on June 13, 14, and 16, 1944, published half a dozen Bradley stories about the rough channel crossing and the hectic mayhem at Omaha Beach. Their chronology was jumbled as the paper published reports in the order available, not in the order written. To achieve continuity, chronological order will now be attempted.

Bradley's account of his landing with the 175th Regiment was written June 7 but not published until June 13. He told how his ship, while waiting to land on D-Day Plus One, had been threatened but not struck by a Luftwaffe air attack. It did its part in shuttling injured soldiers off the beach. *"The wounded were handled skillfully despite the constant rise and fall of the ship. The men were swung over the sides by block and tackle, then carried below on litters to await doctors in the operating room set up in the officers' wardroom or securely bunked in the crew's quarters below.*

"From those not seriously injured we are getting a picture of the early phases of the landing. Troops in the early assault met heavy opposition from enemy cross-machine gun fire sweeping the beaches from low bluffs immediately across the sand. Casualties were sustained in the first assault when boats or men hit underwater obstruc-

tions or mines. Heavy artillery and mortar fire covered the beach in a systematic grid pattern, making the assault on coastal pillboxes and entrenchments most difficult.

"As we watch activities ashore the gray cloud blanket that has covered the Channel areas all day has suddenly lifted, changing the color of the water from a somber hue to a brilliant blue-green. Around us, the hundreds of ships have grown to a thousand and, looking Channelward, we can see convoys of many more on their way.

"Our klaxon has just sounded, and crews have sprung into action stations. As our anchor is heaved word has gone around that we are finally on the way across the narrow strip of water separating us from the beach."

The story Bradley next wrote on June 7, the 115th Regiment's D-Day, appeared in the newspaper on June 13.

"Our turn to run ashore came during mid-morning. Clambering over the side of our LST, we slid down the cargo nets into the small gray craft below that bounced and banged about on the Channel swell. Crowded into the vessel, some two dozen of us were whisked in through the fleet to the beach.

"Wondering whether the sweeper and engineers had removed enemy mines and underwater obstructions, we hung on as the ship bounced over one wave, then through the next. We passed vessels showing obvious signs of hits by enemy shore-fire or underwater mines. Then we were on the beach.

"The Navy enlisted personnel in our craft rammed the light LCVP well up on the sand but even so we found some 20 yards of waist-deep water to wade through when we dashed out of the forward ramp. White tape set up by the first engineer group ashore indicated a path cleared through the enemy mines. To the right and left were American trucks, burned out after receiving direct shell hits. Equipment of all kinds lay scattered along the beach.

"The first dead we saw was a navy man covered with a piece of tarpaulin, lying almost as if he were asleep. Spreading out in a line so that casualties would be small, we started up the beach toward our division command post. The scene through which we passed was one of the most desolate we've ever seen. The few houses along the shore

were almost blown to bits. Up on the hills German concrete emplacements were completely blasted off the ground and mazes of barbed wire entanglements were ripped through in large sections.

"A few yards farther on we came across those dead who hadn't yet been prepared for burial. They were the boys who had hit the beach first, for the most part lads who went in before any of the installations had been cleared out. Some never made the shore, for their white and almost wax-like bodies still had pieces of seaweed hanging from them. Somehow, although many of them were men of our outfit, they all seemed most impersonal. Those first few hours on the beach must have been living hell. And we saw there had been no discrimination in the way the men fell, for the two bars of captains were among the plain uniforms of the privates.

"The object of our first day's march was a limestone quarry off the hillside facing the Channel. There the division command post was set up. A few grimy, unshaven men, the headquarters personnel who had been ashore since the night of D-day, greeted us. Others stretched in or alongside foxholes dug into the hard ground. Here and there pitifully small fires were used to heat the semblance of a noonday meal. We learned that the situation was well under control, that our regiments were well on the way to their inshore objectives."

In the same issue, Watson reported from London that the movement of supplies to Allied troops *"is better than previous experiences had led us to expect."* Having watched the fiasco at Salerno, the *Sun's* military expert told readers there are three distinct phases to an amphibious invasion. First, gain a foothold; second, engage the enemy's tactical reserves to widen the beachhead; third, prepare for the enemy's momentous decision to send in strategic reserves (a step the German high command had yet to take, figuring wrongly that the main Allied thrust would be in the Pas de Calais sector).

In the issue of *The Sun* on June 13 appeared two other Bradley reports, one six columns wide with the headline *"With 29th Division in France"* and the other with the more modest *"Earlier Description of Beachhead Scenes."*

In the latter dispatch, he told of the scene near a coastal village that had just been captured. *"All along the road small groups of peasants walked along carrying a few salvaged possessions. From many miles away we could see columns of heavy grayish smoke still rising from smoldering ruins and, as we drew nearer, dust-laden air made our eyes and noses smart. As we rounded a curve, an infantry-man waved us down. He told us we were in a dangerous spot, several hundred yards from the front and advised parking our vehicle. Piling out, we moved on foot, ready to jump into a deep ditch at a moment's notice.*

"Ahead, officers and enlisted men crouched behind a heavy machine gun dug in beside a former German 88 emplacement. Through a periscope we could see downhill and across a small river that housed the Jerries. A blown up bridge held up the forward movement temporarily. A break appeared imminent with the arrival of the major general commanding the outfit. He called for a quick advance supported by medium tanks. The thundering reports of our artillery indicated that our full weight was being thrown into an effort to breach enemy lines at that point."

The final delayed beachhead story by Holbrook Bradley, written June 9 and published June 13, provided more insights on how to follow a war if you were a combat correspondent in World War II. His comments, like those of Mark Watson, Lee McCardell, and Price Day, would have constituted a useful manual for front-line journalists—if you ever had the time to produce one. Your first obligation was to survive. Your second was to write your head off with your portable Hermes typewriter and get your copy across the Atlantic. Bradley's beachhead stories were delayed for days because a private American company, Press Wireless, had been unable to set up its promised communications operation when the Omaha fighting began. Bad luck followed when an officer heading back to London took his time in getting the Bradley stories on their way.

It was a war in which accredited correspondents wore uniforms, supposedly carried no firearms, got Purple Hearts if wounded, were ranked as officers even though newsmen were always addressed as "Mr.," and often had to find their own transportation by flagging corporals or privates driving jeeps. They slept, often on the ground or in bombed-out buildings, wherever their chosen battles took them.

(*"Those of us in the actual combat zone have little chance to keep up with the progress of the battle elsewhere,"* Bradley wrote later.)

Bradley commented that his Twenty-ninth Division Regiment had moved twice in two days and was ready to pick up again on a moment's notice. By this time it had moved up the bluffs beyond the beach to begin fighting in small villages, obscure crossroads, trails weaving through hedgerows—often with the sound of bombs and firearms not very far away.

"After the first few bomb explosions we learned to relax in our slit trenches amid the pounding of ack-ack nearby and the whiz of flak above us. A few of us even managed to get in five or six hours of sleep. Some of us had a shave and a wash for the first time in many days. Early this morning when we had just finished a breakfast of hot coffee, bacon and hardtack, orders came that once more we were to move on."

As the struggle moved from the beaches to the hedgerows farther inland, fighting continued, often measured in yards. Here's a Bradley description [June 21, 1944] of a typical clash in the slow drive for St. Lo, one in which he had been advised to head down a ravine to watch the action: *"The chatter of machine guns sent us diving for cover. Our artillery thundered round after round into enemy positions. Then came the signal for another attack, and we stayed low as tommy guns and machine guns opened all around us. A few bursts suddenly turned into a deafening chatter as more of our men opened up and the enemy returned fire. Suddenly we got more attention from the enemy. The German machine guns had been making a hellish din on our right but now they became even louder. As we pressed ourselves farther into the soft dirt a spray of bullets went over our heads, clipping off the branches and leaves only a few feet away. The way back led by a series of gates opening into grain fields, each of which seemed swept by machine-gun fire. We dodged low, managed to keep clear of the fire and finally ended up at a side point where litter bearers bring in a few wounded. Back of us the noise of fighting began to die down."*

Another Bradley article on a Normandy firefight appeared on June 28, 1944. *"Most of the men on the front line are accustomed to sleep-*

ing in slit trenches. Then, when the shelling gets close, there is time to roll into the trench for protection. The men in this sector by now have become real veterans of battle. Not only have they proved their ability as tough, shrewd fighting men but they also have knuckled down to the rigors of combat as if such discomforts had always been part of their lives. Men who have fought for 24 or 48 hours or even more hours at a stretch huddle in a trench half filled with water, wearing clothes stained by days of battle. Some have improvised shelter over the trenches—corrugated tin roofing, logs or merely brushwood overlaid with dirt. Soldiers all along the line find these periods of quiet often more nerve-wracking than the heat of intense battle. Perhaps that is why officers have little trouble obtaining volunteers for night scouting and raiding parties. On such missions, action, when it comes, is usually fierce and concluded quickly. On these raids there are bound to be casualties for our enemy is a smart one. But there always will be more men to volunteer."

Alongside the Bradley story, Lee McCardell filed a report from London that mounting air attacks on German oil facilities, transportation points, and armament factories had resumed. For three weeks, the Allied air command had given its full support to the Normandy operation. *"The mounting Anglo-American air offensive had two primary objectives: crippling of the German aircraft industry and disruption of communications. It was part of a concerted plan to weaken the enemy to the point where he would be unable to withstand combined air and land attacks later. Its effects were cumulative."*

As new-fangled German rockets continued to strike Britain, London Bureau chief O'Neill filed a prophetic story [June 18, 1944] warning that in a future war America could be a target for long-range missiles. *"Still crude and unreliable, the robot plane has been no more than a minor military weapon. Given another generation of experiment and improvement and another war to bring it to perfection, it will be something else entirely,"* O'Neill predicted, citing military sources. *"They foresee for the future giant winged bombs capable of taking the Atlantic in their strides, directed by radio control and automatic pilots to precise points thousands of miles distant, potent with destruction and untroubled by an airplane's need to get home again. The flying bombs being catapulted from the French coast have a maximum range of only 150 miles. The first airplane could stay in the air for only a matter of seconds, and now look at the B-29 Super-fortresses."*

While the newspaper would continue to focus on the European theater until Hitler's defeat, it carried its first staff-written report of a battle in the Pacific. Howard Norton, a future Pulitzer Prize winner, was with the U.S. fleet as it sped toward the Japanese-held island of Saipan. *"For the first time we are entering areas populated by Japanese civilians,"* Norton wrote. *"For the first time in the Central Pacific our forces are attacking relatively large land masses where it is possible to develop battles which might last for weeks. This no longer is atoll warfare where small islands can be saturated with explosives and overwhelmed in a few hours by landing forces."*

Thus, in less than a month, *The Baltimore Sun* had established itself as a major player in the European war with its coverage of the Italian campaign, the Normandy invasion, and the ever-growing air war. It had sent a veteran reporter to the Pacific. Bragging rights were justified, and *The Sunday Sun* of June 25, 1944, was not modest about it.

CHAPTER 11

Sun Correspondents on All Fronts

"*From the foxholes of Normandy . . . from the battlefields of Italy . . . from a Marauder bomber high over the invasion beachheads . . . from the front on Saipan, Sunpapers war correspondents are sending eyewitness accounts of the daily drama of the battlefields.*" With these proud words, *The Sunday Sun* on June 25, 1944, adorned an inside page with the pictures and biographical sketches of war reporters whose bylines were well known to the newspaper's readers. It was an apt date for such self-promotion.

Howard M. Norton, an old Asia hand, was at the new beachhead in Saipan, describing the U.S. invasion of the Japanese-held island as "*the biggest battle of the Pacific war to date and probably the toughest.*"

Holbrook Bradley was with the Maryland-Virginia Twenty-ninth Division in the hedgerows of Normandy reporting on hometown troops exhausted by three weeks of constant fighting since D-Day June 6.

Price Day, covering the Italian campaign from the winter stalemate at Cassino to and beyond the capture of Rome, etched the contrast between one Tuscan town bypassed by war and another terrorized and looted by Nazi soldiers.

Mark S. Watson, dean of the *Sun*'s war correspondents, was covering the Allied advance on Cherbourg, the port vitally needed by ground forces still relying on supplies shipped via the beachheads.

Lee McCardell was reporting on the Ninth Air Force as it pounded enemy targets and, like Watson, was writing of the struggle for Cherbourg.

Philip S. Heisler, assigned to the War and Navy Departments in Washington, was in print that day with troubling evidence of Japanese advances on the Chinese mainland.

And Thomas M. O'Neill, chief of the *Sun*'s London Bureau, traced the early planning for Operation Overlord, a task dating back to the perilous days after Dunkirk.

From this mosaic, readers had their choice of vivid writing about the wartime scene. What must have provoked the most attention at command level was O'Neill's scathing criticism of Army Air Force "publicity boys." Excerpts from his dispatch:

"Questions that are searching, explicit and completely new in the brief but brilliant record of the air arm in warfare are being raised here as the result of the experiences since the landing in France and are proving a source of acute embarrassment to the spokesmen of the Air Services Command.

"First, if aerial bombardment is as destructive as it has been represented, how are the Germans still able to bring up very considerable reinforcements across rivers on bridges which have been attacked repeatedly by the air forces?

"Second, if aerial 'pin-point' bombardment is as precise as modern instruments are declared to have made it, why are Germans still able to use launching platforms in the Pas de Calais for those flying bombs?

"These questions come as an unpleasant dose to bombing men who are perhaps much distressed that perfection is demanded of their weapon now it appears as something less than perfect. It will probably turn out that the fault lies not with the bomber but with a vigorous, enthusiastic and able public relations staff which for months has been publicizing the air force with a great deal of industry and ingenuity but with no recognizable restraint."

He went on to say the "publicity boys" had claimed that instrument bombing was as effective as visual bombing only so long as this could not be verified when raids were hundreds of miles away. *"It is different since affairs in France have brought the effectiveness of bombing into the range of the ground forces."*

O'Neill's criticism was targeted at British and American air force commanders who often suggested strategic bombing of enemy industrial, transportation, communications, and fuel targets was capable—on its own—of winning the war. Those in charge of ground and water combat adamantly disagreed. Sometimes lost in the argument was a profound difference between strategic and tactical bombing. For the GIs in the trenches, there could never be too much tactical air power protecting them by blasting enemy forces as they advanced, retreated, or hunkered down.

O'Neill's dressing down of Army Air Force hype anticipated an encounter—a bizarre and hilarious encounter—between the airmen and another *Sun* reporter, Lee McCardell. More on that later.

Once the Normandy beachheads were strong enough to preclude a German attempt to drive Allied forces into the sea, the focus of fighting riveted on two key objectives: capture of Cherbourg, the third largest French port, and a breakout from Normandy at St. Lo into tank-friendly terrain leading to Paris and beyond. *Sun* coverage was intensive for weeks.

First, consider Cherbourg, whose capture required a loop by Allied troops at the beachheads to the right and then north up the Carentan Peninsula. Lee McCardell had attached himself to the 313th Regiment of the 79th Division, an outfit derided because of long training without seeing action. Such derision did not last as the division fought its way up to Cherbourg, thus carrying on a tradition that had entitled it to wear the Cross of Lorraine as a shoulder patch since World War I.

"The drive to Cherbourg had been going full steam," McCardell wrote [July 1, 1944] *"and the 313 was leading the drive. They came through like the older generation of GI Joes who carried* (regimental) *colors a quarter century ago.*

"If we grow lyrical about this, you'll have to forgive us because we followed the regiment into Cherbourg. We know from first-hand observations that it was the first force to smash the enemy's two strong lines of outer defense, and the first to enter the city. It was then 313th's first taste of battle but it is doubtful that the Germans ever suspected that. Once they got going, the regiment fought like veterans. Some died like veterans, too.

"There was the sergeant who caught the enemy's machine-gun fire while leading his platoon in an assault. He called to the men behind

him. *'You guys—don't try to follow me. You can't help me—I'm done for—they'll only get you.' He was dead when a medical aid man crawled out to where he lay."*

After recounting other heroics, McCardell picked up his story with the regiment pulling back 2,000 yards during its Cherbourg drive north to give tactical aircraft the opportunity to blast away at enemy lines. *"The Ninth Air Force dive bombers came in at treetop level to do their blasting job. The bomb release line was marked by white smoke shells fired by our artillery at five-minute intervals. Ammunition belt clips and empty cartridge cases came rattling down on our heads."* The drive then resumed.

Next came a McCardell account of the fall of Cherbourg [June 26, 1944]: *"It was sometime around 3 o'clock this Monday afternoon when some Jerries manning several steel and concrete pillboxes in the chain of Cherbourg water-front defenses hung out a long-sleeved dirty white undershirt. They had had enough. They wanted to surrender to the American Joes, who were attacking from the heights behind the city.*

"When those Germans finally gave up, the American infantry had fought its way through the streets of the waterfront section. A 57mm anti-tank gun was methodically drilling holes in the pillboxes from a point-blank range of about 500 yards as fast as the gunners could slam shells into the red hot barrel. Three thousand captured German POWs streamed out of underground tunnels and ran to American lines waving white bedsheets, towels, and even handkerchiefs," McCardell recounted.

Eager to file his story, the correspondent left the battlefront to hitchhike 60 miles in search of a plane to carry his photographs to London.

A week later the paper printed a letter from the 313th Regiment praising McCardell's *"excellent job of on-the-scene reporting"* from the Cherbourg Peninsula. *"He has gotten the news first hand, on the front lines, without regard to personal danger."* Colonel Edwin M. Van Bibber, of the 313th, wrote his father in Bel Air, Maryland: *"McCardell went right into the thick of it and stayed there. He was unarmed and unattended. No one looked after him except to give him a K-ration once in a while. He is damn good company and a damn good man."*

On hand to watch the arrival of Allied forces in Cherbourg was Mark Watson [June 28, 1944]. From the town's Place de la République, which looks out past a statue of Napoleon, Watson wrote: *"American soldiers and French civilians nearly filled the little square for their joint celebration with music, speeches and expressions of international good feeling."* Such were the shifting moods and vistas of war.

The fighting from the beachheads to St. Lo 20 miles inland introduced Americans to a word—hedgerow (*bocage*)—they would not soon forget. *"Lofty hedgerows surround every farm lot,"* Watson recounted as he faced south. *"They make no trouble for a bulldozer, but they repel tanks with ease and compel the infuriated driver to grope his way to a road or gateway between fields."*

On July 4, 1944, he pointed out the difficulties of fighting in such terrain: *"Whether one is on high or low ground, he is sure to meet Normandy's unending hedgerows which separate the fields from the roads, the farms from neighboring farms and the farmer's own meadows from each other. As most of these farms are worked in small lots this means the hedgerows are often only a few rods apart. They make excellent wind breaks, which is one of their purposes. The hedge itself is of thick foliage and the bushes are rooted in an earth mound which itself is three to five feet high and approximately as thick.*

"The result is that each hedgerow is at one and the same time an admirable barrier against our tanks and an efficient screen for enemy riflemen and machine-gunners, which remain concealed behind each one, firing on our advance patrols until our mortars and Indian-fighting patrols can find the enemy units and exterminate them."

It was Holbrook Bradley's cherished role [July 9, 1944] to describe actual fighting in these hedgerows: *"After picking up our forward company locations, we moved out to find out how the boys were making out. At the next company headquarters, Lieut. Charles Maus, of Westminster, Maryland, sat outside a dugout. All along the hedgerow infantry men were busy digging new trenches or rearranging old ones, drying blankets and other equipment. A few were snatching a late meal. Maus told us he was about to move a couple of hundred yards to check some observation posts and invited us to come along.*

"All of us by now knew that the Jerry machine gunners and snipers cover all the open fields (should) any of our boys stray too far. So we kept cover, hugging a bank along the hedgerow. The lieutenant pointed to a high ridge ahead and said the Germans still held that area. Once or twice we passed men on outpost machine-gun duty. A sudden burst of mortar shell about 25 yards to the right sent us diving into slit trenches along the road. When no more followed we pushed on. Just as we had crossed to a protecting ditch on the other side, a mortar shell burst, this time even closer than the last one. An oil-filled circuit-breaker on a high tension pole above us sprayed us with liquid as a shell fragment knifed through it.

"These are the boys who have fought from hedgerow to hedgerow, struggled from apple orchard to apple orchard. They have lived in shallow trenches. They were dirty and unshaven. Their eyes were bloodshot and their minds often dulled by the incessant pounding. At the end they performed almost wholly by instinct. They got little more than two hours' sleep. Often they went day after day with no rest at all. But these battle-tested veterans inched forward under the hot July sun or in the driving rain to storm the next hedgerow. They took it with bayonets, if necessary, and then dug in to organize for the next move."

Three days later [July 10, 1944] Watson was out on a hedgerow patrol with a major, Robert Serlong, who demonstrated command qualities that drew the correspondent's admiration. The major said the best technique in hedgerow skirmishing was to keep moving and was annoyed that some of his patrols had advanced so far he could not communicate with them. There were casualties and a wounded soldier walked in on his own. Watson reported the following dialogue:

"'Hello boy,' Serlong said gently. 'What hit you?'

"'Shrapnel, sir,' said the soldier.

"'From a tank?' asked the major.

"'Didn't see any, sir.' was the answer.

"'Of course, it wasn't from a tank or you would have knocked it over. Wouldn't you?'

"The wounded boy burst out laughing and forgot his troubles. 'Get this boy over to the dressing station and patch him up,' the major said. 'By the way, do you want to go to the rear or go back to the front?'

"There was a pause of a couple of seconds. 'I ain't hurt enough to quit,' said the soldier. The major grinned."

Such was life among the hedgerows. But the situation within the Allied advance was such that visitors could come over to get a glimpse of the fighting, much to the annoyance of a combat correspondent who had lived in the trenches, eaten cold rations and dodged enemy fire. *"Sightseers and visiting firemen and one-day journalistic wonders pour into the ice-cream front, usually arriving by upholstered plane,"* McCardell jibed. *"They wear neckties and sleep in pajamas and complain about the shortage of clean towels. They demand—and usually get—a private jeep and a chauffeur to take them rubber-necking to Bayeux or Valogneso. They bring back German helmets as souvenirs and tell hair-raising tales about the shells they heard explode in the distance.*

"This dispatch is being written on the ice-cream front in the salon of an army-occupied village overlooking the sunny English Channel, where small fishing boats anchored off the shelving beach roll lazily. Upstairs sits a special service officer with a room full of baseball gloves, movie film and portable radios. Generally speaking, you wouldn't know a war was on."

With three *Sun* correspondents covering what might be called the mud and death campaign, two incidents reflected the fickleness of warfare.

The first was a happy occasion [July 1, 1944]. Let Bradley tell the tale: *"One of the strange coincidences of the war befell this correspondent today. Driving between battalions our jeep almost ran head-on into another headed in an opposite direction on a narrow country lane. Jumping out to find the best way to get by the other vehicle, we found that Mark Watson was a passenger in it."* One is left to marvel how a newspaper with the *Sun*'s limited resources could have two reporters who would meet by chance on an obscure country road in Normandy.

The second occasion took place on July 24, 1944. McCardell narrowly escaped death but an Associated Press photographer, Bede Irvin, did not. Both newsmen were sitting in a jeep covering an operation by the First Army when an errant bomb from an American Marauder exploded nearby. McCardell leaped into a ditch just in time. Irvin reached back to grab his camera, a fleeting but fatal mistake. Four days later, McCardell wrote a tribute to Irvin, calling him *"an honest, gentle, genuine man"* and lamenting how many other good men *"die here in a world awash in tears."*

Always the front-line reporter, Bradley told of a firefight at the entrance to St. Lo before he was wounded. *"We had gone only a few hundred yards up the road when there was a whine of a high incoming shell. We hit the nearest ditch and were showered with dirt and rocks as the explosion almost lifted us back onto the road."* After moving at the suggestion of military police into a nearby cemetery, Bradley went along with a proposal to try to go up the main street to a forward observation post. *"We noticed GIs digging in alongside the road as we legged it up to the corner. Three or four Yanks lay where they had died beside their destroyed tank. All about was more destruction. Down the street we noticed that the cathedral now had only one spire. There were several buildings up the street to the left that seemed still to be in pretty good shape.*

"We decided to make a break for them and landed in a doorway just as all hell broke loose behind us. Looking back we could see great columns of smoke rising from the corner we had just left, and heard more shells landing in the area around the square. We were debating whether to go ahead or turn back." Bradley said they chose the first course and soon ran into further enemy shelling. *"From somewhere in the outskirts came the rat-tat-tat of machine guns and the splatter of rifle fire. A few moments later we were on the street again and heading back to the infantry command post. A few more shells whined overhead and landed 100 yards away with an earth-shaking explosion as the artillery general opened a bottle of wine and passed it around to those who took St. Lo."*

Mark Watson took the opportunity [July 22, 1944] to write a tribute to the Twenty-ninth Division: *"This magnificent unit, which still has in its much altered membership many of the Maryland and Virginia National Guardsmen, who originally composed it entirely, has had an admirable fighting record throughout the Normandy campaign. It was one of the few Allied divisions whose elements landed in great force on D-Day itself. It was the only one of them which almost without relief continued from that day through the final success at St. Lo. Forty-two days later no division in the entire First Army had more continuous service, and it is hard to believe any has a better record. Besides its success at the beaches on and after D-Day it was the 29th which forced the difficult crossing of inundated marshes alongside the Aure River and thus gained entry into the critical town of Isigny, where the capture of flood-control gates finally made possible the clearing of other swamps. Subsequently the division's dogged fighting carried it to the east bank of the Vire River itself and finally it called for a long and costly battle for the ridge behind which St. Lo lies. All this was done by a division which had not seen battles since 1918, when its membership was not of these men but of their fathers."*

Many more would die in future battles.

CHAPTER 12

The Drive to the Siegfried Line

Mark Watson called it a *"dazzlingly swift campaign."* To Lee McCardell it was *"a war of movement on a tremendous scale."* What these two *Baltimore Sun* correspondents were describing was the "dazzling" and "tremendous" Allied breakout from St. Lo to the Siegfried line, from a town but twenty-five miles inland from the Normandy beaches to the German border three hundred miles away. All in little more than a month during the summer of 1944.

The Allied drive in mid-course became two-pronged as several Allied divisions were diverted from Italy to make an almost unopposed landing in southern France. Price Day moved with them. This invasion by the Seventh Army headed northward to achieve a timely juncture weeks later with American armies sweeping northern Europe. Marseilles fell early, but not early enough to feed and fuel and equip massive military forces still dependent on supplies over the beachheads or through the small Norman port of Cherbourg.

The Allies liberated most of France, including Paris (see Chapter 13), before they quite literally ran out of gas near the French-German border. Amidst joys of victory, Allied commanders made some dubious decisions: delaying the use of Antwerp by leaving access to this major port in German hands; sending forces (including the Twenty-ninth Division) into Brittany instead of using such forces for the drive east toward Germany; failing to close the Falaise Gap as Nazi troops escaped from Normandy to fight another day; continuing differences within the high command over single-thrust and broad-front strategy. However, these issues could not dampen summer confidence that the war would end quickly. The tough Normandy campaign was over and Allied troops rolled eastward. Yet autumn brought stalemate and winter much worse. It was a pivotal time when reporters could make their first look-back on the fierce struggle for Normandy

"*During the first seven weeks of Normandy warfare at close quarters, it seemed impossible to drive out the Germans save by pounding them with bombs and shells which resulted in the destruction of cities and farm buildings alike,*" wrote Watson in a retrospective [Aug. 12, 1944] on the battles just beyond the beaches. "*This was true until the German line was smashed and our armored columns began pouring at great speed and overrunning much of France without having to fire at anything save the fleeing enemy on the highways. The happy result is that village after village is quite unscarred and the broad fertile fields of Le Maine are as peaceful and well-cultivated as those of Maryland. The streets swarm with easy-going people engaged in normal activities but quite willing to take time off to wave at the columns of American troops coming up. They also laugh scornfully at trucks of German prisoners being hauled off to the cages, escorted by French guards who do not try to hide their satisfaction.*"

Two days later, he commented that the U.S. offensives "*have been such demonstrations of American mobility as few commands could perform in peacetime maneuvers. Chiefly we maintain unbroken contact with the Germans who unmistakably are withdrawing and compel them to give a large part of their attention to rear guard actions. In all this our air forces are operating almost at will. This is the time when the largest part of victory is available. The more demoralized is our defeated enemy the greater will be his trouble in reorganizing shattered battalions sufficiently to retreat in organized fashion, which is the only way to retreat without disaster.*"

The Watson analysis proved to be uncannily correct during a victorious Allied summer. Leading post-war military experts contended "the largest part of victory" was indeed available. But the autumn and winter would bring countervailing factors to the surface.

Watson had been with British forces after they finally—six weeks behind schedule—captured Caen, a strategic Norman objective invasion planners wanted taken on D-Day itself. Though intense night bombing had broken the resistance of German panzer units, he sadly observed, *"It also broke a good deal of Caen as well."* [July 17, 1944] *"It was with great but temporary relief that I beheld rising above the horizon the two noble Norman towers of the great St. Etienne Abbey which William the Conqueror built for the victory crowning his invasion of England."* He lamented the loss of many other irreplaceable sites: The Church of St. Julian, *"a model of early Gothic,"* the Church of St. Pierre, *"a perfect example of middle Gothic,"* the Church of St. Jean *"whose 13th century design was as gracious as its leaning tower was extraordinary,"* and the University of Caen, whose antiquity was second only to Oxford.

"The dreadful destruction to buildings of the most profound interest to architects, artists and antiquarians cannot be readily wiped from memory," he asserted. *"Time will, perhaps, determine whether so much destruction was necessary."* Like other *Sun* correspondents, he deplored the killing and wounding of civilians caught in the coils of war and marveled that survivors had warmly welcomed Allied troops.

On the other side of the coin, Thomas O'Neill reported from London that Allied ground forces believed tactical air support far behind German lines (causing some of the destruction lamented by Watson) had been of *"decisive importance."* The air cover limited enemy counter-attacks, delayed German reinforcements, and prodded Hitler's generals to put their reserve troops into battle piecemeal—a strategy O'Neill described as *"a form of military madness."*

Bradley remained with the old Maryland National Guard unit, the 115th Regiment of the Twenty-ninth Division, when it established another historic first—first into St. Lo, the long-sought-after hub of Normandy's roadway network. It was the culmination of a seven-week battle that had been planned to last only seven days. The Germans, he reported [July 20, 1944] had retired to hills near the city and immediately started firing on objectives it so recently tried to defend. *"Throughout the first night of the occupation the enemy continued this harassing fire and occasionally snipers peppered our positions only to draw a withering fire in return."*

A poignant postscript to the Normandy battles came from Watson after he witnessed the dedication of a cemetery for the dead of the Twenty-ninth Division [July 24, 1944]. *"Some of the fallen had died in the very meadow where burial took place. After time-honored military honors and a chaplain's prayer, assembled soldiers shouted 'Come on, let's go,' their division battle cry. This cry in the last month and a half has resounded from those ghastly beaches to the battered ruins of St. Lo."* He offered no casualty figures, a censored statistic. Sixty-three years later, Secretary of Defense Robert M. Gates, in a June 6, 2008 ceremony in France, said 9,387 Americans were killed in the Normandy campaign.

In the July 30 issue of *The Sun*, McCardell described the scene in another Normandy village that had suffered terribly. Excerpts:

"The crossroads village is a ghost town. Half its houses are burned shells, their hot ashes still smoldering. Most of the others have been wrecked by shell fire, ransacked and pillaged. Our armor with its umbrella of fighter-bombers swept through yesterday. The Germans bombed the village every night. The bravest of the village firemen turned out in a hopeless effort to save their town. Short strings of thin French firehose, still wet, are stretched along the road opposite the town hall, where a big Tri-Color hanging from a broken upstairs window billows in the breeze.

"A couple of Joes wandered up and down the deserted main street, glass crunching under their feet. They walked around some mowers and hay rakes, standing forlornly among the debris in front of a farm supply store. They peered into a smashed bicycle shop window. It must have been a pretty village, a sort of Frenchmyers, or Jefferson, or Buckeystown, among its rolling hills and orchards. But now it makes you sick at heart to see it."

Three days after McCardell was *"sick at heart"* as he sadly strode through a battered French village, he was happily recounting [Aug. 2, 1944] how, in another Normandy village, this one untouched, he took part in the capture of thirty-five German soldiers eager to surrender. This, of course, was not prescribed behavior for a correspondent who was supposed to be an unarmed observer. But such are the fortunes of war that even the most obedient of reporters, which McCardell was not, could get involved in antics entirely unforeseen.

McCardell's adventure began when he joined two corporals, Pat and Dick, on a Sunday afternoon jeep ride through the French country-

side. They chanced upon *"a charming hamlet of a few farm houses
and an old stone church in a secluded vale."* Its name: Grimesnil.
Soon the three Americans were surrounded by villagers who insisted
on feeding them rich omelets and an endless supply of strong, foaming
cider before leading them to church for a special service in their honor.

Reality returned, in a manner of speaking, when a peasant reported
that there were Germans in a farmhouse a kilometer away who were
anxious to give themselves up. So Pat and Dick, with Lee tagging along,
went after their willing quarry. There they found three of the retreating enemy. *"I have never seen three more frightened men—and I am
talking of the Germans now,"* McCardell told his readers. *"They were
quite terrified. They ran toward us, wailing Kamerad, Kamerad. Pat
and Dick and I would have been fools to have been frightened. They
dropped their hands for a moment and flung open their coats to show
us that they were unarmed. 'Keep your damned hands up,' Pat yelled,
and they seemed to understand. They were three frightened kids."*

The *Sun* reporter got his just reward for this escapade. Back home
in Baltimore cartoonist Richard Yardley drew McCardell, armed only
with a pointed pencil, prodding along four German soldiers with their
hands held high. This incident was cited when McCardell was later
awarded the Bronze Star.

Warfare had obviously entered a new phase when a disappointed
Watson looked back [July 29, 1944] on the American First Army's
failure to *"cut off the avenue of retreat for all the German troops
which we thought we had trapped north of the St. Lo-Coutances
Road."* Failed, in other words, to close the Falaise Gap and encircle
enemy forces. He blamed bad weather. *"Our bad fortune has been the
enemy's good fortune, and it is well known that no one has to dangle
good luck before the German command very long. The speed with
which the enemy began moving most of his troops out of the area
shows that his professional skill in moving men back and covering
their retreat is still one of his most notable qualities."* Watson thus
refrained from direct criticism of the American command by praising the Germans. Some historians have had no hesitation in blaming
Allied generals for frequent failures in shutting traps on nearly surrounded Axis troops.

As the U.S. First Army moved into tank country beyond St. Lo, Watson gave his readers a short description of the battle techniques he saw [July 30, 1944]. *"Our attacking infantry had been hit by enemy shells coming from a long ridge and our dashing little spotter planes had reported just where those strong points were. Even so it was difficult for our artillery to reach them, and diving Thunderbolts were summoned. Over the horizon they came in familiar formation, circled the ridge to make sure of their target, flew out and up some distance, and then come winging in at high altitude for the start of their dive. The leader nosed downward and came in at a rapidly increasing speed until just before it seemed he would crash we saw him release two bombs and immediately afterward pull away to the side. The bombs were on course ahead and struck. There was a pause before their delayed-action fuses worked to permit the pilot to clear the area of concussion."*

After describing two more attacks, Watson said *"our infantry assault troops needed no more help save their own stout arms and stouter hearts. At critical points one saw pierced and burned tanks and the bodies of men who had been unable to escape or surrender. Not only livestock and buildings were destroyed but even orchards were uprooted by bombs. It is one of the saddest sights of war. Normandy, whose sturdy people and productive farms will be most needed in the rebuilding of France, already had suffered terribly. It may be a military necessity for the expulsion of the enemy, but it is a large price which the Norman peasants have to pay for the liberation of the rest of Europe."*

Some days later [Aug. 6, 1944], Watson evoked memories of his World War I service by recalling that during the same week, twenty-six years earlier, German General Erich Ludendorff had identified it as a *"black day"* in which *"German defeat became inevitable."*

Holbrook Bradley's luck ran out on August 8, 1944, when he was wounded after linking up with GIs in a battle to take the town of Vire. His colleague, Mark Watson, wrote in a short follow-up that Bradley had been *"apparently observing proper vigilance (when) a cloud of dust raised by a passing vehicle attracted enemy attention. Several mortar shells were tossed into the area where Bradley was passing."* If this was an attempt to assure Baltimore editors that Bradley had taken suitable precautions, it doesn't quite ring true. Any reader who had been reading Bradley's stories had good reason to hoot, because he constantly risked injury or death to watch front-line battles. His injury, a shrapnel wound in his left thigh for which he received a Purple Heart, was not a minor affair.

Bradley, in his book, *War Correspondent from D-Day to the Elbe*, gave a hair-raising account of what happened on that August day in 1944. He came across GIs who had set up an observation post on the outskirts of Vire. *"'See anything?' I asked. 'Not a damn thing moving out there,' was one reply. 'Maybe the bastards are pulling out' was another. 'They're just lyin' doggo' said a third soldier. I started for the door and focused on a structure about 50 yards away. It looked empty so I started to run for it. I was halfway across the open space when I heard it—the unmistakable sound of a mortar being dropped into a tube. I hesitated for a second. Then there was a smashing blow to my left thigh above the knee, as if someone had hit me with a base-ball bat, and I went down. I tried to get up—and immediately fell flat on my face."*

Watson, taking note of Bradley's return three weeks later to the Twenty-ninth Division as it was besieging Brest, raised an issue that has long excited World War II historians—the Allied failure to cap-ture key ports in Brittany. Watson's words resonate over the years: *"It has been assumed from the beginning that the enemy would offer his greatest resistance in the vicinity of every port. However weak he may appear in the interior of France, once we had driven through his main Normandy line our forward progress against such coastal places as St. Malo, Brest, Lorient, St. Nazaire and Nantes would automati-cally array against us a continuous coast defense comparable to those around Cherbourg. The German command had ample reason to block us from all possible ports."* As it happened, Hitler ordered forces pro-tecting the ports to fight to the last man, a fairly successful policy that played hob with the Allied need for a greater supply flow. Sieges of Brest and other ports siphoned off troops needed for an Allied thrust into Germany that could have ended the war in 1944.

On another front, *"Representing the Combined American Press,"* Price Day filed his first story of the Allied landings in southern France

[Aug. 17, 1944]. He reported the Seventh Army had established a forty-mile beachhead and was moving inland against light German opposition. Naval warships were firing on scattered German strong points.

"The Germans are holding out only in spots and they are rapidly being wiped out," he wrote. *"Elsewhere, counter-attacks are expected but so far none has developed. The sea and sky are almost entirely empty of enemy craft and planes. The few German ships and submarines remaining in the Mediterranean are perhaps awed by the vast armada of American, French, British, Belgian and Greek ships and have stayed away.*

"No German planes appeared today and the Luftwaffe's activity last night was marked by more alarms than excursions. The barrage from Allied warships, transports, and especially built rocket ships that met the planes was potentially the greatest ever seen in any waters, but only a few of the ships spread out hundreds of miles of sea had a chance to shoot.

"Thousands of men and vast quantities of ammunition, food and material pour steadily ashore. The flow is so beautifully organized that on this beach in the central sector the sand is cluttered only by German barbed wire rolled up neatly and laid aside. The loaded trucks are moved directly from the ramps of the broad-prowed landing craft and are driven up a short stretch of sand, checked at a control point and sent in a steady stream along the road.

"American troops come ashore without shouts or fanfare and are moved toward the fluid and expanding front. Veterans of earlier and much tougher amphibious operations are happy the going so far has been easy, but they know hard fighting is ahead and show little emotion."

Paris, too, was in the newspapers. McCardell, also on August 17, reported that Ninth Air Force planes *"continued to tear the German army to pieces,"* thus enabling on-rushing Allied ground troops to mount a *"rapid advance toward Paris."* In 300 sorties, Allies claimed the destruction of more than 200 enemy motor transports and some 60 tanks and armored vehicles. Allied losses: only 13 planes. Regiments were pulled back two thousand yards to give aircraft the opportunity to blast at enemy lines. *"The bombers buzzed into the target area with machine guns blazing. Ammunition belt clips and empty cartridge cases came rattling down on our heads."* Then the infantry charged in a textbook example of how close-in air support assists troops on the ground.

Note his tribute to the Ninth Air Force because it came just three days before McCardell and three other newsmen were ordered back to London by Colonel Robert Parham, chief of public relations for the Ninth. Their crime? They had not devoted full time to his unit, Instead, they had dared to write about the army, of all things, as its armor and infantry raced across France, having left battle-scarred Normandy behind. Jack Tait, a reporter for *The New York Herald Tribune*, who was not one of Parham's targets, broke the story [Aug. 22, 1944] with the kind of cutting sarcasm that is a publicity boy's nightmare. *"The order is the aftermath of a long series of threats indulged in by certain public relations officers of the Air Force,"* Tait wrote. *"Correspondents have been told they must confine the bulk of their activities to coverage of the Ninth Air Force. Those who did not, it was made clear, would have to seek reassignment elsewhere."*

The next day Tait wrote that he and his colleagues at first thought it was a joke. *"It is inconceivable that one group engaged in this war would consider publicity for itself more precious than giving the United States the story of this war, whether it be the air story, the ground story or a combination of the two."* When this bizarre tale hit the newsstands, it aroused howls from the Fourth Estate and, more important, caught the attention of Secretary of War Henry L. Stimson. Suddenly, the Air Force was claiming its only objective was to give other reporters a chance to cover the Ninth—this at a time when there were existing vacancies. Stimson quickly ordered a full report. The reassignment of the four correspondents was put on hold. And *The Sun* ran an article listing thirteen McCardell stories, all of them positive in tone, about Ninth Air Force support of the ground offensive against Nazi Germany. The outcome of this farce was predictable: The newsmen could stay where they were, if they wished, and Colonel Parham was the one who got travel orders. He was instructed to return to the United States.

Meanwhile the new front in the south of France was busy. Price Day reported Allied forces had moved within six miles of the important port of Toulon. *"The ability of the first wave of troops to move so swiftly to their present positions is testimony to the organization of the invasion plan. The inevitable dread of observers in this theater is that any new landing might become another Anzio, but it is clear by now that the present operation is planned more thoroughly and carried out in vastly greater strength than was that bitter venture. The new beachhead is well past the danger point. It would be a distinct surprise if the Germans did not stiffen in southern France, but they cannot push us off as they almost did at Anzio. That the enemy has not yet accepted full battle is indicated by the small numbers of prisoners."*

Acutely aware of French sensitivities, Day pointed to the role of French forces—sometimes cooperating, sometimes competing—in the invasion of the southern Vichy-dominated region of the country. He wrote a profile of General Jean de Lattre de Tassigny, calling him a patriot whose *"principal ambition is the restoration of the honor and prestige of French arms."* His was a career in which he served the Vichy government while seeking its downfall, opposed the Allies until his service to them would enable him to return to France *"at the head of victorious troops"* opposed to the Hitler regime. *"He knows,"* wrote Day, *"that for four years Frenchmen have watched, though in hatred, one of the most efficient armies ever* (the German conquerors) *and set an even higher standard for a* (French) *armée impeccable."*

As de Lattre's forces pushed toward Toulon, Day was with them when they fought for possession of the elaborate Golf Hotel outside that city. During the battle, half of the 280-man defense unit surrendered and the other half was killed. After the battle for the hotel, which fulfilled a fortress-like role, bodies were seen in bedrooms, bar, billiard room, kitchens, lounges, and in blood-spattered foxholes on the outdoor terraces.

Weeks later, having covered the Seventh Army as it swept north from the Riviera coast, Day noted that war damage was slight and the region only thinly occupied by Germans except in the larger cities. Taking issue with the notion that *"Paris is France,"* Day held that the people he had seen in the southern part of the country could be entrusted *"with the future greatness of the nation. Not only have they fought (i.e., cooperated) either actually with the French Forces of the Interior or by assisting the FFI, or merely by non-compliance with German orders and desires, they have also, in these comparatively lucky sections, suffered greatly.*

"Many of their young men have been murdered by the Gestapo. Many others, some not so young, are engaged in forced labor in Germany. Others, in thousands, are simply missing. The result has been not as the Germans planned, the breaking of the people into submission. The Germans, with their utter inability to project themselves imaginatively into the minds of other people, made a mess of trying to link the French to the Reich. On the darker side, many French, who from fear or weakness or hopelessness tried to get along with the Germans because they were by nature fascist or criminal, actively assisted the Germans." Always even-handed in judging the French, Day took issue with "prophets" who said France was finished as a great nation.

The Sun on Aug. 21, 1944, published an article by Watson that combined military analysis, descriptions of battle scenes, personal observations about the horrors of war, encounters with French civilians in places rich with French history, praise for American soldiers, and disappointment with objectives unattained. His story started by striving to put a gloss on the much-lamented Allied failure to close the Falaise Gap before thousands of Nazi troops escaped from Normandy eastward where they would fight again, often with serious consequences. Note Watson's subtlety:

"That yawning gap from Argentin to Falaise is closed. Patrols from the British on the north and Americans on the south had made earlier contacts along the roads connecting these two ancient, long-embattled towns, but the Germans were finally driven out only this morning." "Finally driven out" was not the fate planned by the Allies for the almost encircled German forces. Defeat or extermination or incarceration of entire Nazi divisions was. *"A considerable number of Germans had made their escape through this gap,"* he wrote. *"However, before they left the Allies had killed or captured a good many of their companions."*

Since Watson was with U.S. troops as they fought north from Argentan toward their meeting with British soldiers moving south, he chose to describe battered Argentan after the tide of battle: *"It is a pity but war crushes ancient and lovely monuments and the most useful of lives as swiftly as it destroys the meanest hovel and the most worthless of humans. It pays no heed whatsoever to which shall be taken and which shall be left. Argentan's 6,000 residents could not believe that the war's most violent eddies would totally pass communities a few miles away and yet swirl around their own town."*

It was *"dotted with those mournful items which mark the tide of receding battle—ruined houses and barns, splintered trees, dead cattle and occasionally German dead as there had been no time to bury. This in an historic town reaching back to the father of William the Conqueror."*

Watson described his impressions of the village priest, the village doctor and the village mayor, all of whom had stayed in their city while most inhabitants fled: *"One was Father Rattier, who could not leave his flock—and who, in all truth, when I asked him why he remained with a bandaged head, admitted he would not leave his church. Another was old Dr. Picot, who stayed to meet that little flock's material needs. A third was Mayor Silvestre, who apparently feels about his city as a ship captain feels about his ship. These men even the German troops saluted. That they were not killed was a miracle."* The priest told him of being struck by stones as he lay abed in his church, but added, *"'We Frenchmen are happy to be free.' I think he controlled his emotion better than I did my own,"* the veteran reporter confessed.

Then came the most tragic part of his story. Watson heard an explosion when he entered the town and ran to the lane from which the sound came. *"Our soldiers were staring in sudden horror. Almost at our feet, by the door of a house, was a tangle of four figures, a man, a woman, and two little girls. They had apparently been just about to enter the door when one of them exploded a mine or booby trap. One of the little girls and her father had bought the worst of it. Their clothes were in shreds. The child was mercifully unconscious and so motionless we thought she was dead until we heard her gasping. The sister was less hurt and screamed to her father lying in the lane on his back, and feebly moving one arm and the stump of another. The young wife, with that incredible bravery of women, was clinging to her senseless baby with one arm and trying to raise the ghastly wreck of her husband with the other. I cannot bring myself to describe what five minutes earlier had been the face of her man. It was a positive relief to quit that street of horror and rejoin tankers at the edge of town."*

CHAPTER 13

Race into Liberated Paris

After spending most of June and July fighting their way into Normandy, Allied forces in August broke out of that province and swept into tank country on the high road to Paris. It was an exultant moment for *The Sun*. In an era when it considered *The New York Times* as the only newspaper worth emulating, the liberation of Paris gave *The Sun* a dramatic opportunity to outshine its "good, gray" competitor. And it did so with enough resourcefulness and luck to make the last week of August a triumph that ought to be remembered as long as presses roll in Baltimore.

Lee McCardell was the first American reporter to get into the French capital ahead of the authorized U.S. entry. He did so by befriending five members of the French resistance who gave him a ride on the roof of their Citroen as they raced into Paris one day ahead of General Charles de Gaulle's forces. *"It wasn't the easiest method of travel but the driver was in a hurry to get home,"* McCardell wrote.

His colleague, Mark Watson, was hardly to be outdone. Riding into Paris next day with a U.S. armored column, he found himself the only fluent French speaker among his fellow Americans seeking directions to the Eiffel Tower. Desperate to join the victory parade, U.S. officers installed Watson in a car at the head of the column. *"That is the sort of thing a newspaper correspondent dreams of but usually encounters only in the movies,"* Watson mused.

On August 28, 1944, Baltimoreans awoke to read a six-column front page headline: *"Two* Sun *Correspondents with Allies Entering Paris."* Just below appeared an unusual home-office box. The

McCardell-Watson race had turned into an unintended intramural competition, *"McCardell by a Length"* was the small headline. *"Lee McCardell beat Mark Watson by a day,"* the paper declared, tongue in cheek. *"McCardell, going in with the French in a somewhat unofficial fashion, entered the capital on August 24 while Watson, traveling with the Americans, entered the city August 25. But McCardell's first dispatch reached the Sun office in so short a time before Watson's that a photograph was needed to determine the winner."*

More to the point, the stories of both reporters carried Paris datelines. Not so with *The Times.* In that crucial liberation week, the New York paper did not have a single staff-written story from inside the city. The nearest it came was a *"NEAR PARIS"* dateline. Otherwise *The Times* relied on the Associated Press, the United Press, and staff reports from Supreme Allied Headquarters.

What happened? Weren't New York reporters supposed to be everywhere? This author learned the answer only when, six decades later, I chanced upon an account of the recapture of Paris by A. J. Liebling of *The New Yorker* magazine. Both he and Harold Denny of *The Times* had been caught in huge traffic jams along all roads leading to the French capital on liberation day. Denny, after coming across some Germans *"saw he had a scoop of historic proportions since he was the only* (sic) *correspondent for a daily publication present,"* Liebling wrote. So Denny tapped out his story, gave his dispatch to a public relations officer and then suffered a correspondent's worst nightmare. The press center at the Hotel Scribe managed to lose *"poor Denny's exclusive* (sic) *eyewitness story,"* Liebling wrote. *"At any rate* The Times *never received it. The big* (Times) *story about the surrender was an Associated Press dispatch that read as if it had been assembled in London."* All this on the same day the *Baltimore Sun* had two bylined dispatches by reporters who had much more to write about.

First let McCardell begin his story: *"It took me six days to reach Paris, traveling at times behind various reconnaissance and armored elements and finally entering the metropolitan area yesterday with tanks of a French armored division."* [Aug. 28, 1944] He described the five members of the French Forces of the Interior (FFI) that he had fallen in with as guys *"in summer sport clothes"* who really knew their way around.

"One afternoon they took us to call upon Danielle Darrieux, the French actress living in retirement outside Paris. They took us one night to the home of Andre Berthomieu, a French movie director, and his wife, Leni Norro, a French actress. We spent three nights in country inns and a fourth in a lavish country home of a lady who embarrassed us with apologies. Germans had run off with all her sheets and best wines." In this name-dropping piece, McCardell also informed Baltimore readers that near Rambouillet he had encountered the great American writer, Ernest Hemingway, an old hand at conflict. McCardell was worried that other correspondents might beat him to Paris. Hemingway assured him that would not be the case, and he was right.

Watson was not to be outdone in high living. After arriving in Paris in the spectacular fashion mentioned above, he got himself a front-row seat at the historic Hotel Crillon to witness the surrender of the German headquarters command. He described this as *"the main act of the day,"* adding: *"It was the end of the Master Race in the City of Light and it did not look at all like the visions Hitler had painted."* Old friends welcomed Watson and some of his fellow reporters to their home, gave them the use of a porcelain bathtub, and *"seated us before the first white table cloth, shining silver and glasses and china any of us had seen since quitting London."*

Despite these high jinks, there was a war on, and McCardell told of passing through the village of Monfort-LeMaury near Versailles. *"The day before after a small American patrol had passed through, the villagers hung out all their flags. That night the Germans came back, shot the Maire and his wife and burned his house. We understood then why French villagers were sometimes cautious."*

He also described evidence of combat even as the Paris celebrations began. French artillery was shelling German batteries in the Bois du Boulogne and the areas around the Auteuil race track. *"In several instances crowds mobbed individual German prisoners and snipers. Police had to fight to protect the terrified Jerries."* Watson heard rumors shots were fired at General Charles de Gaulle when he attended services at the Cathedral of Notre Dame. He reported that two French priests present at the ceremony had confirmed the stories. When visiting Notre Dame himself, he saw *"chairs were still lying around overturned in the two side aisles"*—signs the de Gaulle party had moved quickly outside the line of fire. Those firing on de Gaulle were described as Germans, or Communists or Vichyites—perhaps all three—as the general took control of the city.

Both *Sun* reporters marveled at the exuberance of Parisians when columns of American troops finally entered their city. Their welcome was *"hysterical,"* wrote McCardell, *"even while the streets still echoed and reechoed with the last hopeless resistance. I felt like I had been moving in a dream. Crowds of men, women and children were screaming 'Bravo,' throwing flowers at columns of Allied tanks, half-tracks and jeeps. Tears were running down many a Parisian's cheek. Tears ran down my own once or twice."*

Watson made a similar observation as he told of racing to keep up with the American Fourth Infantry Division, which had been given the honor of leading the official U.S. entry. *"The citizenry tossed flowers and swarmed over every truck or jeep that stopped, deluging non-reluctant soldiers with enraptured kisses."* He told of meeting a Frenchman, a fellow veteran of World War I, who had lost a son in the current conflict. *"This day is the first day of joy I have had since my boy's death,"* he told Watson. French crowds taunted and threatened terrified German soldiers. They shouted *"Assassins . . . Pigs . . . Thieves"* and *"a few other expletives that would startle a Pratt Street longshoreman."*

Paris had been a scene of sporadic street fighting for days as a German withdrawal hung in the balance and the Resistance forces were divided between Communists and Gaullists. All were at least united in hunting down Vichy regime collaborationists, a quest that resulted in gunfire at the Chamber of Deputies, a last retreat for Vichy police units. As for girls who had been friendly with German occupiers, their reward was a shaved head. Watson told of one girl who was left with *"a small double clump of short hair in imitation of Hitler's moustache."*

Watson wrote that *"there is no doubt that the city's enormous resources as a rail and road center will prove valuable for the coming phases of the campaign."* But he also told of growing supply difficulties as Allied armies rushed eastward, beyond Paris. Only later was it learned the great French capital had escaped the fate of devastated Warsaw when the German commander decided to prove himself a European—repeat, a European—daring to defy Hitler.

The next day *The Sun* carried reports by Watson and McCardell warning that the Paris situation remained dangerous and uncertain. The French Resistance and German authorities had agreed on a three-day armistice during which German troops would leave the city. *"Time will tell whether the Paris committee was wise in granting the armistice at all,"* Watson commented. McCardell, for his part, reported rumors from Paris alleging outright combat between Nazi troops. But in the end, Paris remained intact—one of the great achievements of Western civilization. It was a heady moment in the war, with Price Day reporting from Marseille that Germans were disorganized and offering only token resistance to the Allied offensive in southern France. *"The present advance is in fact hardly a military campaign at all in many places. It is an expedition through friendly country."* He warned, however, that the Germans still held one-third of Marseille and had a battery of two hundred guns in the port area.

By September 1, these precautionary comments terminated. German forces were in retreat in many areas, leaving vast quantities of military equipment, food, and other supplies to rapidly advancing Allied troops. From the front in southern France, Day reported: *"Remnants of the German 19th Army, after a painful crossing of the Drome River, limped toward the area southeast of Lyon to join other depleted and motley units. Of the Germans who escaped the debacle, many were on foot, their vehicles lying in a gigantic junk pile. Elsewhere throughout the northern half of the liberated territory, other Germans were also afoot because their vehicles had run out of gas or oil. Abandoned and intact cars and tanks are found in increasing numbers. In one area northeast of Grenoble the farmers disclosed that the Germans took their butter to use as motor lubricant. It is increasingly clear that except for the 19th Army, which retains a measure of cohesion, Germans in this area are in a state of confusion, out of touch with each other and ignorant of the disposition of the Americans, French regulars and Maquis troops"* (French guerrillas).

War is not only a tale of clashing armies. For *Baltimore Sun* war correspondents operating largely on their own, it also was a tale of individuals whose singular fate could mean life or death, good or bad luck, courage or cowardice, grand adventure or crushing misfortune. By happenstance, on September 3, 1944, the newspaper published two articles by Day that ran the gamut of human emotion. Filed in different places on different dates, they both arrived in Baltimore in time for the big Sunday edition. First, a tense horror story from Grenoble, a city captured by Allied forces moving north from the Riviera invasion:

"In miserable and rainy twilight, against a wall of a shabby metal works on the outskirts of Grenoble, six young men found guilty six hours earlier of treachery against France died before a firing squad. More than 10,000 citizens of Grenoble, packed in balconies, clinging to roofs and sneering from beneath a black flood of umbrellas that eddied through the streets leading to muddy Champs Bouchayer, cheered as a long line of Maquis sent a single fusillade into the men who, by their own admission, had born arms as members of the hated militia (of the Vichy government). *The execution was scheduled for 7 o'clock. At three minutes to seven a black windowless van pushed its way through the crowds and through the lines of Maquis who had tommy guns cocked and pistols in hands. Within two minutes of seven, the men, ranging in age from 17 to 22, had walked firmly and rapidly to six L-shaped steel posts standing some six feet out from the wall and spaced 15 feet apart. Five of the men wore dark blue clothing, the other a brown coat and light trousers. One was red-headed, the others dark. They were not blindfolded. All faced the firing squad with open eyes and with their hands tied with new thin rope behind their backs. Precisely at 7 o'clock, without formality, a line of Maquis wearing the ridged helmets of the French army, fired. The man on the right end fell first, knees forward and legs buckled under him. The next four men slumped slowly. The last man stood until after the coup de grace, and still remained half standing until the rope was cut away."* One is left to wonder how these young men

would have lived their lives if war and German occupation had not intervened.

In the very same issue of *The Sun,* Day had a long sprightly interview with Gertrude Stein, the celebrated American writer and conversationalist who had spent the war in obscurity at the foot of a mountain in the lower Alps: *"A stocky little woman with close cropped gray hair and lively brown eyes looked happily at the small task force of unarmed, worn, dirty and unshaven war correspondents. 'Can you get it through your thick heads how wonderful it is to see American children?' We told Gertrude Stein how wonderful it was to see her. For the past four years of war the author of* Portraits and Prayers, Four Saints in Three Acts, The Autobiography of Alice B. Toklas *and other volumes; one of the most brilliant of modern critics; friend and sponsor of Picasso and Hemingway, and proponent of the theory that 'a rose is a rose,' that 'pigeons on the grass are melancholy,' and that 'the world is round' has been living in this out of the way corner. She, Miss Toklas and a white poodle, Basket II, haven't been hiding exactly. They simply haven't let anyone know where they were. The villagers knew, but they didn't tell.*

"At one time, as an eminent American citizen, she was offered a chance to get out. She thought it over and turned it down to stay with France through its abysm from which she never doubted for a moment it would emerge. By staying she got one of the great stories of the war, for it was in the region of cloud-filled valleys and rugged peaks that the Maquis (French guerillas) arose in their fullest strength. She started her story in Paris on the day the war began. For almost five years the manuscript was kept in illegible shorthand so it couldn't be deciphered if it fell into hands of Germans during the four times they occupied parts of her house. The Stein book is tentatively titled 'All the Wars I've Known.' Its opening sentence: 'I do not know whether to put in the things I do not remember as well as the things I do remember.'

"Then she rattled off some of her observations:—'I've more relatives in Baltimore than I can count.'—'Germans do not do anything incorrect. It's only that they're there, like a blight.' Of some German occupiers who meekly obeyed her order not to sleep in her library,

'The only trouble with them was that they had a key complex. Germans always go off with all the keys. It is a strange complex in the German mind. As far as I can make out, it consists first of the fact that they want to have control of the key, which gives them a feeling of being master, and, second, no matter what they're the keys to, it gives them some sense of security. Every time after the Germans have been here I had to have a whole set of keys made.' About the black market—*'The first year of the war was horrible. France almost starved. And then the black market got going. Don't misunderstand about the black market in France. It was for the poor as well as the rich. Every railroad worker lived on the black market. It saved France. I've spent most of the past four years walking from house to house and village to village getting some food here and some there. So has everyone else, and we've not only lived, but especially in farm country, we've lived well.'* Day reported that *"when Miss Stein had a problem with money, she sold a Cezanne portrait of his wife, one of two paintings she brought with her from her collection in Paris. The other, Picasso's great portrait of herself, hangs without a frame among the steel engravings which adorn the walls of her rented house."*

Back to the war: Lee McCardell once again was writing about how correspondents covered the conflict [Sept. 4, 1944]: *"Wars are now moving with such dispatch on such a vast front that scores of newspaper correspondents pouring into Paris from London have only the vaguest notion of what's going on. If the situation seems confused to newspaper readers at home, they should have the satisfaction of knowing it's the same way here. Separated by vast distances from the press censors, radio transmission points and—most important of all —the briefing officers who formerly filled in the war story for them, all are trying frantically to piece the story together."* Holbrook Bradley, sixty years later, told this writer the business of getting his copy to the paper was often uppermost in his mind. Not only were his D-Day dispatches held up—a terrible disappointment. Since he typed on single sheets of paper (no carbons), a lost dispatch was a loss forever. There were no rockets from Baltimore about transmission difficulties. The only message he got from the home office was to keep his head down, an instruction he knew he could ignore.

As the Allied offensive swept across France, Watson reported from Soissons *"the farther one advances in this dazzlingly swift campaign the clearer is the evidence of the demoralized state of the enemy. Our infantry and artillery have been able to move in the armor's trail, consolidating its gains and establishing a firm wall to block the enemy's retreat."* In the same issue of the newspaper, McCardell reported that engineers building advance airfields for the Ninth Air Force had been hard put to keep up with the advancing front. *"The construction battalions now are leapfrogging each other. Their reconnaissance teams are well beyond Paris in the race to keep the fighter-bombers on the heels of our armored columns and motorized infantry now rolling toward the German border."*

A new theme crept into Watson's reportage in mid-October when he was writing about Aachen—this time not as a military objective waiting to be taken but as a German city now under the occupation control of American forces. Here was a great opportunity, he wrote [Oct. 15, 1944] to demonstrate how the U.S. would administer conquered territory and populations. *"Our performance in that stage is inevitably being witnessed by the Germans in the immediate area and their impressions are inevitably being communicated in one way or another to millions of Germans in the cities which lie on the other side of the combat line."* Occupation control must serve the military campaign, he asserted, citing the old army dictum that *"one of the prime requisites for success in the forward areas is orderliness in the rear."* Watson estimated there were still 10,000 German civilians in Aachen who had defied Nazi orders (obeyed by 150,000 others) to evacuate the city. Some were the likeliest candidates *"to accept our domination"* having gone through a screening process whereby *"a good many dubious sheep and undoubted goats"* have been left in prison camps. To perform police duties, 80 persons had been selected as "reliable" and had been outfitted with new uniforms—blue jackets and red-striped pants—that drew the envy of the populace.

Nazis had long boasted they had brought order out of chaos after coming to power in the early thirties. Watson wrote: *"If now the American administrators can demonstrate that they, too, can and without savage oppression likewise establish and maintain civilian order, there will be a political victory which, in after effects, may prove commensurate with the military victory itself."* The Sun's military expert said the army's program might not satisfy Americans who think *"every German should be exterminated"* or others who believe convinced Nazis will *"immediately yield to generous treatment and become reformed characters." "The army is following a middle path which seeks to separate known goats from potential sheep. They are endeavoring to keep the goats isolated to provide the sheep with an opportunity to demonstrate their tractability and their willingness to live at peace with the world."* In assessing damage in Aachen, Watson reported that while many water mains were shattered, schools were more in need of teachers than repairs.

During this optimistic period before the storm, Day and McCardell came up with vignettes mocking the Germans. Day told of a trio of would-be deserters, one of whom had a safe-conduct pass that had been dropped on enemy positions. But there was a problem. *"They understood that they had only one ticket among them. Could they surrender on that, or should they go back and get two more?"* McCardell described a German veteran of World War I who had attempted to surrender but his commanding officer was a *"stinker"* who would execute his whole squad to prevent defections. The vet defected anyway and, *"ironically enough,"* in the same locality where he had surrendered in the last war.

There would be precious little time or inclination for Allied troops to belittle the German enemy in the grim weeks ahead.

CHAPTER 14

Hardships and Haunting Memories

As Allied armies raced past Paris on their exultant five-week march to the Siegfried Line, they passed Verdun in a blink. Verdun, where in the First World War the French and the Germans had fought their longest sustained battle, where they had bled one another white over a no-man's-land that in the final analysis had hardly shifted. *"On these blood-drenched hillsides, nearly three decades ago, the German army of the First World War was flung back in defeat after sacrificing 300,000 of its own men and exacting also as great a toll of the French defenders,"* Watson wrote [Sept. 4, 1944]. *"Only a little distance from Verdun itself—one of whose streets is named after the American 42nd Division of the other war—are the heights above the Meuse and the dense Forest of Argonne in which the Americans made their largest sacrifice and gained their most glorious success under Pershing. In this war our march past Chateau Thiérry, Soissons, St. Mihiel and the Meuse has been a far easier enterprise.*

"The journey from Laon has been something of a sentimental affair, for in its course we touched at a great many places well-remembered from our days under Pershing. This time, instead of being spaced over a long campaign, they were compressed into a single day's travel. Not through mud but over smooth highways and not past ruins but through the smiling agricultural fields of Champagne, where happily the most of the grain crops have come to harvest too late for the Germans to carry it away with them. There are scars which trace back to the First World War. West of Fismes, whose name is familiar to many a Maryland veteran, we came to a silent memorial beside the road bearing the familiar insignia of the American Fourth Division,

which had fought along the Aisne-Vesle with great gallantry in the other war. Over the highway we at last came in sight of the noble towers of the cathedral of Rheims, which dominates the whole plain. It was a singular experience to see how much the freedom of Rheims means to France as a whole. We had not yet reached the city when we met a parade of French citizens carrying the flags of France and the Allies and coming to a proud salute. The great cathedral will presumably always wear honorable but melancholy scars of the other war when the German bombardment destroyed its famous glass and much of the incomparable sculpture which made this cathedral one of the marvels of all time.

"East of Rheims our advance had continued at great speed and as we crossed the Vesle and lesser rivers on the trail of our troops it was with the continuous memory of the difficulties which attended the American advance in the other war when the German army was still fighting with all the ferocity of which it was capable. At length the deep green of the Argonne Forest appeared on the horizon of Argenna where 22 of Pershing's great divisions had been engaged and where they suffered 119,000 casualties. Among those were two divisions largely composed of Marylanders of whom a fair number still lie in the Romagne cemetery near Montfaucon with 20,000 other American dead.

"As one approaches Verdun now it is a different thing from the years of the other war. In 1918 the city was still largely a shambles from the long bombardment. Today it is rebuilt. It must be remembered that when France mistakenly put its trust in the Maginot Line it scuttled the great fortress at Verdun, whose giant circle of forts had proved its merit so unmistakably in 1916–17. Verdun has figured in history in many ways but never more gloriously than it did in the other war. Along the road which leads from fort to fort I came on another spot of which I had not thought of in years. Here stood the little hamlet called Fleury lying so close to Fort Veux that upon it fell numbers of German shells intended for Fort Veux. Day after day they fell and month after month so that when I was here in 1918 what was once Fleury was mere churned earth. Not only had houses disappeared, but stones were not recognizable as stones for only pebbles

were left. Worse still, not a tree remained, not a stump or a twig that would say this was once a wood. Even in this war I have not seen such total and absolute destruction.

"Today the whole ghastly scene was revived in memory for I passed a monument on which was inscribed: 'Ici Fut Fleury'—'Here Was Fleury.' It was never rebuilt. Perhaps there is no better monument to the awfulness of modern war."

Three weeks later [Oct. 1, 1944], Watson was still in the same region, this time even more autobiographical. From Chaumont not far from Verdun, Pershing commanded an American army of two million men. *"Memories of that achievement remain so vivid to an older generation as to encourage the use of two days away from the Siegfried Line for sentimental exploration of the area which held the news headlines a quarter of a century ago."* Watson referred again to *"the heroic military performances"* of World War I doughboys in places he was passing through twenty-five years later. He told of Domrémy where Joan of Arc was born and whose *"hillsides are still dotted with sheep descended, no doubt, from Joan's own flocks,"* and of Chaumont, the Pershing headquarter town, where *"there is no difficulty in picking one's way through narrow streets. The journey was immediately continued to the old barracks where the headquarters had been. The central building, which held Pershing's office and those of his central staff had been set afire so that the roof had fallen in and destroyed the fourth and third floors. The small cage that I had occupied at the time had been charred to a crisp. The old general's old office had not been reached by the flames, but it and most of the others had been 'decorated' by the Germans with the usual mottoes and drawings. There was small resemblance to the busy hum of American offices in those days when Col. Hugh H. Young and many other Baltimoreans found business there.*

"There remained only one other point of interest, the chateau in which I had been comfortably billeted at Chaumont. There were misgivings immediately on passing the great stone gate, for in other days Chaumont du Bois had been a place of singular beauty. Now it was unkempt and along the winding roads were those untidy foxholes which German soldiers had for use against American aerial bombs

which never came. Where once there had been a tennis court, it was 'overgrown.' The great pool was quite empty, and the warning cry of peacocks now no longer sounded as I turned into the lane."

Early September 1944 was a moment in the European conflict when the Anglo-American coalition, from the top down, believed the war could be over before the end of 1944. It was not a totally flawed calculation. The German army had suffered huge losses during and after the breakout from Normandy, leaving the Nazi homeland apparently scantily defended. But at this critical juncture the Allies overran their supply capabilities, thus giving Germans the opportunity to reorganize and rebuild their forces. What had seemed a rout turned into a stalemate, with the Rhine tantalizingly close and yet so far, far away.

At Brest on the westernmost part of the Allied invasion of Northern Europe, Bradley had been covering the American siege of that port, one of several Hitler had ordered defended at all costs. In a dispatch written September 10 and published September 15, Bradley made it clear that at last Brest's days of German occupation were numbered. He reported that more than 1,500 Germans had surrendered and resistance had been reduced to a small force combating American troops and French Forces of the Interior, the famous FFI. The Brest Fort still had a month's supply of food and ammunition, but its grounds were pockmarked by bomb and artillery shell craters. German prisoners said they just could not take incessant pounding any longer. *"As we watched the sunset from the lighthouse at the tip of the (Brest) peninsula last night, the absence of battle noises seemed strange in the light of the fighting that has taken place there during the siege,"* wrote Bradley. *"From the ancient church, perched on the cliff's edge, came the sound of French peasants who already are returning to their homes, some of which are still smoking."*

Next day appeared a Bradley dispatch of continued fighting. *"There were sounds of scattered rifle fire as we headed along a trail littered with discarded American and German equipment. There was a continuous rustle overhead of our artillery shells as we followed the trail along a telephone line. There was also continuous thudding as these shells landed up ahead and filled the air with dirt and flying debris. Soon reports of the battle came back over the wire and then two GIs appeared herding ten dirty, grimy, apparently dazed Heinies up the path. They had taken them as they stepped out of the hedge and none seemed sad about being captured. All along the path we found foxholes. They were dirty, filled with straw and usually contained a blanket, a mess kit, gas mask, a rifle and sometimes some ammunition.*

At a few spots there was American equipment—some covered with blood, some just discarded to lighten packs while following the wire up a narrow trail. Someone made the remark that the wire didn't look American when the leader of our party spotted a German lying in a hole in front of us. He had just finished saying the Heinie was dead when he raised up and another German appeared somewhere behind him. We backed off expecting a hand grenade but none followed. Dave Scherman of Life *magazine yelled in German for the Germans to come out with their hands up. Just to back him up our guides fired a couple of shots up the path and more Germans came waving a white flag and clasping their hands over their heads. This caused us to take another trip back to deliver the prisoners to the command post, which we did, and then started hunting for more. This time we ran into one of our platoons and finally got to the front lines. From here we could still see flights of dive bombers circling the burning city, looking for spots that needed their attention. Whenever such an opportunity presented itself a ship would peel off and come down screaming, with all its machine guns chattering, strafing and bombing at the same time. What remained of the garrison was still holding out but taking a pounding."*

The end of the siege of Brest came on September 18, 1944, freeing the Twenty-ninth Division to move across France to the rather static front near the German border. *"Brest proved to be one of the toughest nuts to crack,"* Bradley wrote. *"It was a tough slugging match that meant a constant drain on our own men and supplies. The end came suddenly when we blasted our way into the town, which had become a mass of smoking ruins.*

"With only a few days to clean themselves and their equipment, the men of the Blue and Gray were on the move again by jeep, truck and French boxcar. Moving (far eastward to) *the First Army's line with the 30th Infantry and the Second Armored Division north of Aachen, the*

29th slammed into one of the toughest fights of the war—the initial breakthrough of Hitler's main defenses. Back in England the slogan of the division was '29th Let's Go.' Since then the 29th has gone farther than a lot of its men ever dreamed was possible and has achieved a record which is envied throughout the army."

With winter closing in on embattled front-line soldiers [Nov. 6, 1944], Lee McCardell's constant interest in the welfare of ordinary GIs triggered an angry, sarcastic critique about the army's way of outfitting them. Excerpts:

"The announcement that every American soldier is to be issued a wool sleeping bag with a water repellant case revives the old question as to why it took the army's masterminds three years to get wise to the fact that the Joe's antique bedding was inadequate for winter weather over here. Most Joes' private opinions are that the masterminds for these decisions spent too much time in the hotel bedrooms of Washington, London, Algiers and Naples and too little in foxholes on the front line, where management never turns on the steam heat.

"The average Joe's winter bedding has been a bitter joke ever since the war began. In the field it usually consists of two blankets and half of a canvas shelter tent. Try sleeping out in your own back yard with this combination some cold night.

"In dry weather Joe doesn't bother to pitch a tent. Wet or dry, if he is in a foxhole, he doesn't dare; he simply spreads his shelter half on the ground and spreads his blankets on top. In wet weather when he pitches his tent he must either put his raincoat under his blankets or roll them up in the mud. The only sleeping bag Joe has ever had is the one he makes for himself by sewing his blankets into a sack contrived by sewing up his shelter half. And when he does that he sews himself out of a tent.

"The canvas leggings Joe wears have long caused him a pain in the neck. Leggings get wet. Leggings' laces break. Soldiers in the Mediterranean theater got tired of wearing wet leggings and tying up their broken laces. They called on the nearest village shoemaker and had him sew six inches more leather on top of their GI shoes. This proved so practical that the masterminds in the army finally took the hint and started issuing high-top combat boots to certain troops.

But thousands of Joes in France are still struggling with wet canvas leggings.

"*Thousands of infantrymen have been shivering in light field jackets issued to them by their rich uncle. It's utterly impractical for Joe to wear a long army overcoat in the field. But during the European winter he will never manage to keep warm in that field jacket even when it is reinforced by a GI sweater. Many artillerymen and most men of the armored services are issued warmly lined combat jackets with knitted collars and cuffs. But for some reason these garments are not issued to infantrymen. Practically every officer in the army and war correspondents, many of them quartered in permanent buildings and working in warm offices, have managed to wangle the combat jackets for themselves. But Joe—well, there just aint any for him.*"

In the same issue of *The Sun*, Price Day recounted the ordeal of a veteran infantry battalion cut off for more than six days from the American Seventh Army in France. "*They were under such heavy fire that their wounded could not be evacuated. The men who fought through to them met some of the bitterest resistance the Seventh Army has had. Those of the 'lost battalion' who could walk out today are haggard and weary. Some are in their teens and some in their middle thirties, but except for a boy here and there who could not grow a beard they all look the same age. Their eyes are hollow and their cheeks scooped with hunger. When one of them grins it is not an easy grin. It is like the cracking of a mask. For five days they were without food of any kind. They drank dark, grayish water dipped from a swampy bit of forest which they call 'mud puddle' and sometimes they had to fight their way to that. Unable to use axes because the noise of chopping would disclose their position, they felled four and five-inch saplings with their pocket knives, muffling the trees in blankets as they lowered them into place above their soggy foxholes. Time after time they tried to break through the encircling Germans but their losses were heavy and they became progressively weaker. Through pounding rains and swirling fogs with one day of cold sunshine and two nights of colder moonlight they held out. Finally P-47 fighter-bombers dropped new batteries for the single radio they had (plus) K-rations, medical supplies and fresh water for the wounded. They were dropped on the day the Germans made their last and strongest attempt to crack the defense. The men on the hill fought from dawn to dark. In the midst of that fight the first of the relieving Americans arrived to be greeted with handshakes, hugs and kisses.*"

The combination of McCardell's lament for cold infantry men and Day's story of heroic fighting by cold infantry men cut off for days from food and decent water must have been heavy reading on a Monday morning back home in Baltimore.

The following Sunday, Armistice Day 1944, McCardell offered more details on the burdens of infantrymen. The scene was in the rain-soaked woods and fields east of Nancy: *"The muddy army bivouac areas are reminiscent of those winter quarters which the artists sketched 80 years ago illustrating the Civil War. The soldiers are building log cabins and wooden shanties. Many of the soldiers do their own cooking. Between meals they huddle around open camp fires, trying to keep dry. They do their own washing and hang it out to dry, a demonstration of extreme patience these damp, foggy days.*

"The troops in the front lines live in foxholes bordering the barbed wire concertinas, usually two men in one hole to keep each other company. The foxholes are half covered by timbers and earth and big enough for one man to sleep under this shelter while the other keeps watch. The highest ground in this region is boggy. A well-designed foxhole has a seepage pit at one end from which the tenants haul the accumulated water at hourly intervals. There is no hot food on the front line. The men up there subsist on cold K rations, burning the paraffin-covered cardboard container to heat cups of water for instant coffee. As long as he is on the front line the wise infantryman stays in his foxhole during daylight. It isn't safe to stick his head out if he is under enemy observation. He is too apt to draw artillery fire. Patrolling is the only organized activity along this part of the front right now and it is strictly an after-dark operation. The object of the patrol is to slip across no-man's land, reconnoiter the enemy lines and bring back a prisoner or two."

On October 2, 1944, Price Day and Mark Watson reported toughening German battle tactics along the broad front from Aachen to the Swiss border. Watson described the situation as *"almost stationary warfare"*—words that could equally be applied to the World War I scenes he had been writing about. Day wrote the Germans were hitting small American advances with *"every kind of fire, small arms, automatic weapons, mortars, flak wagons, light and heavy howitzers and guns. Some of the German fire is in the form of tree bursts—projectiles which detonate on contact and shower the forest below with pellets. The effect is that of an airburst and foxholes offer little protection. Whenever the Germans are thrown back they are almost certain to attack again at night or early in the morning. Our line troops are getting little rest, Germans creep close if they can and then rise from their place of concealment and charge, running, shouting and shooting. With some this is fanaticism, for some of the prisoners are among the finest of the Nazi troops, but other, less imposing prisoners sometimes say SS men moving behind them threaten to shoot any man who falters."* Watson, for his part, reported small but hard battles involving the First Army in the north—this taking place in downpours similar to those mentioned by Day. The tone of both articles made it clear that the days of headlong advance across France were in the past.

Day had a grand time in the next issue of the newspaper [Oct. 3, 1944] telling of a rear-echelon major who had joined three experienced reporters (including himself) and was gung-ho to *"go through a mine field under fire"*—something he felt would be a great story. *"By now he was clearly convinced that we were cowards,"* Day related. *"We were beginning to smart a bit—we were also beginning to think hard thoughts about people who make trips to the front and other thoughts both gentle and bitter about men who have no choice and who must go through and face enemy fire whether they like it or not.*

"From then on the major divorced himself from us, partly because we were always having to go back and file stories and partly because we weren't bold enough for his taste. At dusk we saw him again at a high point from which the Germans—out of ammunition after all—had decided to descend and surrender. It was a wild and romantic setting in the midst of unpeopled hills and the major was standing on a rampart talking to a pretty plump Maquis girl in a tight jersey and slacks. From one hand dangled his war loot, a pair of fine Ger-

man binoculars—damaged beyond repair." This was Price Day at his best—always gentle, always ready to see the comic side of things, always ready to insert his needle into the rears of people who probably wouldn't know they had just been skewered.

Lee McCardell and Holbrook Bradley, on October 5 and 6, 1944, were in *The Sun* with stories describing the Maginot and Siegfried Lines. Though both articles were written in October, they were in sharp contrast. McCardell's visit was a peaceful excursion to a French fortification that since its capture in 1940 had been turned into a German sightseeing mecca. Goebbels, Goering, Keitel, (not Hitler) and thousands of German soldiers had visited. Now that it had been captured by Americans it had American visitors. When McCardell arrived, he found a sign saying "Ring the bell." This he did and was greeted by a French janitor/tour guide who had been left on the job by the opposing sides. He charged them both for his services. *"After the Germans captured the Maginot Line in the summer of 1940"* McCardell wrote, *"they dismantled most of its forts. But this one was preserved with all its plumbing and machinery in working order, just as the Nazis had taken it. It was kept as a sort of Nazi museum piece."* The visitors walked down stairways and tunnels. To provide electricity for the installation, McCardell was shown *"vast catacombs equipped with large diesel engines, batteries of dynamos and enough transformers, switches and cables to illuminate the entire city of Paris."* After observing kitchens, sleeping quarters, hospital facilities and gun positions, ventilation systems, and trains with miniature cars *"the motorman sounded gongs and off we went traveling a mile or so to remote gun positions and turrets. The Germans,"* McCardell wrote, *"had captured the fort by attacking from a direction in which its fixed guns could not fire."*

Bradley's story about his visit to the Siegfried Line also asserted that it, too, had been taken from the rear. *"We were surprised by finding it only a series of pillboxes arranged for interlacing fire. Most of us had expected something on the order of the French Maginot Line. Seized two days ago during the first heavy fighting as the line was breached, this pillbox had been one of the main strong points serving to back up smaller forts. Inside, the fort seemed similar to many of those we have taken earlier in the campaign. There were two main rooms, evidently used as sleeping and messing quarters for the garrison. Heavy steel doors separated each room and we saw each door guarded by a small aperture through which the entrance could be covered."*

Near the Siegfried fort visited by General Omar Bradley the sounds of nearby battles raged on. Mark Watson had reported [Oct. 5, 1944] that American forces had breached the Siegfried Line on a crescent-shaped front three miles long. *"The fact that in this narrow area we have expelled the enemy from his concrete, permanent positions and driven him into temporary foxholes has a pleasing aspect—enemy troops, in that case, are experiencing the same discomforts which are suffered by our troops in the way of mud and cold."*

CHAPTER 15

In the Foxholes

From the vantage point of well over half a century, it is well to read Mark Watson's extraordinary dispatches leading to the Battle of the Bulge as a mystery story with a surprise ending. The difference, of course, was that Watson didn't know the ending any more than did his readers. He and the entire Allied command—the generals and their top intelligence officers—didn't know that on the night of December 15–16, 1944, the Germans would launch a huge offensive that was Hitler's last big shake of the dice. As American forces reeled backward, a new phrase entered the language: "The Battle of the Bulge." For four cold, dark, bloody weeks, a period punctuated by what the GIs called *"Black Christmas,"* hopes for a quick victory over Germany disappeared into despair—despair that lasted until a month later when the German advance became another retreat, and, unfortunately, another escape from Allied encirclement.

Though Watson had dropped tantalizing, on-target clues of coming trouble in the weeks leading to the Bulge, he never solved the puzzle. But he did write remarkably prescient dispatches that foretold the disaster to come. For the issue of November 20, four weeks before the German attack, he warned of a new enemy buildup in troop concentrations all the way from the stalemated German battle lines eastward to the Rhine:

"What they are manning them with is a question the answer to which will be disclosed as the fight goes on. The presumption is that the rapid reshuffling of forces has provided the enemy with reserves of tanks and infantry divisions which he will be able to put in our path

and with which he undoubtedly will counterattack at his own time and in his own manner."

A week later [Nov. 26, 1944] he contended the Allies had miscalculated the quality of enemy reserve troops. He cited stiffening German defenses:

"It would be a mistake to think of these local defenses as mere isolated examples of courage and perseverance. They are part of the whole complex system of German defenses. If one of these defenses holds firm, it may provide a base for a flanking attack on us, or if three or four of them wear down our strength sufficiently they may succeed in weakening us in a critical place and thereby make possible a really grand-scale counterattack designed to hurt us severely.

"We have taken a great many counterattacks but they have been on a small scale. But if these small enemy counterattacks are so combined that they inflict upon us severe losses in an area where we are not too strong anyway, we may expect the enemy to mass remaining strength against us in that area."

There are notable clues in these passages. While Watson seemed to accept the widespread notion in Allied ranks that German strategy was basically defensive, he saw the potential for *"a really grand-scale counterattack,"* something the Germans had not been able to launch since the landings at Normandy. While he intimated the Allies did not know just what forces the Germans were amassing, he pointed to their *"rapid reshuffling of forces"* and their *"reserves of tanks and infantry divisions."* This proved a lot more accurate than the complacent U.S. command tendency to consider the enemy broken, a notion Nazi generals described (after the war) as accurate in September but not in December. By then, considerable forces had been shifted from the Russian Front. And while Watson did not mention the Ardennes Forest by name, he warned that an offensive could come *"in an area where we are not too strong anyway."* The Ardennes clearly qualified since it was a lightly manned sector at the vulnerable juncture of two American armies.

On November 19, he wrote, *"there is no hint of any considerable* (German) *retreat in depth or breadth"* and any pullbacks would be largely for the purpose of straightening battle lines. The next day he advised readers to beware of any assumption that the battles on Germany's western border could lead to the kind of breakthrough the Allies had achieved at St. Lo the previous summer.

These articles, alone, would have justified the Pulitzer Prize for Watson's war reporting. But, of course, he wrote much, much more. As far back as early September when the Allies raced to the German border and then stalled, Watson filed a story from *"near Aachen,"* the first large German city to fall into Allied hands. He told of a Nazi order for civilian Germans to evacuate territory west of the Rhine. *"The German government, it now appears, is determined to refuse surrender and to maintain a defensive war for the largest possible time,"* Watson wrote. He identified a September 12 order from the *Gauleiter* of the Cologne-Aachen area that concluded: *"Whoever hinders the evacuation or attempts to avoid evacuation not only endangers his own life but will be considered a traitor by the public and will be treated accordingly."*

Such an evacuation, he wrote, *"is the very thing a military command would particularly avoid"* because it would clog highways required by German forces. *"It illustrates perfectly the Nazi leaders' determination to make a military sacrifice of any character if necessary to carry out the fanatical views of the Nazi party. It is presumably an effort to keep that maximum of the 'master race' together for whatever fate awaits them."* Watson may have sensed the Bulge offensive was Hitler's own idea, one rejected by several German generals who believed (correctly) that the loss of manpower and equipment in such a battle would lead to the collapse of the Nazi war machine.

On September 18, 1944, Watson reported the Germans had launched a heavy, unanticipated counterattack against American forces that had breached the main Siegfried Line near Aachen—a clear sign the German headlong retreat across France had come to an end. *"The attackers came forward in a series of the heaviest artillery support we have met in a month,"* he wrote. *"It was extremely rough business. A senior commander declared that today's fight was not one bit easier than our original head-to-head battling on the beaches last June."*

Watson pointed out the Germans had opened the way to the U.S. capture of Siegfried strong points by leaving defenses to untrained troops. *"It was this grossly insufficient manning of the Siegfried Line which made it seem likely that the enemy was committed to abandoning his West Wall and conducting his main defense on the Rhine,"* he wrote. *"Today's vehement attack, which was not a holding action at all but a genuine assault, compels revision of that judgment. The tremendous resurge of strength—perhaps too late—illustrates again a military failing of which our enemy has been guilty repeatedly. That is his determination not to yield ground quite soon enough and thus is ultimately unable to extricate himself save at severe loss."* This was a prophetic comment on the ultimate result of the Bulge.

Two days later, Watson continued his description of the battle for Aachen. *"Wave after wave of admirably disciplined German troops came once more in a new assault upon high ground which our American veterans had taken last Sunday. But as they reached the bottom of the valley and started upward toward our positions they met such a hail of rifle and machine-gun fire that it shook even these seasoned German troops. Nevertheless, with splendid dash they kept on coming, running a few steps, flinging themselves down and firing while they regained their breath, then rising and running forward again. At each interval fewer men regained their feet. As they drew nearer, our men added to the previous small-arms fire volleys of hand grenades, some of which missed the forward ranks of the enemy and rolled downhill to explode among those following.*

"When the fight was over not a single American fire trench was taken but German dead lay within ten feet of our parapets and were strewn thickly down the slope of the field. The German unit engaged in this ferocious assault is made up of excellent troops with such a high record that one of the prisoners proudly gave our Americans sincere if reluctant praise, saying 'This is the first time our regiment has ever been stopped by small-arms fire.'" Watson described the Aachen front as one of major importance; if the Allied breach of the West Wall became large enough it could make the rest of the Siegfried Line useless.

By the beginning of October 1944, Watson said the Allies were taking a breather resulting in *"almost stationary warfare"* along the broad front from Aachen to the Swiss border. After citing weather as a complicating factor, Watson focused on logistics—a subject that often figured in his reporting. Military authorities had encountered *"the most intolerable strain"* in trying to sustain troops with ammunition and fuel as they raced toward the German border. *"The army's need to bring up the supplies in an increasingly huge quantity called for by the immense forces, parts of which are 300 crow-flight miles from Normandy and 50 miles further from Cherbourg, which is the first big French port to come into our hands. What stopped the army's advance was not the Siegfried Line but the plain need for getting our supplies restored to a proper basis. Our relatively light activity had reduced front-line consumption of supplies; our supply services had been able to improve greatly all the port installations."* [Oct. 8, 1944]

Tapping once again his firsthand knowledge of World War I operations, he recalled that General Pershing had been able to use the six great seaports of southern and western France, plus a rail system that was relatively unhurt. *"In this war Americans and British alike had to bring in all the goods over bare, wind-swept beaches until we could win Cherbourg. Germans had demonstrated great skill and persistence in clinging to the French ports of Brest, Lorient and Havre. It is now entirely proper to discuss certain phases of that problem which are less familiar to the layman—and indeed to a good many combat soldiers. Staff officers have the responsibility of seeing to it that the field commanders entrusted with a vital combat mission are assured of fuel, ammunition, transport, food, maintenance and all other needs just as essential to the mission as our men, guns and planes."*

In a passage that resonated after the Battle of the Bulge erupted, Watson noted that the Germans, too, were taking a breather. *"It is, of course, unfortunate but inevitable that while we are catching our breath, a fugitive German army is similarly engaged. We are now opposed by a foe who is stronger than when he was in flight."* Price Day, reporting from the Seventh Army farther south, wrote of Germans hitting small American advances with *"every kind of fire, small arms, automatic weapons, mortars, flak wagons, light and heavy howitzers and guns. Whenever the Germans are thrown back, they are almost certain to attack again at night or early in the morning.*

Our line troops are getting little rest. The Germans creep as close as they can and then rise from their place of concealment and charge, running, shouting and shooting."

Watson reported [Oct. 11, 1944] American troops had surrounded Aachen *"save for a small gap of a mile and a half which is completely exposed to our fire."* Next came a U.S. warning that the city would be destroyed unless it surrendered. His article reflected an American desire to establish a precedent for the taking of other German cities. But the Germans had vowed *"we will fight to the last man"* and, as it happened, they held out until October 21. As the siege continued, he vividly described an American attempt to end the fighting by sending in a truce team: *"Thus far, only three Americans have made their way into the middle of the city. They were blindfolded. They left their companions behind them and were waved forward by watching Germans. On stating their desire to deliver a message to the German commander they were led to a house where their eyes were uncovered and a young German officer greeted them stiffly with a Heil. After delivering letters to the commanding German, the three Americans were given passes allowing them to return to their own lines. All this with a handshake and an* Auf Wiedersehen." The next day [Oct. 12, 1944] Watson reported the German reply to the American ultimatum: a counter-attack as two relief columns tried to fight their way into the city only to be raked by American fire. The U.S. forces then began their promised bombardment of Aachen, which Watson viewed *"as a fine city with numerous industries, admirable buildings and parks, vestiges of ancient baths built by discerning Romans and, of course, Aachen's cathedral or minster built over Charlemagne's famous octagon chapel."*

On October 13, Watson told of further bombardment from a number of observation points around the ringed city: *"It is a painful thing to see a city being battered to bits, but, in all candor, one must admit the pain is more controllable where the city's destruction is dictated by its own masters. The German high command is still bent on holding Aachen (but) there is no doubt that Aachen is doomed."* When the city surrendered ten days later, Watson wrote: *"it had been clear for three weeks that Aachen could not be retained but in spite of this the German command sent small relief columns in rapid succession.*" When Watson visited the city he noted the damage was not as severe as he expected and the cathedral was only partly damaged. In describing Aachen's formal surrender [Oct. 22, 1944] Watson said the German commander, *"carried it out with great punctilio."* Having been given permission to make a farewell address, the commander told his men that surrender was a breach of orders necessitated by the fact that the Americans had cut off his supply of ammunition as well as food and water and he was powerless to fight any longer. He then added he would have liked to close his remarks with a cry of *Heil Hitler* but Americans had strictly forbidden that conclusion. Then he added coyly, *"but we can do it mentally."*

Relatively late in the European campaign, the Germans introduced jet aircraft, a development that would change civil and military aviation forever. Had they made this breakthrough a year earlier, a rejuvenated Luftwaffe could have challenged Allied domination of the skies during the Normandy landings and after. Even so, Watson warned [Oct. 24, 1944] of a Luftwaffe *"revival"* based largely on jet aircraft. The Messerschmidt 163 fighter and the 262 fighter-bomber had already made their appearance, attaining speeds of more than 500 miles an hour. The comparative lack of maneuverability of these aircraft offset some of their speed advantage by requiring far wider loops and turns. Allied planes had shot down a few. Watson cautioned, however, *"it would be foolish to ignore the fact that all these developments may well have a considerable effect upon our own air campaign. They have been in use for too short a time to permit anything except tentative judgments as to the planes themselves or as to tactics which their odd qualities will impose on them. These tactics, in turn, will necessarily influence the counter-tactics to be used against them. German hopes have been that the new Luftwaffe types would be able to overcome the Allies' present enormous superiority in the air."*

Watson saw a necessity for continued heavy bombing not only of Ruhr manufacturing targets that had been hit again and again but of new targets *"for it is in these centers that the enemy is producing all these new types of airplanes and whatever mystery weapons he may have up his sleeve."* Only after the war was it learned that German jets would have been deployed earlier in far greater quantity and lethality but for a fortunate mistake by Hitler himself. *The Oxford Companion to World War II* stated, "Hitler foolishly demanded a modification (of the planes) for bomb-carrying which delayed production, and it was not until March 1945, far too late to have much effect, that all Me262 resources were devoted to fighter defense of the Reich."

On November 1, 1944, Watson showed his skill as a military analyst by citing the vital strategic importance of the Scheldt estuary leading to the port of Antwerp. While the allies had long held the city of Antwerp, German control of the estuary and Walcheren Island had prevented use of the port and denied Allied forces much-needed supplies in their thrust toward Germany proper. *"The Germans' ability to block our maritime approach to Antwerp harbor through control of the banks of the Scheldt seems about vanished,"* Watson noted. *"This is an end the Allies have long sought and for which they paid a considerable price. At times this fighting has been as fierce as any these Allied units have encountered since Normandy. The stakes are very large. The Allies need the port facilities of Antwerp for supplying their forward armies. This supply need has been great and nobody knew this better than the Germans. Throughout the campaign the Germans have shown consummate skill in delaying our use of the large continental ports to supplement traffic through Cherbourg and over the Normandy beaches.*

"It must be made clear, however, that even the expulsion of the last German from Walcheren north of the Scheldt will not suffice. The presumption is that before we can move a single cargo into Antwerp with munitions for our troops along the Siegfried Line many obstacles and mines must be cleared from the crooked channel. The effect which this can have on General Eisenhower's campaign is unquestionably very great, for it is a well-known fact that our principal handicap this past month has been the severe strain put on our supply system."

The same reasoning was responsible for Germany's successful assaults on the British airborne division's short-lived bridgehead at Arnhem. Had the Allies been able to strengthen the bridgehead they could have routed the Germans fairly quickly from a large part of the Dutch seacoast. This was made impossible by the firm stand of the enemy at Arnhem. After the war, some historians blamed British Field Marshal Bernard Montgomery for giving priority to what proved to be his disastrous attempt to reach Arnhem instead of solving the Scheldt/Antwerp problem.

On Armistice Day, 1944, Watson lamented lost hopes that the war could be ended by then. The enemy, he warned, *"has regained his breath, firm footing and much of his confidence. Our supply system was magnificent during the Normandy campaign. Had it been able to meet the stupendous strain of September demands, one dares to suppose that our astonishing rush would have continued and we would have been on the banks of the Rhine. Had this taken place, who can say what would have happened by November 11. Or had Hitler, Himmler and the handful of other Nazis been proven mortal. Or had the terrors of the Gestapo not cowed all the anti-Nazi sentiment in Germany as no other people in the world can be cowed. Or had the weather been a little kind to us. Here are several might-have-beens, and every one of them went wrong. That succession of mishaps totaled enough to blast the fondest hopes of the Allies for a victory in early November. Now we have been reminded that destiny is not controlled by hopes but realities."*

At this stage of the war *The Sun* was making full use of its four correspondents in the battle for Germany. Holbrook Bradley, back on the continent after his shrapnel injury, disclosed that the Twenty-ninth Division (his first love) had been part of the Allied drive which first penetrated the Siegfried Line. *"To the men who recalled struggling ashore against a hail of fire on the Normandy Beaches, the break through the Siegfried Line was the culmination of a personal battle which began at Vierville, carried on through St. Lo, Vire and Brest, and will be completed only with entry into Berlin itself. For the men of the 29th the road across the continent has been a rough, hard fight. Troops wearing the blue and gray shoulder patch were among the first to hit the beach as the 116th Regiment fought its way ashore in the gray light of dawn on that morning which now seems part of the distant past.*

"Stalemated above St. Lo, the 29th was given the job of taking that rail and communications center, which proved a vital hinge when

Lieut. Gen. Omar N. Bradley's troops broke Marshal Erwin Rommel's line above Coutances. For a time it looked as though the division would join the rush for Paris but the high command needed a force to reduce the strong (enemy) garrison at Brest, and the job fell to the 29th. The rest proved to be one of the toughest nuts to crack. It was a tough slugging match that meant a constant drain on our own men and supplies. The end came suddenly on September 18 when we blasted our way into the town, which had become a mass of smoking ruins.

"With only a few days to clean themselves and their equipment, the men of the Blue and Gray were on the move across France by jeep, truck and French boxcar. Moving in on the First Army's line with the 30th Infantry and the Second Armored Division north of Aachen, the 29th slammed into one of the toughest fights of the war—the initial breakthrough of Hitler's main defenses. The 29th has gone farther than a lot of its men ever dreamed was possible and has achieved a record which is envied throughout the army."

Because so many of the troops in the Twenty-ninth came from Baltimore and the entire state of Maryland, this dispatch must have been widely and avidly read by friends and kin back in the States who, for security reasons, had long been denied the details Bradley at last supplied.

December 1944 issues of *The Sun* began with stories from the four correspondents of tough fighting, small gains, and enemy counterattacks near the French-German border. Mark Watson caught the mood in a dispatch about continued fighting near Aachen. He described eastward advances as *"slow and arduous"* and said *"most of us had hoped for larger results from a mid-November artillery barrage."* The last two weeks of fighting had been *"hard to bear"* as American troops encountered *"industrial communities whose stone cellars provided a continuous chain of strong points for the enemy's defense"* and *"mine-choked and mortar-showered woods where our task was a test of strength, courage and endurance."*

Lee McCardell reported a dozen enemy counter-attacks against the Third Army, Holbrook Bradley a ceaseless exchange of fire from medium and heavy guns on the Ninth Army front, and Price Day a rear-guard resistance of German troops in the Alsace sector.

In more detail [Dec. 1, 1944], Bradley described a drive toward Koslar, a town on the highway leading to Cologne. *"Koslar once had a population of over 5,000 civilians,"* he wrote. *"Today American troops are the only persons seen about the deserted streets. Cows, horses and pigs are running wild about the village. The buildings are of brick and cement construction and many have been reinforced to make them shell- and bomb-proof. The cobblestone roads which a short time ago echoed to the tramp of German boots and the rumble of enemy tanks now are broken up by shell fire and are littered with discarded equipment."*

Price Day came up with an insightful piece about the ambiguous position of Alsatian civilians who found their often-disputed region under French rule in 1918 and German occupation in 1940. Excerpts:

"'We want to be French,' a man from Molsheim said. 'We are glad to see you—each time. But why don't you stay?' His wife brought out the family album. Almost half the pictures were of men in German and French uniforms. I understood her to say that one of her brothers was in the French army and one in the German army, that her father had fought for Germany and her grandfather for France. The 11-year-old daughter spoke no French at all. Two days later in a village south of Strasbourg I asked a group of small children if any of them spoke French. They were gay, healthy, bright-looking children but at the question their faces went blank. Then one boy ventured a tentative answer. 'Ja,' he said."

All Alsatians wanted to know what would happen to them, Day stated. *"The answer cannot be simple. The problem of Alsace will not be solved by the mere moving of the boundary line of France again from the Vosges to the Rhine. The truth is that the rushing current of the Rhine, one of the world's strongest military barriers, is no cultural barrier at all. The Rhine valley is of one piece, composed of two almost identical halves, split by the river. It is a geographical entity, and the people living in the two halves go by almost identical ways of life, and in the long run have the same economic interests.*

"What the ultimate solution may be, I, for one, am unable to imagine. I only know of arbitrary changes of international borders and

shifts from one official language to another." Day lived to learn the *"solution"* he yearned for. It was the rise of a Pan-European mentality and an American-Soviet nuclear duopoly that kept Germans and French at last from fighting one another. Alsace-Lorraine faded as an ignition site for conflict.

On December 8, 1944, Bradley filed one of his patented dispatches of American infantry in action. It was an indecisive probing action in the German border city of Julich. The Ninth Army attacked German troops bivouacked in a Sportsplazt converted into a strong defensive position. Bradley was not only there, he was one of the first Americans in the town. And the Twenty-ninth Division newspaper, "29 Let's Go," ran a paragraph giving him full credit as a front-line *Sun* correspondent always on the lookout for GIs from Maryland.

A light-hearted story that turned, in retrospect, into a heart-wrenching tale was filed by McCardell just days before Germans stormed through the Ardennes Forest to launch the Battle of the Bulge. It was a feature on *"lucky guys homeward bound, safe and sound, for 30-day furloughs in the good old U.S.A."* McCardell said they were rolling into an Army Replacement Depot somewhere in France. *"As far as they're concerned, today is Christmas and tomorrow will be Christmas, too. From the muddy battlefront of Lorraine, directly home on short notice."* He quoted Sergeant William T. Kenney of 3110 Batavia Avenue, Baltimore, married and the father of an eight-month-old baby: *"'I just couldn't believe it was true when I first heard it.' Three days later, all new furloughs were cancelled."*

In one of the last pre-Bulge battle scenes, McCardell described fighting by General George Patton's Third Army as it advanced slowly into the German Saarland. *"Muddy roads twisting eastward over the hills and down to the river bank are a blind man's routes. Through ghost villages of conquered German Saarland, where fantastic shadows of burned and broken buildings mark gloomy streets even darker than open roads, they cut their speed to five miles an hour. The only sparks of light are those leaking weakly through broken shutters and blacked-out windows."*

McCardell then describes an anti-tank unit that has crossed the Saar River on a ferry and is slogging its way toward battle. *"Nobody stops. The line keeps moving. You are blowing hard now, wondering if you will ever get across the stretch of sticky marsh, mud and darkness, wishing that you dared to stop long enough to pour water out of your squishing shoes.*

"You don't stop. You would be lost in the night if you did. There are no landmarks on this black wasteland except the glow of fires to the east. Then your feet hit a hard, stony road unexpectedly. Shadows of dead houses and garden fences loom up on either side. You are in a street tripping over rubble and broken wires, crunching broken glass underfoot. You've reached a town. The dark street is lined with tanks, trucks and jeeps. Men you've been following disappear into a dark house. The captain tells you the place you want is in a cellar. You feel for the outside cellar door in the dark. The cellar is crowded, smoky, dimly lighted, with a low ceiling not quite high enough for a man to stand upright. The dirt floor is littered with coal, rubbish and dirty mattresses. The air is rank with the smell of soldiers who have not had their clothes off for weeks, whose wet shoes and socks are drying at their feet.

"But after the mud, darkness and flame-lit smoke and burst shells of the night outside, that cellar is heaven." And heaven it would remain in the mind's eye of thousands of American soldiers as the worst of the European war was about to begin.

CHAPTER 16

Black Christmas
in the Bulge

American troops came under fierce German bombardment on the Ardennes Front as the Battle of the Bulge began at 5 o'clock in the dark morning of December 16, 1944. It was midnight then in Baltimore, plenty of time for a news flash in the morning papers. But *The Baltimore Sun* night news desk had no way of knowing about the surprise attack by thousands of German troops and tanks, wiping out lightly manned U.S. positions. No wire service alerts announced the greatest American intelligence failure since Pearl Harbor.

Top Allied commanders did not anticipate the enemy offensive. British Field Marshal Bernard Montgomery had said the previous afternoon that the Germans *"cannot stage offensive operations."* Lieutenant General Omar Bradley's G2 (Intelligence) had dismissed warnings from a lone colonel by saying, *"It is now certain that attrition is steadily sapping the strength of German forces on the Western Front."*

As a result of such complacency, it took Supreme Allied Headquarters in Paris at least a day to recognize the alarming situation. Newspapers, often hampered by censorship and news embargoes, were well behind the curve. On December 16, the lead headlines in *The Sun* and *The New York Times* dealt with the Philippines. *Sun* correspondents Day, McCardell, and Bradley wrote, respectively, about Seventh Army drives, Third Army's gains, and fighter-bombers in action. All reflected a belief the Allies were on a continuing offensive.

The next day, December 17, *The Times* remained focused on the Philippines, relegating a staff-written story about "German Assaults on 1st Army Front" to page 19. *The Sun*, to its credit, was more perceptive. It ran this streamer headline on the top of its front page:

"Nazis Launch Dozen Counterattacks on First Army Front." Then followed an Associated Press dispatch that, considering the circumstances, was a fairly coherent account of bewildering events.

Mark Watson, on assignment in Brittany, was not at Supreme Allied Headquarters, Paris, to file. This was ironic since his earlier dispatches, far more than pronouncements from high-ranking military leaders, had reflected concern about growing German capabilities. (See Chapter 14.) Soon he was on the main story [Dec. 21, 1944] in which he posed *"the inevitable question in the civilian mind: How could this violent change in the military situation come about with so little apparent warning?*

"The fact is that warnings have been issued from time to time by sober and competent commanders who have known the enemy's thrifty use of his tanks, artillery and planes was not at all a sign of his total exhaustion but rather for his saving them for a bold and determined use at the proper time and place. That time would be when the Germans were ready and the place would be at a point where the Allied line is not at its strongest.

"Whether we should have been able to foresee this time and place of the enemy's attack and forestall it is, at present, not so important as to how quickly and fully we can remedy the situation. There will be a better grasp of the whole affair if we recognize that the German command remains one of the greatest military machines of all time and that this present stroke, like so many in the past, has been skillfully planned, industriously prepared and executed thus far with the greatest adroitness and resourcefulness.

"Whatever may be the German manpower shortage—and it is serious—the German command has managed to use field defenses to replace manpower as fully as possible. Therefore, he has stored up everything in a reserve which he has carefully guarded, equipped and armed. And lately he has been able to concentrate and fling into action one mighty effort. He was able to mask his concentration and forward movement under these mists which have so gravely interfered with our bombing and scouting planes. He has been able to move five or six Panzer divisions and an uncertain number of infantry divisions into this gigantic offensive.

"How long he is able to keep going we are yet to see. One word should be said about our own failures to block this rupture by our lines in Luxembourg. We had been conducting our offensives to the north and south and because an offensive must be pushed with great strength it was obvious we had to have our strength along the Roer and Saar rivers. Relatively, our strength in the intervening sector must have been weak—certainly too weak to resist any such gigantic shove. We remain strong to the right and left and there is no present indication that either shoulder is weakening.

"It therefore becomes a question of how quickly our own forces can block off the intrusion of the infantry columns. It is apparent that the narrower the breach can be kept, the better are our chances to subdue the flow of enemy troops through it. Whatever our ability to engage, hold and batter down the enemy columns, it would be ill-advised to think we are likely to have any outstanding good news for some time to come.

"Granting this, it is still a fact that the distant prospect is by no means unfavorable. Our resources are still superior by far and, this being the case, our desire remains to get the enemy into an open fight this side of the Rhine rather than let him remain on the entrenched defensive and force us into continuing costly, grinding attack. Certainly we would have preferred to have that open fight in an area of our own selection rather than in this deep zone.

"Even so, if we can establish and hold onto new lines, we will regain the advantage we once had and lost—namely of having the bulk of the enemy's strength in a battle of maneuver where we are certain that our American commanders are a fair match for the enemy's best. It is likely that only this will bring the war to an end. It may be that only through some such unhappy business as this present seeming catastrophe could that ultimate solution be brought to pass. Of this we will know much more ten days hence. If in that time we can get a fair amount of good flying weather much that now looks dark will look much brighter."

In the next day's *Sun* [Dec. 22, 1944] Watson wrote that First Army troops were preventing the enemy from widening its fifty-mile-wide salient into Belgium but warned *"we have not done so well in the center"* where, among other things, the Germans had cut the Bastogne-Liege road and increased their penetration to twenty-five miles. He also lamented that weather prevented the flight of a single U.S. aircraft. *"Transportation facilities are just as important to the German army as they were to us in our own breakthrough last summer. One dares to forecast that the time will come when his relative weakness in transport will prove his greatest handicap."*

This analysis of a battle still unfolding stands up remarkably well after the passage of so many years. The work of historians, the release of official after-battle reports, the publishing of memoirs confirm the swift-moving developments Watson described under deadline.

What was to be a terrible Christmas for tens of thousands of American soldiers figured hugely in December 24 *Sun* staff dispatches of Watson, McCardell, and Day. Watson praised those soldiers who *"stood like a rock"* and prevented the Germans from making a breakthrough across the Meuse River and as far away as Antwerp. *"There is no Christmas holiday for those heroes,"* he wrote. *"But admiration for them and gratitude to them and pride in them and in men like them should be at the heart of every Christmas holiday-maker in America."*

McCardell, a reporter never reluctant to bare his own feelings, wrote a widely noted letter to his children that *The Sun* published on its front page the day before Christmas: *"The real name of the town where I am is Luxembourg, but on Christmas Eve I'd rather call it 'Toyland.' With its funny little houses, its sharply pointed twin church steeples, its bridges standing on high, slim, graceful arches and its tiny trolley cars, Luxembourg really looks just like Toyland. Luxembourg is built on steep hills overlooking a river valley just as Ellicott City overlooks the Patapsco River. But Luxembourg is much older than Ellicott City. There are ruined castle towers on some hills. The little river winding along is crossed by beautifully carved stone. Yesterday it snowed and now Luxembourg looks exactly like a little town in a Christmas garden underneath a Christmas tree. It looks as if it had been covered with dabs of white cotton and powdered with the same kind of sparkling artificial snow we used to buy at the ten-cent store for our Christmas garden. The tiny trolley cars look exactly like the little trolley car we had at grandfather's long ago.*

"Once upon a time, a happier Christmas time, we all went to Keiths on Lexington Street to see a moving picture entitled 'Babes in Toyland.' There were some robot soldiers who frightened the people in Toyland. They frightened you too, Abby. You were a very little girl then. You hid your face and held my hand tightly. Do you remember? Well, this Christmas some robot soldiers of Hitler, grown men old enough to know better, are frightening the people of Toyland—I mean Luxembourg. But I don't think the German soldiers will ever get here because our American soldiers are fighting hard to keep them out.

"This isn't a very happy day for anyone to be spending Christmas Eve, especially when they are so far away from home. It's cold and wet and muddy and tonight it will be dark and lonely out there where our soldiers are fighting. There will be no candles, no Christmas music, except perhaps a little that a few soldiers may hear on the radio. When I was out there yesterday I saw only one Christmas tree. Some soldiers posted along a road had set it up on top of their cannon which was aimed toward Germany. They had no Christmas bells and no tinsel with which to decorate it but I think it was the bravest Christmas tree I have ever seen. In the majority of the poor little country villages where the armies have been fighting, there aren't even any shop windows. They've all been smashed to pieces. Houses have been burned and blown to bits. Their broken furniture is scattered all over the streets.

"We've forgotten to ask how Santa operates in Luxembourg, but from the looks of this Toyland he'll be doing the best he can. Not that there are many toys in the shops, but the shop windows are the gayest and brightest we've seen this side of the ocean. There are Christmas trees with glittering bells in these windows. There are little pasteboard Santa Clauses. There are red candles and little packages of ginger cakes tied with colored ribbons and sprigs of evergreen and tinfoil Christmas stars. I am most fortunate to be in Luxembourg on Christmas Eve. So many other homesick fathers will be in muddy foxholes tonight. It makes me ashamed to look around my hotel room, clean and tidy, with white-painted woodwork and carpeted floor. My bed has clean white sheets and a soft white pillow. However homesick I am, I will not be wet or cold or hungry. In a world of miserable men

this Christmas, who am I that I should be comforted by the knowl-edge that my three children will sleep this night in warm, dry beds; that you'll wake tomorrow morning, bright-eyed, in a cheerful house with a roof and all its doors and windows? So many, many other children of Europe will sleep tonight in houses without roofs, without doors or windows. Many will sleep on straw in cold, damp cellars, where Santa Claus will never find them. In fact, though this is the third Christmas I have been away from home, I think it will be the happiest I have ever spent. Not the merriest, mind you, but the hap-piest. Happiest because God, by being so good to you, is being good to me. At least there is peace this Christmas in your world of men of good will. Good night, God bless you as bountifully as he has blessed me. And a Merry Christmas. Dada."

In post-holiday stories [Dec. 26, 1944], all four *Sun* correspondents described why the yuletide had come to be called *"Black Christmas"* by soldiers in the trenches.

"This has been one hell of a Christmas," wrote McCardell [Dec. 26, 1944]. *"It has been a magnificent winter day of bright sunshine and freezing temperatures along the pine-clad Ardennes, white with snow where the American troops are fighting to beat back one of the main thrusts of the German counter-offensive. But there is no Christ-mas spirit out there so far as the soldiers are concerned.*

"Snow-covered hills and deep little valleys have been noisy all day with machine-gun and artillery fire. Dirty brown smoke from burn-ing villages bombed and strafed by our fighter aircraft smear the blue horizon of the Christmas sky. The fighting is slow and confused by the fact that many Germans still are wearing American uniforms, driving captured American trucks and using American tanks. The country over which the battle is being fought is extremely rugged, with high wooded hills and steep ravines. It is distinctly not what a soldier in a tank division would call 'good tank country.' Christmas dinner for the men was cold canned C rations of meat and beans."

Price Day, with the Seventh Army the day before Christmas, described a moonlit Christmas Eve as *"an unquiet one. . . . There is no snow but the moonlight falls almost as cold and white as snow. For the first time this winter the canals here are frozen over. The water in the shell and bomb craters and in abandoned dugouts and foxholes has become thick ice. The churned mud of the fields and roadsides has stiffened, holding impress of the last vehicles to pass through before it froze. Only the swift streams remain fluid.*

"*Strasbourg, where, according to the story, the custom of the Christmas tree originated, spreads dark and ghostly under the early moon, the frail spire of its cathedral pointing up to the stars. Elsewhere, on the roads behind the front, traffic is being carefully checked by MPs carrying ready tommy guns. As they stop the vehicles, other men with tommy guns crouch to one side, while armored vehicles watch from the other. It is certainly not an atmosphere of peace.*"

With Day reporting about action south of the main Ardennes, Holbrook Bradley filed from north of the Ardennes along the Roer River. "*Doughboys, standing guard duty, stamp their feet to keep the circulation flowing. Overhead a million stars glow in the cloudless night, casting a cold gleam on the barren fields and battered villages where the American and German infantry hold forward lines a scant thousand yards apart. A couple of olive-drab riflemen sit in a slit trench with eyes fixed on the river 300 or more yards away where shots a while ago told them the Germans were still on patrol. Just a few hours back these boys sat around coal stoves in cellars behind the lines reading letters from back home and perhaps opening a Christmas package.*

"*These bright spots are few and far between along this part of the front. Muddy foxholes and earth-walled dugouts furnish little chance for Christmas festivity. Soldiers must move carefully to avoid the watchful eyes of the enemy out across no-man's land.*" Bradley listed the names of almost fifty servicemen from Maryland and Virginia he had encountered.

On the other side of the globe, "*somewhere in the Pacific,*" *Sun* war correspondent Philip Heisler was also contemplating that Christmas Eve moon. Aboard a mighty battleship with its 16-inch guns projecting over the heads of a Negro stewards' choir singing "Silent Night," Heisler wrote the following: "*The moon shone down on the decks where the men sprawled in the faint breath of a humid breeze. There was a faraway look in their eyes as they turned their eyes sky-*

*ward and listened to the old familiar words. From the gray shadows
of other ships nearby came faint whispers of their carol singers."*

So rolled the dice of war. At midnight, cooks and stewards went
below deck to begin cooking a Christmas dinner of turkey, creamed
mashed potatoes, asparagus tips, fruit cup, ice cream, and coffee. Certainly a festive feast compared to cold canned C-rations choked down
in freezing temperatures by G.I.s caught in the deep snow and darkness of the Ardennes Forest.

In one of the angriest pieces he wrote during the whole war, Mark
Watson used words like *"defeat"* and *"misery"* and *"tragic"* to
describe American failures during the Battle of the Bulge. Though
unstinting in his praise for the fighting doughboys, Watson turned
caustic in asking questions and complaints that have intrigued military
historians ever since. Someone in the Allied command, he wrote:

"Totally failed to recognize the immense strength which (German
General Karl) *von Rundstedt had assembled east of Luxembourg.*

"Failed to recognize the imminence of the attack.

*"Failed, consequently, to place sufficient defensive force in front
of this impending onslaught, probably because of our concentrations
in the Roer and Saar valleys.*

*"Failed as a substitute measure to protect roads and mountain
passes with anti-tank artillery in sufficient quantity or with defensive
road blocks or mines."*

As a result of these failures, the Germans had seized the offensive the
Allies had held since their breakout from Normandy in mid-summer,
Watson declared. He contended the Allied command had *"totally
failed"* in devising *"scientific defense"* tactics that the Germans had
used time and again. The result: a *"great victory"* for the Germans.

Watson speculated (accurately) that the grand plan for the German
attack through the Ardennes—the same route the enemy used with
great success in June 1940—might have come from *"none other than
Hitler."* The Germans had driven to within four miles of the Meuse
River and, if it had succeeded in this objective (which it did not), it
could have advanced to Brussels or Antwerp or Paris.

The *Sun's* military correspondent had long warned his readers
about the expertise of the German armed forces but this was the first

time he had been so harsh in criticizing the American high command. *"While we have successfully channeled the enemy drive and prevented its spread to the north and south, which was vitally important, we have not been able to block its progress westward or even to prevent its steady building up of strength for future progress."* Warning that the Germans might pair their Ardennes attack with a new drive elsewhere, he lamented, *"the fantastic cloud of optimism which seems to be concealing from some of our people the grave aspects of this battle. We even hear that people who ought to know better are advancing the sugary theory that we have done an adroit job of luring the enemy into a position where we can destroy him."*

Thus, Watson was accusing the high command of propagandizing the American people with a *"fantastic cloud of optimism"* while *"concealing the grave aspects of battle."* Such barbs must have troubled military brass, coming as they did from a reporter respected for his knowledge of war and his sympathy for officers responsible for thousands of lives. As one reads his copy at this critical moment of the war, he seems so taken aback by battlefield defeats that he anticipates a second major German attack elsewhere. It never came.

As the Battle of the Bulge started to turn in the Allies' favor, some of Watson's pessimism faded. He wrote he had long believed the Germans would be plagued by the same factors that had slowed the Allies: a shortage of fuel and other supplies. He took heart when the German advance stalled just four miles from the Meuse River, Hitler's first objective. One probing German patrol had simply run out of gas. And he was unstinting in his praise for *"the gallant resistance of our troops among Monshau, St. Vith, Bastogne and Echternach"*—places that still resonate in Army lore.

Typically, McCardell was in a hurry to get into Bastogne, the scene of storied resistance by encircled American troops whose commander, General Anthony McAuliffe, rejected a German demand for surrender. Germans desperately needed possession of that vital center of the region's transportation web. *"When I was in Bastogne yesterday afternoon, Germans still encircled the city save for one narrow corridor through which this back road runs. But today it was possible to enter the city by another highway,"* McCardell wrote.

He told his readers that a 36-hour news blackout imposed by the Allied command had permitted only the sketchiest news to get out. *"That blackout must have been a source of considerable anxiety and apprehension at home. It was a tense, apprehensive time for all concerned. We heard more rumors than the home front did, but we enjoyed the sight of confident troops in action to meet the emergency."*

On the last day of that historic December, Watson reported the German advance was over. *"Von Rundstedt most surprisingly fails to move forward or attempt to enlarge his spearhead. It is now apparent that he is going no further with his offensive as originally planned. Slowed at the very outset by the strength of American resistance and by the Air Force's systematic punishment of his essential supply lines, he was unable to make the initial success which was essential."*

The January 3, 1945, edition of *The Sun* reflected growing confidence that American forces were beginning to go over to offense. Watson wrote that the brighter outlook showed Bastogne's value. *"In our hands it has been a firm barrier to the whole German offensive. In the enemy's hands it almost certainly would have let von Rundstedt push his left column all the way through to the Meuse."*

In an accompanying dispatch McCardell was even more optimistic. *"It may be a little premature to write off von Rundstedt's winter offensive as a tactical washout, but the failure of the Germans to break through the Bastogne corridor, to broaden the original salient of penetration, or to push further west does not indicate that things are going too well with them. Our fighter-bombers are still swarming over the enemy during daylight hours. Our artillery can easily cover the neck between the Bastogne bulge and our northern front, less than 15 miles at its narrowest point. Moreover, the Third Army is still whittling away at the southern German flank. The battle here may well be the beginning of the end of an action that will be the highwater mark of the German winter offensive."*

From the southern Seventh Army front, where German-French rivalry was endemic, Price Day observed [Jan. 4, 1945] that *"the people of Alsace are wiser in the ways of war than civilians ever should be."* His dispatch began with a glimpse of a village where a middle-aged woman was peeking from a second-floor lace-curtained window.

"The woman watches the military traffic on the highway, noting the types of vehicles, their number and whether they are loaded or empty," wrote *The Sun* correspondent. *"Above all, she notices which way they are going.*

"Some Alsatians were remaining in their homes, others trudged south and west, away from the fighting. The region had just been captured by the Allies but the inhabitants had been warned by retreating Germans that they would be back. Some Alsatians were eager for the return of the Germans, others unable to care, and some feel a sensation not far from panic. It's not too difficult—in fact it is difficult not to—imagine the anxious family conferences that have been taking place behind shuttered windows.

"Should the French flag be taken in? If the Germans happened to return, there would be those eager to denounce every person in every house that had flown the tricolor. What of souvenirs received from American soldiers? What of Marie's Allied currency in the family cashbox? What of the young son who was proud of being the best student in his class in the French language? What of the people in the next house who had not been friendly to the Americans? What would they tell the Germans if the Germans came back? Whether their fears are justified or not, their melancholy migration is a sight no American who has seen it will forget."

Two days later [Jan. 6, 1945] Watson reported why those villages described by Day had reason to be fearful. In Alsace scattered German attacks had increased to a point where they could be labeled an offensive.

Correspondents on the front lines found themselves scooped when what they had withheld for two weeks leaked out back in the States: command of the U.S. First Army had been shifted from Bradley to Montgomery. In other words, from an American general to a British general, from an advocate of a broad front to one favoring a single thrust. *"It is hardly necessary to dwell upon the well-known characteristics of Bradley and Montgomery to make the point that their handling of situations is essentially different and to suggest that after seven months these differences are well-known to the German command,"* Watson wrote [Jan. 3, 1945].

Edmund Duffy (1899–1962) was cartoonist for *The Baltimore Sun* from 1924 until 1948, winning three Pulitzer Prizes, in 1931, 1934, and 1940. His third Pulitzer was awarded for his October 7, 1939 cartoon entitled "The Outstretched Hand of Peace," showing Hitler's hand dripping blood as he made spurious peace offers after invading Poland. The small nations he had subjugated are shown cowering at Hitler's feet. Duffy's somber cartoons chronicling the cataclysmic struggles of World War II are regarded as his finest work. Courtesy of *The Baltimore Sun.*

As London Bureau chief during the entire war, **Thomas M. O'Neill** reported the Blitz on London, followed British government policy, and served as a conduit for reporters on the continent. After the war, he became the newspaper's top political columnist. Courtesy of *The Baltimore Sun*.

The doyen of *The Baltimore Sun*'s correspondents, **Mark S. Watson** had acquired his insight into military strategy on the staff of General Pershing's army in the First World War. In 1944, he won a Pulitzer Prize for his World War II reporting. Later he was the first journalist to receive the Presidential Medal of Freedom, the supreme civilian accolade of the nation. When he died, the Pentagon press room was named for him, a deserved tribute from his newspaper colleagues. Courtesy of *The Baltimore Sun*.

Lee McCardell filed deeply personal accounts of the war in Europe, always chronicling the hardships and heroism of the ordinary soldier. He and Price Day were among the first Western reporters to describe Nazi atrocities. After the war, McCardell served as bureau chief in both London and Rome, covering the Middle East and North Africa from Rome. He ended his career as assistant managing editor of *The Evening Sun*. This photo shows how layout staff indicated crops with a grease pencil. Courtesy of *The Baltimore Sun*.

Price Day, a future Pulitzer Prize winner and *Sun* editor-in-chief, reported the Italian campaign, including an eyewitness account of the fall of Rome. He was with the Seventh Army when it landed in southern France, then followed the war into the heart of battered Berlin. This family snapshot showing him in his wartime uniform was taken the day he left Baltimore, on December 8, 1943. Courtesy of Katherine Day Slevin.

The "young whippersnapper of the group," **Holbrook Bradley** went ashore with the Twenty-ninth "Blue and Gray" Division on D-Day Plus One, was wounded in Normandy, but unofficially checked himself out of hospital to rejoin the division in its fight through Europe. After the war, Bradley left the paper and went to work for the State Department. In his 90s he wrote a vivid memoir of his wartime experiences, published in 2007. Courtesy of *The Baltimore Sun.*

In this Edmund Duffy cartoon, "A Fine Idea for a Title," Hitler ponders the invasion of Italy as a spectral hand extends a copy of Edward Gibbon's cautionary book *The Decline and Fall of the Roman Empire*. Courtesy of Edmund Duffy Cartoons CC 1, Rare Books and Manuscripts Department, Milton S. Eisenhower Library, the Johns Hopkins University.

In addition to filing dispatches, *Sun* correspondents took their own photographs that were transmitted back to the paper through the military's own wire service. As Holbrook Bradley waited in the landing craft off the Normandy beaches on June 7, 1944, he took this photo of the Twenty-ninth Division preparing to go ashore on D-Day. Courtesy of *The Baltimore Sun.*

Edmund Duffy portrays Hitler looking out across the English Channel on wave after wave of the Normandy invasion in a cartoon, "Waves of the *NEAR* Future." Courtesy of Edmund Duffy Cartoons CC 1, Rare Books and Manuscripts Department, Milton S. Eisenhower Library, the Johns Hopkins University.

Lee McCardell captured this shot of the Seventy-ninth Division Infantry hiking up a Normandy lane towards the battlefront. Courtesy of *The Baltimore Sun.*

McCardell caught this scene of French civilians in Normandy sharing a road with American soldiers. Courtesy of *The Baltimore Sun.*

McCardell sent home a photo of Army nurse Lieutenant Mary E. Andrew of Federalsburg, Maryland, washing her socks in a helmet. Courtesy of *The Baltimore Sun.*

Infantry of the Yankee Division manage to get some hot food during the bitter winter of 1944 in the Ardennes. Lee McCardell, who filed several dispatches criticizing the army for not providing the men with adequate food and clothing for the freezing conditions, took this evocative photo near the village of Berle. Courtesy of *The Baltimore Sun.*

Four Yankee Division soldiers seek shelter in a shell hole that had damaged a village house. Always meticulous in reporting the names of ordinary GIs so that their relatives could read news of them, Lee McCardell identified three of them as Staff Sergeant Martin Cohen of 2126 Walbrook Avenue, Baltimore; Floyd Sumner of Cedar Grove, North Carolina; and Private Dillard Yarbrough of Grand Saline, Texas. Courtesy of *The Baltimore Sun*.

Holbrook Bradley snapped a scene of the Twenty-ninth Division in Julich, showing a wounded man being carried out on a stretcher improvised on a jeep. Courtesy of *The Baltimore Sun.*

McCardell's most harrowing photos were shot on April 29, 1944, in the Bavarian village of Neunburg, where an American corps commander forced the villagers to exhume the bodies of 160 Jews who had been massacred by SS guards and thrown into a mass grave. A series of photos shows the villagers, mostly women and children, carrying the open coffins down to the village cemetery and laying them on the ground prior to a dignified re-burial service conducted by a U.S. Army chaplain. Courtesy of *The Baltimore Sun.*

When covering the closing phases of the Italian campaign, **Howard M. Norton** scooped the world on the death of Mussolini. In the Pacific, he witnessed the Saipan invasion and narrowly escaped death when a Japanese shell hit his subchaser, killing most of its crew. After the war, Norton won a Pulitzer for investigative reporting of Maryland government scandals. Courtesy of *The Baltimore Sun*.

Lee McCardell is shown taking the surrender of a bunch of Germans at the point of his pencil.

Mark Watson, the oldest of the correspondents, endures the hardships of the front lines in dashing style, while the youngest, Holbrook Bradley, crouches over his C-rations while thinking longingly of crab cakes.

Price Day requests an army press officer to find him the complete works of Shakespeare.

In a composite sketch that appeared in the paper on Sunday, August 6, 1944, *The Baltimore Sun's* other political cartoonist, **Richard Q. (Moco) Yardley** (1903–1979), drew several of his colleagues in action on the front lines. Courtesy of *The Baltimore Sun* and Susan Yardley Wheltle.

Philip Heisler went ashore at Iwo Jima and gave a riveting account of riding out a typhoon on a destroyer. He later served as managing editor of *The Evening Sun,* for thirty years. When he retired in 1979, he tacked up a letter in the newsroom. "I avoided the goodbyes because I was afraid I might tarnish the tradition that all managing editors are tough, hard-hearted, and unsentimental warlords." Courtesy of *The Baltimore Sun.*

An isolated Hitler sees his world disintegrating around him in this Duffy cartoon entitled "Berchtesgaden Sunset." Courtesy of Edmund Duffy Cartoons CC 1, Rare Books and Manuscripts Department, Milton S. Eisenhower Library, the Johns Hopkins University.

While part of this shift represented an Eisenhower attempt to placate the ever-demanding Montgomery, Watson held that it nevertheless made sense, that it unified command of the Allied troops north of the Ardennes salient. *"The military situation is much too important and serious to be disturbed by matters of international jealousies,"* Watson asserted. *"It is not the first time that large elements of our troops have been under British command or British troops under American command. There will probably be a great many more such minglings but publication of such events is one question on which ordinary caution compels us to bow to the judgment of the military command. The question of who is commanding a sector is of very great importance in enabling any competent commander to judge his opponent's intentions. The cases most familiar to readers of American history would be those of the Civil War. The commanders of both sides had been comrades since West Point days. Lee, in particular, showed great acumen in surmising what McClellan's temperament and habits would lead him to do in like circumstances."*

The issue of *The Sun* dated January 7, 1945 was a banner day for McCardell, who filed one story on current battles and another story on what happened to beleaguered units of the Pennsylvania-based Twenty-eighth Division, the first target on the night the German offensive began.

First, the current battle description: *"The hilly terrain in what GIs call 'mountain goat' country was not unlike but more difficult than that encountered by American troops in Italy. It was inaccessible to vehicles, except for the narrow, winding, ice-glazed road with treacherous hairpin curves turning and twisting under enemy observation."*

Second, writing history only a month after the December 16 enemy attack: *"The 28th, sister division to Maryland's 29th, had landed on the Normandy beaches on D-Day and had fought through St. Lo and the Huertgen Forest until they got to Clervaux for supposed rest and rehabilitation."*

Instead, McCardell wrote, they encountered *"floods of infantry, screaming, shouting, laughing and acting as no other German infantry had acted before. The men who faced them swore they were doped or drunk, or both. The defense put up by the 28th delayed the German advance long enough to enable the 101st Airborne Division to occupy and hold the vitally important crossroads town of Bastogne. Well dug in, the Americans held their fire until the oncoming enemy infantrymen were within 50 yards. They racked 'em and stacked 'em until the Nazis were clambering over their own dead. Still another outfit on the main road to St. Vith fought two columns of German tanks all night and the next day. At midnight Sunday, the American commander radioed his battalion headquarters that the situation was critical, his men outnumbered, surrounded and almost out of ammunition. He was ordered to withdraw. He replied, 'We can't get out but we'll make them pay.'*

"*At 4:30 Monday morning a young lieutenant came on the radio to report his men fighting from house to house with no ammunition except hand grenades. 'We've blown everything there is to blow. I don't mind dying. I don't mind taking a beating but we'll never give up to these bastards.'* "

Another McCardell vignette: "*Cannoneers of a field artillery battery fired their guns at constantly decreasing elevation and when the Germans threatened to overrun their position they grabbed rifles and carbines, jumped into foxholes and fought as infantry. They beat back five attacks until their ammunition ran out.*"

And a scene at Clervaux: "*Headquarters personnel, rear-echelon typists, military police, waiters, engineers, stragglers and others fought something approaching guerrilla warfare for the next three days. Finally, orders came to withdraw toward Bastogne. A convoy had to fight its way through enemy roadblocks. A few stragglers drifted in for days after, suffering from hunger and exhaustion and trench foot.*"

Nine days later [Jan. 16, 1945] McCardell wrote a riveting story about the plight of soldiers fighting in the Ardennes Forest in the dead of winter. Excerpts:

"*You have to see it to believe it. If you can imagine an army fighting its way through the mountains of Garrett County in mid-January, with ten to twelve inches of snow underfoot, the trees encased in frozen sleet, the temperatures four to five degrees above zero, the skies overcast with the constant threat of more snow—if you can imagine this you'll have some idea of the ordeal through which the American troops are passing.*

"But that's only part of the picture. *You must blacken the snow with greasy soot where enemy shells have burst. You must drop frozen bodies with waxen faces in the drifts along the back roads where burial parties have not yet passed. You must people the pine forest with cold soldiers in shallow foxholes, their fingers numb and their toes frostbitten. You must picture tanks crawling across unbroken fields of snow, the dull clank of their tracks over the snow-caked bogie wheels muffled and remote. You must see infantrymen gloved and bundled against the stinging cold, weighted down with ammunition and weapons, toiling across hilltops, knee-deep in snow.*

"When the dreary winter afternoon's cold, unfriendly half-light fades across these frozen hills, you must see the infantry men drop their gear in the snow, get out their shovels and dig in for the coming night—dig through a foot of fine, dry, sifting snow and another foot of hard frozen earth. You must feel the bite of the icy Ardennes mist that rises now from the snow to fill the hollows among the hills and cling to their heights like thick, gray, frosty mildew. You must get stuck in one of these drifts, get out and push or shovel a path for your jeep while the snow beats into your face like a desert sandstorm. You must try keeping warm in a freezing countryside whose houses have been stripped of their doors, window glass and roofs. You must try to keep warm in unheated truck cabs, tanks, half-tracks and open jeeps.*

"The correspondents attached to the Third Army average eight or nine hours a day in jeeps getting up to the front and back again to town where press censors and radio stations are located. We live the life of Riley compared with that of the average GI in combat on the battlefront. I wish we could do justice to his fortitude. To keep my aging bones warm, I go forward wearing heavy GI winter underclothing, a wool-lined combat jacket, felt-lined flying pants, a wool-lined trenchcoat, a muffler, two pair of heavy woolen socks, felt-lined galoshes, a fleece-lined helmet and two pair of woolen gloves.*

"No GI is so warmly dressed. I don't have to sleep in the snow or eat cold rations. And I never return to my warm, lighted quarters at* *night without a deep sense of my own unworthiness and shame. After dark, there's no light in the cold, lonely foxhole in the pine forests. There's no warmth except that of the bodies of the living men who sleep there in their overcoats and lie awake waiting for the dawn. It's a long wait."*

In a piece marking the end of the Battle of the Bulge, almost precisely a month after it began in mid-December, Watson must have been aware that once again the Allies had failed to complete an encirclement—this time of thousands of Germans escaping the huge territory they had carved out in their Ardennes offensive. These enemy troops would fight another day.

The *Sun* military correspondent complained that *"the Germans usually move more quickly than we do in spite of our manifest superiority with which to do most of the moving. The explanation does not lie wholly in the fact that all techniques of warfare are practiced habitually by the German general staff and only in wartime by our own, save fleetingly and on a small scale. Also responsible is the elaborate character of our equipment requirements and supplemental comforts. They are far greater than those of the Germans, Russians or Japanese and they tend to slow our movements. This is recognized by our officers who still feel these items produce better soldiers and are worth preserving even if they are embarrassing in moments of stress."*

CHAPTER 17

Slogging Ahead

"Don't be surprised if an unarmed correspondent jauntily comes at you from the enemy sector inquiring, 'Anyone here from Baltimore?' It'll be 'Brad' Holbrook Bradley, Baltimore Sunpapers, who Saturday got out ahead of our right flank, got back safely, and then was the fourth man into the Julich citadel, dashing in with the First Squad."

—From the Twenty-ninth Division Newsletter,
"Twenty-nine Let's Go"

In Bradley's account of the capture of the Julich citadel, there was no hint that troops of the Twenty-ninth had recognized his daring. But there could be no doubt in the mind of *Sun* readers [Feb. 26, 1945] he was observing fierce combat from the front line:

"Sniper fire from the citadel made the open area immediately in front of it rather unsafe so we crossed over the piles of brick and masonry to a house from which observation was possible," he wrote of the Twenty-ninth Division assault. *"Machine guns were already at work on the entrance and a few seconds later the heavy grilled doorway collapsed. The run across the park to the shell holes where GIs crouched seemed more than the 50 yards it was. Almost as the fire ceased, the order came over the radio for the assault platoon to take off. Lieut. Clay S. Purvis, of Charlottesville, Va., from K Company of the 116th Regiment, yelled 'follow me' and took off through smoke and dirt toward the bridge over the moat. Even as the first men hit the bridge, sniper's bullets kicked up dirt at our feet.*

"Then we hit the main gate and were inside a tunnel. There was a constant chatter of machine guns and the occasional carrumph of larger guns as we moved on through the tunnel. Inside the fort we found piles of rubble, broken bricks and masonry. Three German staff cars stood at one side—blown to bits. Less than ten minutes after the first man entered the citadel, a patrol had already reached the far side. There was still very much of the sound of battle as we pulled out of the citadel. Already the eyes of the artillery, the division Piper Cubs, wheeled and turned over Julich and beyond, spots they never would have flown over two days ago." Bradley's story ended with the names of nineteen GIs involved in this small victory.

Decades later, in his memoir of his wartime experiences published in 2007, Bradley recalled being with troops of the 175th Regiment, Twenty-ninth Division, as they crossed the Roer River to reach and occupy Julich. *"The trail we were following led across several hundred yards of muddy fields, through a stretch of swamp bordering the road near some demolished houses. It was eerily quiet as we crossed a quagmire of vegetable gardens without a shot. But then, as we approached the building line, the enemy opened fire with a deafening blast. Capt. Ben Pollard hit the ground instantly, and three of us followed him as a hail of lead cracked over our heads to slam into the brick side of a house. Apparently, the Germans had held their fire until they spotted us, and then opened fire again. But diversionary fire from men behind us gave the break we needed, and the four of us were on our feet, stumbling through knee deep water over barbed wire to reach our forward command post."*

Compare this to his real-time copy [Feb. 26, 1945]: *"Capt. Ben Pollard of St. Dunstans Road, Baltimore, was about to take off to find a pillbox so we decided to follow. We suddenly stumbled on a dead Yank who lay in a contorted, crumbled heap, his blood-filled helmet on the ground beside him. Men of his platoon picked up their dead companion and carried him to one side. As we stood by, we noticed the dead youngster's crumpled clothing, and his disordered dirt-filled hair. There has been little glamour to this operation, but it was most important. There was no blood-tingling bayonet charge, no flag-waving, no cheering. Just another routine rush from one broken-*

up house to another." Bradley evidently was in no mood to spare the folks back home the horror of war as seen in the death of one lone infantryman.

The town of Julich was just one of many enemy strong points in the so-called "middle ground" between the Allied front line and the west bank of the Rhine River. Unlike Cassino and St. Lo and Bastogne, its name would hardly resonate in American memory. This was land that had been fought over for centuries, its inhabitants having to settle for rulers of great variety. What was to happen in the first three months of 1945 never got world attention comparable to the Normandy landings, the liberation of Paris, or the Battle of the Bulge—at least never until the American First Army grabbed the Remagen Bridge over the Rhine. This spectacular breakthrough opened the way for sweeping drives into the heart of Germany. Nevertheless, the battle for Julich and many other places in enemy territory was brutal—and decisive. *The Baltimore Sun*'s frontline reporters saw and told of a slogging, miserable conflict that helped bring an end to the European war. Mark Watson, the dean of the four-man *Sun* squad on the continent, was not with them. After a long stint of duty reaching back to the North African campaign, he returned to the States in late January on a well-deserved furlough. His place at Supreme Headquarters was taken by Price Day, a development that unfortunately reduced the paper's presence in the trenches to Holbrook Bradley, and Lee McCardell. But both had proven records for producing reams of good copy, and they carried on as the colorful veterans they had become. And in the Watson tradition, Price Day wrote broad analytical articles about the conflict on the Western Front.

In summing up the historic seven months that saw Allied armies sweep from Normandy to the German border, Watson wrote [Jan. 21, 1945] that the U.S. performance was *"much more successful than any of us would have dared to believe."* After making that positive assessment, however, he laid out lessons learned, some highly critical. He noted Allied forces were *"badly surprised"* when the Germans launched the Battle of the Bulge and *"destroyed half of one of our new divisions and badly mauled others. It cannot be denied that we also greatly underestimated the enemy's ability to train his new* conscripts. *Some of the Allied mistakes were made in the higher ranks of the command, and they were costly. We were not prepared for any such blast."* He did not name names.

The *"joyous optimism"* prevailing from July to September 1944 was replaced by *"deep depression and concern,"* Watson wrote. *"The reverses of October remind us that our enemy is dangerous and threatened to transform our winter of discontent into one of plain misery."* Not until the gains made by the enemy were wiped out shortly after the new year were the Allies reassured the German army's temporary triumph had ended as a resounding strategic defeat. The enemy had won no new soil and lost irreplaceable men and machines.

In a follow-up dispatch from London, Watson focused on the *"Russian steamroller"* and posed a question that has intrigued historians ever since. Why had the Germans put up such an *"indifferent defense"* to the Soviet advance, even to the point of moving crack divisions from the Eastern to the Western Front? In his answer, Watson asked another question: *"Is it possible that the German high command has become so desperate that its judgment is faulty?"*

"If that is the case," he continued, *"we may indeed be near the point which the Allies attained in October 1918, where we had actually won yet did not know it until the next week brought the German collapse. It therefore has become a question only of the day when the German will to fight will finally be paralyzed through the loss of the German power to fight. Just as it was in 1918, it is still a question of when it will come."*

Taking on his new role of military analyst on the spot, Price Day speculated [Feb. 2, 1945] that a German January offensive well south of the Ardennes may have been in hopes of a quick victory against the American Seventh Army. A mix of veterans of Africa, Sicily, and Italy, the Seventh "stopped the Germans" first in the Hardt Forest, then in Hardt itself, then *"for twelve bitter days in the little towns of Hatten and Rittershofen and finally along the Moder River where the Germans tried to establish a beachhead."* Such specificity could have come only from a reporter who had seen the American effort to halt a German effort to reoccupy Alsace.

In another analysis, Day described how the tide had turned so quickly in the Allied favor: *"In a way that could hardly have been predicted two weeks ago, the war in Europe has become a single great battle, with events in the East and the West, in Norway and Italy, more closely interlocked than ever before. Until last summer, the continent of Europe was a land of vast spaces over which our military thinking operated at great and often extreme range. What happened in one spot was felt more slowly elsewhere. Today's attack by 1,000 B-17s on the heart of Berlin has as its primary effect direct support to the Red Army. In this, as in many other things, it is almost as if the strategic picture had suddenly contracted, as if the war against Germany had become one complex tactical operation. The enemy is on the defensive everywhere, which means the Allies choose their moves."*

On the actual battlefield, however, the change in the tides of war was obscure to soldiers fighting to keep alive. *"These are monotonous, dreary days,"* Bradley reported [Feb. 14, 1945] from the Twenty-ninth Division near the German border. *"For the better part of a week rain has pelted down on roads and fields already covered with deep, thick, sour mud, the result of a thaw a week ago which melted several inches of month-old snow. Men and equipment alike are now generally covered with grime. The battle-scarred towns seem more desolate than ever, for piles of rubble and wreckage are still found everywhere, covered with a mass of decaying wood, plaster and the remains of household furnishings. Cobblestoned and brick streets have been cleared to a certain extent by engineers but the recent bad weather has turned most of them into rivers so that slime is scattered on personnel, equipment and buildings by passing vehicles. For the past three months most of the personnel of the Blue and Gray Division have been living in the basements of houses. With typical GI ingenuity the men have fixed up these 'dugouts.' It is not unusual to find a doughboy stretched out full length on an inner-spring mattress or an overstuffed easy chair with his feet up to a glowing stove. Adding to the difficulties of terrain, climate and all other aspects of war is the fact that the outfit has seen little action during the past two months."*

From another front, the Saar River crossing to the south, McCardell recounted another tale of frontline battle. *"The moon had gone*

*down under a cloud and it was good and dark now along the river.
The infantry lay still in the ditches on either side of the road or flat on
the narrow strip of ground sloping to the muddy river bank. This was
the first river crossing many had ever made. They kept their heads
down. The guns roared in the hills behind them and the river valley
shook with fire and thunder.*

*"The first wave ought to be across now. You lost interest in every-
thing but the depth of the nearest ditch. You hugged the ground and
prayed as you only pray when under artillery fire. The infantry slung
their rifles, dumped mortars, machine guns and ammunition into
assault boats, picked up the heavy boats, four men to hand grips on
either side, and started down the slope to the river bank. Machine
gun fire was coming back from across the river. But evidently the
infantry had landed on the far shore and was going through barbed
wire. One soldier had been hit. He was crying like a child. He had
gotten it in the leg."*

While McCardell and Bradley continued their battlefield coverage,
Day offered a military assessment of the situation as seen by Supreme
Headquarters in Paris. *"Unless Hitler can soon send more divisions,
a few weeks at most should find Allied forces along the Rhine from
Trier to Emmerich. Certainly, the enemy will delay our advance as
tenaciously as possible, but not to the extent of engaging in a battle
of attrition west of the Rhine. The enemy has not been able to build
up a strong counter-attacking force. While most of the enemy's troops
continue to fight with determination, apathy among German troops
is definitely apparent. Two lines of defense now lie between us and the
industrial mass along the Rhine. The chance that either line will hold
for long seems slight."*

As March 1945 began, Allied forces had recovered all territory lost
during the Battle of the Bulge and had fought across the Roer and
Saar Rivers and other natural barriers. The German army started to
crumble. McCardell reported [March 1, 1945] that Bitburg, a fair-
sized town between the Rhine and the Eifel Mountains, had fallen to
Patton's Third Army. *"Much of the original town had been reduced
to rubble by American Air Force bombs weeks ago. Only about six
German soldiers and the same number of civilians were found among*

the ruins. Bitburg is the worst battered city of its size to be occupied by Third Army troops on this front. Not one house has escaped shellfire or bomb damage. The center of the little town looks like a municipal dump, it walls almost leveled, its streets choked with rubbish and debris. The civilians found in the town were badly frightened and loath to leave the cellars in which they had sought protection. The brownstone brewery, where they were assembled under guard—its tall chimney is a Bitburg landmark for miles around—seems to have been the biggest thing in a town which appears to have been highly prosperous in peacetime.

"One of the first infantry men into town last night was Private Arthur Mentzel, 3422 Keswick Road. Today Mentzel was helping guard Bitburg's remaining civilians in the town's brewery. North of Bitburg, troops of the 87th and 4th Infantry Divisions fought against strong points of resistance.

"Singled out today for special attention by the 87th Division headquarters for 'individual courage and devotion to the platoon he was assigned to lead' was Sgt. Charles Register of Baltimore. Nicked in the arm by a German machine-gun slug as he jumped over a roadblock in an attack on an enemy machine-gun nest, Register stayed in the fight until it was over before he permitted his wound to be dressed. After the aid men had patched up his arm, Register resumed leadership of his platoon and fought throughout the remainder of the day's action."

Thus McCardell continued his war coverage of Maryland men in combat.

The next day [March 2, 1945] Bradley was with the Twenty-ninth Division when it attacked the town of Rheydt. As he turned to talk to a man by his side, *"a shell from a Jerry self-propelled gun smacked not ten feet away. The three of us nearest the concussion were hurled to the ground. At the impact, the man on the left yelled he had been hit. He had half a shoulder torn away, his collarbone broken with jagged edges showing. There were a couple of more shells. The man on the ground was already being bandaged, the medics calling for a litter squad to evacuate him before too much blood was lost."*

The rolling Allied offensive next captured Munchen Gladbach and Trier. Bradley reported that the advance had been so quick thousands of Munchen Gladbach civilians were still in the town. In contrast, McCardell wrote that most of Trier's population had fled. Both reporters told of German civilians waving white flags and trying to be friendly with occupying troops. These were two very important cities. Their fall prepared the ground for one of the most spectacular feats of World War II.

CHAPTER 18

Across the Rhine

With Holbrook Bradley assigned to the Ninth Army in the north and Lee McCardell with the Third Army in the southern part of the broad Allied advance into Germany, the big headline event of March 7, 1945, occurred in the center. There the First Army captured the Bridge at Remagen and the first Allied soldiers planted their boots on the east bank of the Rhine. The beachhead they established anticipated the war-ending sweep that followed.

The Sun had no eyewitness at Remagen for this historic event, an exploit later to be celebrated in books and films. But Price Day caught up [March 10, 1945] with a story that clarified details of the crossing. *"The Remagen Bridge is an iron railroad structure, one of the two tracks which were passable. On Wednesday afternoon (March 7), after a charge along 18 miles of road, it (a U.S. contingent) reached the bank of the Rhine to find the bridge standing. Company A of the 27th Armored Infantry Battalion was immediately sent across. A few surprised Germans in the vicinity attempted to set off prepared demolition charges but failed and fled. The armored infantrymen reached the far bank, climbed the steep cliff and established the first beachhead across the great river."* He reported the American presence was *"strong and growing,"* but cautioned it was *"a long way from a concentration of supplies and men."* Day speculated, correctly, that it could become *"a major factor"* in later war developments.

The Sun's correspondent at Supreme Allied Headquarters, Price Day filed an optimistic report [March 11, 1945] asserting that the first phase of the spring offensive had *"gone better than had been hoped— and hope was high for we knew we were strong and the enemy was weak. We did not know a month ago quite how extremely weak—taking the western front as a whole—he was."*

Meanwhile General George Patton was capturing large chunks of land still held by the enemy west of the Rhine. Lee McCardell filed this colorful story [March 15, 1945]: Patton's armor *"broke loose in the Eifel and came boiling down to the Rhine at 40 miles an hour to overrun German bivouac areas. Captured German soldiers are still being counted. Ordnance collecting teams are just beginning to gather up captured enemy equipment. The corralling of hundreds of horses used by the Germans is still a problem almost as big as that of handling misplaced civilians.*

"As in Normandy, the engineers are using bulldozers to clear the muddy, narrow roads cluttered with smashed German equipment. Ten days after the breakthrough, German stragglers are still crawling out of cellars, haymows and stone quarries to give up. Little groups of would-be prisoners still march unguarded to our rear looking for someone to accept their surrender.

"The larger towns of the Eifel have been bombed but the villages of stone, half-timber and pink plaster houses with gaily painted shutters have not been touched by the destruction of war. Traditional cloaked and bearded Germans still tend flocks of sheep in the deep green vales among the hills. In sharp contrast to the highly modern industrial area of the Cologne Plain, the Eifel comes closer to the old fairy-tale Germany. Supposedly simple peasants hang out their white flags and then stand gaping with much the same interest and awe that people watch circus parades.

"And, believe me, it is something to gape at. Our soldiers are not very pretty. Dirty, muddy and tough-looking, their automotive equipment alone, for sheer weight and volume, is a terrifying spectacle of the Western world on its way to war. From the American point of view, the breakthrough was a 'cavalryman's dream' come true. Tanks, mechanized cavalry and armored infantry tore up one road and down another. They literally ran over surprised German columns on the march. They could have massacred those trapped against the river."

Continuing his coverage of Patton's offensive, McCardell described the surrender of a number of German officers in a village near the

Rhine [March 17, 1945]. *"All the German officers were spic and span, freshly shaved, carefully brushed. Their general turned out in wraparound leggings, long green overcoat and a German overseas cap. The Americans who gathered around them were covered with whiskers and mud. They had not washed or shaved for a week. They had no time."*

The commander of the task force that captured the German officers told McCardell this story: *" 'Dirty and muddy as I was, I certainly felt like hell when I saw that general and his officers all slicked up. They gave me the old Heil Hitler salute, damn them. The general was an arrogant cuss. He and his party evidently were on their way to the Rhine with expectations of catching a ferry to the far shore. They had arrived by automobile in the village where they were captured and had taken quarters in its Gasthaus. Half empty glasses of beer and a plate of German crumpets were found on the taproom table set for the general's party.' "*

With Patton's army racing to its massive Rhine crossing on March 23, 1945, McCardell offered a gripping picture of Mainz, one of the largest German cities on the west side of the river yet captured: *"This Rhineland city, in which 7,000 people were killed within 15 minutes during an air-raid last February 27, is occupied today by doughboys of the 90th Division. Of the 150,000 peacetime population of greater Mainz, more than 50,000 remain. Many of these are living in abject squalor amid the ruins of their town, without light, water or gas. If you ever visited Mainz as a tourist you will remember it was a cathedral town, the place where you caught the steamer for a daylight trip down the Rhine to Cologne. It was a town of comfortable hotels and fairly good restaurants. The cathedral, characteristic of Rhenish Roman art, still stands, one of the least damaged buildings.*

"There were no boats on the Rhine today. The steel spans of the railway bridge lie in the river like a crushed Meccano toy. The hotels and restaurants are heaps of rubble or burned out skeletons, looking like Baltimore after the 1904 fire. Many weary women carry buckets of water drawn from a common tap. We saw three items of food.

"First, a paper bag of apples. Second, a lapful of tiny potatoes being peeled by a woman living in the dirty barracks just outside the

cathedral. Third, a small bag of unappetizing crackers which two young girls were eating while they watched American soldiers. I saw only one woman and three or four men who looked as if they belonged to the well-to-do class. The great mass of the people remaining in Mainz obviously are the poor members of the working class. Many are living in half-ruined over-crowded rows of cheap flats. Others are living in the cathedral itself, in shanties and dugouts and in dilapidated wood barracks.

"The city's air-raid shelters are some of the crudest and deepest I have ever seen. I saw women washing clothes in the big basin of stagnant water under the wall of the cathedral. One group of young people was stretched out on the ground taking a sunbath in the park. There wasn't much left. The limbs had been stripped from the blasted trunks of the trees. The exploding bombs had cut down shrubbery. The twisted tail fins of those bombs were still lying around and little clumps of violets bloomed amid the debris."

PATTON'S 3D ARMY CROSSES RHINE, SECURES BEACHHEAD, PUSHES INLAND

So shouted the front-page *Sun* headline on March 24, 1945, as the Third Army stormed across the great river barrier without the loss of a man or firing of a single shot. In contrast to the surprise crossing of the Remagen Bridge by a single company of doughboys, this was a huge invasion by forces that had built up inexorably as they battered through the Saarland and elsewhere. Mark Watson, still in Washington, wrote that *"the Allied supreme command now has eight field armies (Canadian, British, French and five Americans) firmly placed on the Rhine for a distance of 250 miles, from Arnhem to the Alps."*

So swift had been the advance and so paltry the German resistance, Watson continued, that *"we have magnificent troops far from exhausted physically, their morale actually heightened by great successes gained at small cost. Allied attack strength in the west has gained its greatest height at the very time when German defense strength has sunk to its lowest."*

In assessing what he called *"one of the most brilliant campaigns of the entire war,"* Watson said the Allied high command had been able to minimize casualties and save fuel, ammunition, and equipment for later operations. Meanwhile enemy communications had been paralyzed and its armies uncoordinated.

Price Day, reporting from Paris, suggested that even Frankfurt was now threatened (an accurate forecast) but cautioned that the enemy could still muster forces to cause *"painful days."* Nonetheless, the two analysts left readers with the impression the end of the European war was but weeks away.

From farther north along the Rhine, Holbrook Bradley was an eyewitness to the Ninth Army's crossing near Duisburg [March 26, 1945]: *"There was little to indicate one of the biggest operations since D-day was about to begin. The colonel preparing to take off for the river front suggested we* (reporters} *come along as this was the best opportunity of seeing how the operation would be carried out. For a moment the mass of armor, assault boats, bulldozers, amphibious craft and the profusion of material overshadowed us. Then we, too, were moving and were lost in the steady stream of men and vehicles.*

"There were heavy flashes and earth-shaking concussions to the north of us as the British artillery went into action in support of the Commandos who were then crossing the Rhine below us. In the bright moonlight every figure, tree and house seemed to stand out almost as if it were day. This made us rather uncomfortable as we walked along the top of a dike only 60 yards from the river and less than 400 yards from the German positions. The American batteries opened up behind us with an ear-splitting roar that seemed almost on top of us. There seemed to be no response from the Jerry gunners, so we took a chance of lying on the top of the dike to watch the shelling. For the next hour until the jump-off, it seemed as if every piece of artillery in the entire American army was cracking behind us, sending steel by the thousands of tons onto the German held ground.

"Engineers had brought fast storm boats and smaller assault boats to the back edge of the dike. Now, as 2 o'clock approached, doughboys, packs on their backs, rifles or heavy weapons over their shoulders, filed forward in silent columns. Suddenly, as the hands of our watches pointed to H-hour, the artillery as at one command ceased, then went into action again with increased volume. At the same moment, the first boats were lifted over the dike and carried down to

the water's edge. To those watching from the top of the dike it seemed almost like some fantastic Hollywood set.

"The first boat could be made out halfway across the 300-yard width of the Rhine when a green and then a white flare shot up from the German-held ground. This seemed a miracle following the saturation of artillery that was still going on. The sound of a patrol clash showed that some of the Krauts still held out, probably in cellars, but they must have been groggy. As the boats continued to stream across the Rhine the men of the leading units were soon lost in the smoke-filled darkness. A couple of hours later the situation had settled down to a well-defined bridgehead attack that was progressing smoothly.

"Shortly after 5 a.m. the colonel felt the battalion had advanced enough to warrant moving the regimental command post across. As an alligator driver gave us a lift across the river there came a familiar whine and carrump of Jerry artillery as three shells crashed into a levee 50 yards from where we stood. There were a couple of casualties when the smoke and flying debris cleared away, but down at the river's edge the doughboys were loading as if nothing had occurred, even as a couple more rounds landed downstream from us.

"From the first moment we hit the beach it was evident why the men had no tougher time getting in. The ground seemed excellent for defense but the Krauts never had time to prepare it properly and, as a result, all opposition was from a few hastily dug ditches, firing positions and outposts. There were few mines, little or no wire. One Yank lay face down in the mud where he had fallen. A shell crater beside him showed he fell to artillery rather than infantry. In a trench were a couple of dead Germans, probably ordered to hold out to the last regardless of the cost—and they paid in full.

"German gunners back from the river were going through the usual routine of throwing a few rounds into every village and crossroad as we moved up. Files of prisoners under guard of doughboys came down the road, but the only other signs of life were barnyard fowls wandering aimlessly through the ruined houses and a couple of gaunt pigs rooting in the shell-torn gardens.

"As the infantry continued to push into Germany, by H plus seven

hours some elements had moved almost 5,000 yards. Those of us at vantage points on the ground could watch flight after flight of cargo planes carrying in British and American paratroopers who jumped behind German lines to confuse the issue further."

With bridgeheads securely in place east of the Rhine, Mark Watson reported that Allied forces were in position to conquer vast swaths of enemy territory [March 27, 1945]. *"The primary aim of these grand-scale offensives is not to encounter enemy resistance and batter it down, but rather to find a soft spot and race through it at top speed. Once clear of enemy restraint, our armor is expected to go as far and as fast as it can go without losing its own contacts and endangering itself either through lack of fuel and ammunition or through exposing its flanks to destructive enemy action.*

"Each ten-mile advance by 100,000 men uses up a large quantity of gasoline which must be made good. Also it adds ten miles to the distance which trucks must cover and ten miles to the distance which returning empties must traverse. It also adds ten miles on the left flank and ten on the right which our supporting troops must consolidate to say nothing of the whole interior space which must be swept clear of enemy troops and even enemy civilians who are disposed to make trouble.

"In brief," Watson observed, *"swift and superb have been our breakthroughs and bright as is the future of General Eisenhower's drive, this must not be thought of as a mere parade."*

Day, in a dispatch from Allied Headquarters in Paris, likened the onslaught of American and British forces sweeping toward Germany's heart to a flood. *"One way to comprehend what is happening would be to take a plaster relief model of Germany and feed water into it from the west. Over the broad Westphalian lowlands, through the Hessian Gap into Bavaria, and along the valleys that pierce the hills of central Hesse the Allied armies pour steadily. Groups of Germans forming for counter-attacks are overrun. Other groups, small and large, are bypassed and cut off. Enemy formations that might have been shifted to areas of immediate danger find their routes of travel cut. Already a number of natural features along which the Germans might* have hoped to establish momentary stabilization have been passed over and through. Even the German methods of delay by demolition are breaking down.

"The capture of 30 gasless tanks southwest of Siegen was more than an isolated instance; it was a sign and a portent. The fight cannot be long in the west of central Germany and it will be hardly a match in intensity with the battles of late 1944 on the Western Front. On March 1, the enemy forces in the west totaled fewer than 70 divisions. In the opening 25 days of March he lost an average of one division per day. A reasonable estimate at this moment would be that the German effectives in the west number about 250,000 men. The rest of the 1,250,000 Germans in uniform are not fighting troops. If the enemy is to stand at all, if he is to gain any capacity for regrouping his armies for defense, he must draw from other fronts. In Italy, 23 or 24 German divisions are committed. If a plan to pull out altogether were put in operation now, it would be completed too late to affect the war. The enemy cannot get out, cannot dare, with his slow and limited transport. In Norway there are fewer than 15 divisions able to get out, like those in Italy, only in a thin stream. The German troops now in Norway will have no effect on the events of central Germany.

"There remains the Eastern Front. It is likely that those (German troops) that do come west will be committed piecemeal and be frittered away. Whatever reinforcements Hitler may feel he can afford to send to the west will not have any great effect on the pace of our progress. The pattern of today's fighting will be largely the pattern that will be seen from now to the end of organized resistance—a powerful striking force led by armor with the infantry following closely behind. These operations are a process of knifing and circling and cutting off and doing a thorough job despite our speed, as we go ahead. Most German soldiers will go on fighting till they are told to surrender. It is likely we will have to go on with the systematic annihilation of the German army that is now in progress."

With German soldiers surrendering wherever they could find a captor, McCardell offered some goings-on around Giesen, a town in the path of General Patton's all-speed-ahead Third Army [March 31, 1945]. He began with a vignette involving a sole German soldier: "A *few miles above Hanau, a German soldier steps out into the middle of the highway when he sees your jeep coming. He raises his hands above his head. He stands there motionless on a hillcrest, silhouetted against the sky like a cardboard cutout. He is waiting to surrender.*

"*He has taken off his side-arms and dropped his rifle. He wears only his haversack, his canteen and his gas mask over his uniform. He has thrown away his helmet. He has his peaked gray felt cap on. He stands at attention, heels close together, hands over his head. Your jeep driver swerves to keep from running the German down, as you speed past him. He executes a sort of about-face, still at attention. With a puzzled expression on his face he watches you drive on.*

"*You pass whole companies, marching back in step under guard of two or three bored GIs. White flags hang from the windows of all houses in the little German towns along the road. Streets are full of townfolk.*"

McCardell later encountered quite a scene in a place called Friedberg: "*The town was full of German soldiers, the cleanest and neatest German soldiers you have ever seen. Garrison troops no doubt. They walked about the streets as if nothing had happened, gathering up their suitcases and haversacks, and eventually assembling in the barracks yard for formal surrender.*"

CHAPTER 19

Witness to Atrocity

Price Day was one of the first American civilians to glimpse the horrors of the Holocaust. The dateline was November 28, 1944, more than four months before large Nazi death camps were overrun by Allied forces deep in Germany and its conquered territories. So great was Day's revulsion and disbelief as he looked at Nazi instruments of mass murder that he evidently restrained his reporter's instinct to lead his story with hard news of what his eyes told him. Reading his story decades later, when the Holocaust was known in all its monstrosity, one senses Day's hesitation or, at least, his discipline, in dealing at that moment with a subject almost beyond comprehension. He was, after all, not a shock journalist. And so he started gently, obliquely, almost taking his readers by the hand as they walked into nightmare.

"The people who lived on top of the mountain that rises above the town of Natzviller could look out on what must be one of the loveliest views in the world," he began. *"Natzviller lies halfway between burned-out St. Die, to which incredulous refugees are still returning, and Molshein, a Germanic-looking medieval city on the Alsatian plain where the first little group of liberating GIs are feeding a monkey in a proprietorless café. The miniature town itself is pleasant from above, but it is the peaks of the Vosges range, covered with evergreen and with heavy frost sparking in the cold sunshine, that made the view worth traveling far to see."*

Then, ominously, the tale darkens.

"Those who have been looking at it for the last three years did travel far—some from Norway and Russia and Holland—but they didn't travel by choice. The fifteen-acre expanse of camp is inhab-

ited today by one man, an aged Alsatian who, though he has trouble speaking anything but German, is able to explain that he worked as a laborer around the camp while the Germans and their non-criminal prisoners were still here. This man (note Day's careful attribution) *says that from 5,000 to 6,000 people were shot here in the last three years and their bodies burned in the establishment's crematorium. I cannot vouch for the figure. I can merely report what I saw."*

And what this *Sun* correspondent saw were one-story wooden structures with barred windows surrounded by barbed wire. *"Here, those in confinement were kept crawling through a three-foot steel door into four by four cubicles with concrete floors and completely white walls and no heating. On a terrace below sits what was the camp's more serious business of killing people. Here, one room is filled with urns of two types, metal and real pottery. A pair of long black rubber gloves lies on the floor and another pair lies on a table. Another room is half-filled with coal, with a shovel standing upright in it. Next to this, with ashes over its bottom to a depth of five inches, is a steel chamber capable of holding the body of a man or woman. It has well-made doors at either end and an efficient system of drafts. Beside it lies a steel frame for sliding bodies into the chamber and a pair of tongs like ice tongs but stronger. My informant said the tongs were used for handling bodies before they were placed on the frame. Since capacity of the crematorium was one body at a time, the room below, which is reached by steps from outside, was used, I am told, as a repository for bodies waiting until their time came. I was also told* (again note the careful attribution) *that it was as they were forced down these steps that the victims were shot in the back of the head. These particular facts I cannot check, but I think that the process must have been different since on the floor within the cremating chamber are two rooms which seem to have been used to prepare the victims for their fate.*

"The first holds a big decontaminating chamber surrounded by a pile of thousands of shoes—but again I do not know that the shoes belong to the persons who were killed, although the Alsatian says so. In the center of the room stands what at first looks like an operating table, but is tilted and slanted toward the end. Toward its center runs

a series of grooves, like those in a steak platter. They meet a central groove leading to a drain. At the foot of this obscene structure is a wash basin, with water still running in it. What purpose this could have served other than to hold the bleeding bodies of people who were being stripped for cremation, I cannot imagine.

"I believe this camp, from which all prisoners were taken last week to Germany, was a place of wholesale murder. Nothing else could explain the elaborate and efficient arrangements. It is its very efficiency—an almost incredible neatness—that makes the spine turn cold. If there were traces of blood, if the bodies or bones were left about, it would somehow be less shocking, and the notion of a special table for the bodies of those murdered is modern proficiency perverted beyond the comprehension of an ordinary observer."

Price Day was no *"ordinary observer."* He seems to have constructed this dramatic story to convey his personal revulsion in a way that was bound to horrify his readers. Even six decades later it continues to shock even though the stupefying details of Natzviller were minuscule compared to what the world would soon learn at Auschwitz and so many other huge killing grounds. The Nazis indeed plotted mass murder with the *"elaborate and efficient arrangements"* and the *"incredible neatness"* that a *Sun* reporter was one of the first to report.

If Day did not see the dead bodies of Nazi victims, McCardell did. It was months later in early April 1945, and in the town of Ohrdruf, another German village, like Natzviller, that achieved unwelcome notoriety. There was, however, an important difference. There was but one inhabitant left in Natzviller, and he obviously did not approve of what had happened. Ohrdruf fell to onrushing Allied forces, who soon learned of a tale of Nazi sadism and murder. The town's inhabitants professed to not having known of the atrocity on its outskirts.

In his story printed on April 7, 1945, McCardell immediately took his readers to the death scene: *"There on the blood-soaked ground before you lay the bodies of 31 miserable men. Each had a bullet in the back of his head. They had been shot three days ago by SS guards, you were told. You had heard of such things in Nazi Germany. You had heard creditable witnesses describe just such scenes. But now that you were actually confronted with the horror of mass murder, you*

*stared at the bodies and almost doubted your own eyes. 'Good God,'
you said aloud. 'Good God.' Then you walked down around the corner of two barren, weather-beaten barrack buildings. And there in
a wooden shed, piled up like so much cordwood, were the naked
bodies of more dead men than you cared to count. 'Good God,' you
repeated. 'Good God.'*

"*These dead, more horrible in death than any carnage you had seen
on a battlefield, belonged to German Concentration Lager North,
S-3 at Goltha. Until three days ago, when the camp commandant
grew uneasy over the approach of Lieut. Gen. George S. Patton's 4th
Armored Division, 2,000 prisoners, Germans, Czechs, Serbs, Yugo-
slavs, Russians, French and Belgians, were held there under a guard
of 150 of Hitler's SS men. Many were Jews. A few were non-Jewish
prisoners. All were males. The youngest was a Jewish boy, 16 years
old, who had been in the camp four years. The health conditions in
the camp were appalling. It was being swept by a typhus epidemic.
The deaths from typhus averaged thirty per day. The prisoners had
been dying at that rate for weeks.*

"*The dead were stripped. They were numbered with a black crayon
scrawl on their naked skin. They were carried down into the charnel
house, a wooden shanty, beside the latrine. Here they were stacked
like slaughtered pigs and sprinkled with lime. When the shanty was
filled, the SS men backed up a truck and other prisoners loaded the
corpses onto a truck. The truck hauled the bodies out of the camp
to a pit in the woods two miles away. Here the bodies were burned.
The prisoners who survived said 3,000 to 5,000 had been burned in
the pit.*

"*Tanks of the 4th Armored were drawing closer every hour. The SS
guards were eager to take off. One man in the burial detail hid under
a bunk in the barracks. Another ducked off into the woods. Fourteen
escaped. They told the German interpreters their story. The Americans hesitated to believe it. Major John R. Scotti, of Brooklyn, N.Y.,
the command surgeon, was sent out to investigate. The dead were still
there. 'I couldn't believe it even when I saw it,' Major Scotti said. 'I
couldn't believe that I was there looking at such things.' Other prisoners had been flogged to death or shot, so many that they couldn't*

remember the number. *Others had disappeared in small groups from time to time.*

"The prisoners said the camp had several means of torture. On one occasion the officials had made them stand for attention continuously for 24 hours. At the end of the stretch one of them remarked: 'Ha! You like it, yes? You may stand at attention ten hours longer.' On days when small groups of prisoners were selected for the mysterious mission described by the guards as 'labor in underground shelters' the commandant lined up the entire population of internees held in 'protective custody' under the Nazi law. Then he lighted a cigar, strode up and down before the assembled prisoners, puffing the cigar violently. He looked them over, and finally stopped before one group. He would take the cigar out of his mouth, and flick ashes at the group and say: 'Those.' The prisoners in these groups were taken away. None who remained behind knew what happened to them. Those selected for 'labor in underground shelters' never returned to Concentration Lager North S-3."

Note the difference in the structures of Day's November story and the one filed by McCardell the following April. In the intervening period, world awareness of Nazi state-sponsored mass executions had grown exponentially. Thus, the two *Sun* war correspondents were addressing an audience much changed and increasingly outraged. Whereas Day took a slow pace in leading up to the shock of Nazi horror (*"The people who lived on top of the mountain could look out on one of the loveliest views in the world"*), McCardell had no hesitation in slamming home the stark reality of what he saw in his very first sentence. (*"There on the blood-soaked ground before you lay the bodies of 31 miserable men."*) In the bulk of their stories, these seasoned reporters often resorted to staccato sentences to describe the scenes before them. There was no need for embellishment. Adjectives were limited.

McCardell could not get Ohrdruf out of his mind. His anguish and a chance encounter of war would not let him. Early April found him near Erfurt where, for the first time, he met survivors of Auschwitz, the most notorious of all Nazi charnel camps, with a well-designed capacity to gas, strip, plunder dental gold, and cremate thousands of victims daily. Jewish international organizations, it was later learned, implored the Washington and London governments to bomb the hell out of Auschwitz to halt its deadly operations even though many prisoners would die in the attacks. Allied authorities thought they had more pressing targets. So the killing went on to the end.

One of the Auschwitz survivors McCardell interviewed was *"a stubby little gray-haired Jew"* who was also an alumnus of Ohrdruf where, he said, 3,400 died within four months, most of them beaten, starved, and worked to death. Then McCardell took up the tale [April 12, 1945]: *"Yes, you knew about Ohrdruf. You'd been there. You'd seen the bodies, or what was left of the bodies. Prisoners at Ohrdruf had been marched away in groups of 100 each guarded by four SS men, when American troops had captured the neighboring town of Gotha."* Four survivors speaking with McCardell told him they were part of the last group to leave Ohrdruf. *"In the darkness of a woods where they'd been bivouacked their first night out of camp, the four escaped. They had been recaptured the next day by Volkssturm troops, but the officer in charge had let them go. The four fugitives lost their way, walked back into the German lines, were recaptured a second time and thrown into a cellar in the village of Neudietendorf, about five miles southwest of Erfurt.* (Note McCardell's attention to authenticating detail.) *Here the Americans found them, gave them soap and razors, took them to an abandoned German house and told them to throw away their filthy prison garb and dress themselves with any decent civilian clothes they could find. One found a gray homespun suit and a pair of high black leather boots. Another found a bright plaid silk necktie. But their shaved heads still marked them as prisoners. And on their right forearms each still wore his blue tattooed prison number."*

Dr. Bela Fabian, 56, of Budapest, a novelist and former president of the Hungarian Independent Democratic Party, was an Auschwitz survivor. He had been sent to Auschwitz where he received the tattooed number, B-12305. *"The officer in command stood on a ramp where the trainloads of incoming Jews arrived at the camp and by a simple gesture of his thumb indicated those who were to be gassed and those who were to be held as slave laborers,"* McCardell wrote. *"'We were asked about our age,' said Dr. Fabian. 'I lied about mine and said I was 46 because I knew that anyone over the age of 50 would be sent to the gas chamber immediately. I was passed into the camp but a close friend who was by my side, Stephen Farkas, did not know about this distinction. He gave his correct age and they took him away. I never saw him again. Of 150 children sent to the camp, all but 50, who were kept as runners, messengers and servants, were sent to the gas chamber without question. All young mothers who refused to leave their children were gassed. The strong and healthy ones and the good-looking women, including mothers willing to abandon their babies, were kept. On one occasion I saw 1,000 Jewish boys, 14 and 15 years old, loaded onto trucks and taken to the gas chamber and crematory. They knew where they were being taken and that this was the end. Some of them began to weep like little children. One of the boys, the son of a Hungarian lawyer named Wienberger, stood up in his truck and made a speech, telling the others, 'Brothers, we should not cry. We are dying for the betterment of mankind.' It is impossible to describe the conditions under which we lived. They were incredible. I have seen men, strong as steel, broken down completely within six weeks after they arrived.'"*

McCardell identified other Auschwitz survivors, one of whom, Meyer Heinz, took up where Dr. Fabian's tale had ended: " *'The people were pulled out of cars onto a ramp as soon as the train arrived. All their baggage and personal belongings were taken from them and placed in special enclosures where the bags were broken open and the contents distributed into bins—one for women's dresses, one for children's clothes, one for food and so forth. The inmates were herded into another enclosure where they were stripped and their heads were shaved. They were also deloused, so to speak, and given striped prison uniforms. The only personal belongings they were permitted to carry into the prison with them were eyeglasses, belts and shoes.' "*

By the time Allied forces were rushing into the German interior, seizing evidence of war crimes before its perpetrators had time to cover up, American and British newspapers were full of German atrocity stories. What had been a subject often relegated to short articles on inside pages—an approach encouraged by the Roosevelt and Churchill governments—was now the stuff of large headlines and vivid photographs day after day, so much so that some readers grew weary. McCardell, ever sensitive and sympathetic, exploded [April 22, 1945]: *"Perhaps Americans are tired of reading these atrocity stories. God knows we correspondents are sick of writing them. We are sick of seeing these people, sick of listening to their tales. But they belong to the Nazi wreckage, laid bare by the ebbing tide of war on the battle front. And the tide is still running out."*

While the tide was still running, McCardell was still writing. From Fuchsmuehl, a Sudetenland village peopled with well-fed German-speakers, the *Sun* reporter described the plight of thirty-two American GIs captured during winter warfare in the Ardennes. *"All were suffering from malnutrition. They told the usual story of hunger and mistreatment in German prison camps. They made a long, forced march to the rear through snow, with little food and rest. Jewish prisoners were segregated along with other 'undesirables.' Early in February the prisoners were marched to Burga where they were put to work with political prisoners under SS guards digging underground tunnels, presumably for underground factories. The prisoners were kicked, cuffed and beaten with rubber hose. Their rations consisted of one liter of watery soup per man per day, sometimes with turnips or potatoes and one two-kilogram loaf of bread per day for five men, with an occasional measure of margarine and sugar.*

"Of the 350 men in the original group, 47 died while working in the tunnels. The prisoners were quartered in unheated wooden barracks and, except for the wood they stole, they received no fuel throughout the winter. Two weeks ago the prisoners were marched from Burga to Hof. By that time the Americans were so desperate for food that they were stealing rations from each other. 'We were so close to starvation that it was every man for himself,' one of the prisoners said. The day before the Third Army reached Hof, the Germans evacuated their prisoners, including many so ill and weak from malnutrition that they could not walk. These were loaded into horse-drawn wagons, 20 to 30 to a wagon, piled on top of each other.

"We saw some of these men last night—mere human skeletons suffering from advanced stages of malnutrition. Plain starvation would

be a better word. Their bodies were caked with dirt. Some were cov-
ered with sores. Their clothing was infested with lice. Nobody knew
how many Americans had died on the journey. Estimates ran as high
as 50."

However riveting these stories, McCardell's passionate coverage
of Nazi atrocities is most remembered by a tale in which American
military authorities took immediate action to humiliate Germans who
professed ignorance or indifference to the fate of Hitler's victims.
The date was April 29, 1945. The German village was Neunburg, in
Bavaria. The mass deaths were especially poignant because the end of
the war appeared so near. *The Baltimore Sun,* on at least three widely
spaced occasions, has reprinted McCardell's words. This, without
apologies, is a fourth:

"The little men of Neunburg, who say they did not know what
went on in the Nazi concentration camps, know now. So do the wom-
en and older children of Neunburg. By an order of an American corps
commander, they served as pallbearers today at a mass funeral of 160
Jews, who, suffering from slow starvation, had been shot and killed
by the SS guards one week ago in a woods overlooking Neunburg.

"Every man, woman and child above the age of five in Neunburg
who was able to walk attended the funeral by military order. They
stood in the cemetery with the mutilated and emaciated bodies of 160
murdered Jews lying in front of them in open coffins. They listened to
the statement, in German, read over the loudspeaker. They were told:
'You have been ordered here to look upon this indisputable, this grue-
some evidence of barbarity, and to be solemnly told that the people of
the world hold the Germans responsible for this horrible crime that
has resulted in the death of these innocent men. The German people,
all of you, conspired to tear these wretched victims from their homes
and families—from their wives, children, and other dear ones in for-
eign lands. You conspired to transport them here to work as your
slaves in your factories, your farms, and your homes. None among
you raised his voice or arm in protest. You were content to profit by
their blood and sweat and misery.'

"Many of the Germans standing in the little cemetery, among the
marble monuments and well tended burial plots of their own dead, had

heard the indictment before. At least they had heard it indirectly when American soldiers, aghast at the murder of the Jews in the woods above the town, had asked them, 'Why? Why?' All over Germany that question is asked every day by the Americans. Almost always the answer is the same: 'I don't know anything about it. I am only a little man.'

"But the little men of Neunburg know about it now. The women and children know about it. And to make sure that there was no misunderstanding, they were required to file past the open coffins of the 160 murdered men when they left the cemetery. Neunburg, a country town, lies in a pretty green valley dotted with lakes and surrounded by wooded hills.

"A week ago, a column of prisoners being moved eastward under SS guard from Buchenwald and Flossenberg concentration camps halted on a road about a half mile west of Neunburg. The 160 half-famished prisoners, reduced to skin and bones, were shot and killed there. They were the bodies of Polish, Hungarian, Rumanian, and Yugoslavian Jews. They had been hastily buried in two pits—or rather the bodies had been dumped into two pits like so much garbage and covered with earth. The Neunburg folks were ordered to open the graves and remove the bodies. The bodies were ghastly to behold but no different than those of other SS victims found at Buchenwald, Ohrdurf, and other German prison camps. All must have been close to death from hunger before they were killed. Most of them had been shot; others appeared to have been brained by clubs and rifle butts. Some had their eyes gouged out. They were dressed in the filthy rags of striped prison garb and broken wooden-soled shoes. A few were barefooted. Dirty pots and pans from which they had been fed had been tossed into the pits with them. The ground where they had been shot down was still gory from their wounds. The empty shells of the cartridges, which had killed them, still lay among the gore.

"An American army corps commander ordered the 160 bodies reburied decently by the townsfolk of Neunburg and directed that the entire town should attend the funeral services to be conducted by United States Army chaplains. The hour for the funeral was set at 10 o'clock this morning. At 8 o'clock this morning, every man, woman, and child of Neunburg, with the exception of the toddlers and a few

aged, infirm and ill adults, lined the main streets. Many of the children were under five and one mother carried a year-old baby in her arms.

"The 160 rough wooden coffins, built by village carpenters, had been stacked in the fork of the crossroads just west of town. A group of about 100 liberated slave laborers and surviving stragglers of the ill-fated march from the prison camps—it was from these stragglers that the Americans got the first-hand eyewitness account of the mass shooting—were also in the street. They marched up the hill to the pine woods where the exhumed bodies lay on the floor of the forest and held Jewish funeral rites there. Then the male inhabitants of the village started up the hill, each group of four men carrying an empty coffin from the pile at the crossroads. They carried them in the old-fashioned way on two sticks, one fore and one aft, and two men on either side.

"The burgomaster, who had arranged the details, had hoped to have at least 700 men serve as pallbearers, but there were not that many men in the village. About 50 of the coffins were carried by women and half-grown boys and girls. They walked up the road in single file, turned off into the pines and there the Jewish men of the group who had held the service were waiting to lift the corpses into the coffins.

"The Germans accepted the task stoically. Several of the women faltered and wept and one fainted with hysteria, but the others struggled along with set faces. Some had come up to the pinewoods carrying umbrellas and pocketbooks. Now they had their hands full with the weight of the body in the coffin they carried. They tucked their pocketbooks and umbrellas in the coffins beside the dead and took to the stick. 'It's pretty tough on the women,' remarked one American who watched the cortege move out of the pines. 'It was tougher on the people in the woods—the ones they were carrying out,' replied another. The bodies were heavy for the boys and girls. It took six to ten to carry a coffin. The road winding down the hill to the village was slippery and muddy and the women pallbearers worked in relays spelling each other along the way back into town.

"The funeral procession stretched out for more than a mile. The Neunburgers not needed as pallbearers packed the sidewalks of the village main street, looking at each body in its open coffin as it was carried past. The American soldiers watched them, too. Some of the

Germans carrying the coffins plainly felt humiliated, others bore up proudly. The Neunburg Catholic padre, a tall, dignified man, was among the townsfolk who watched the procession. He strode along the street slowly, gravely and sadly looking at each body as it passed but he took no part in the services at his graveyard. They were conducted by Captain Barnabas E. McAlarney of Chicago, Catholic chaplain of a tank destroyer group, and Captain Dean W. Geary, of Altoona, PA, Baptist chaplain of a Negro ordnance battalion."

Sixty years later, on May 1, 2005, *The Sun* published a story by reporter Todd Richissin describing a visit to the scene of the crime, a visit to the insignificant little town of Neunburg, a Neunburg that physically showed little change from the photographs taken so many years earlier by McCardell.

Interviewing Mayor Wolfgang Bayerl, who was born a year after that awful long-ago Saturday, Richissin found none of the Holocaust denial attitudes that still haunt this twenty-first century world. *"What happened is not just something that we should not forget,"* Bayerl said. *"It is something we cannot forget."* Recalling how the Americans forced the townspeople to conduct the mass burial of the Jews killed in the nearby forest, he said: *"What the Americans did here— maybe that could be considered harsh. Then I think what happened, and what the Nazis did—these human beasts I call them—and I think maybe the Americans had the right idea."*

Richissin provided details of how the Neunburg massacre came to pass. On April 20, 1945, a Friday, the Nazi jailers marched 17,000 inmates out of the Flossenburg concentration camp as Allied liberators drew near and prodded them on a long march through different routes in the Bavarian woods. Their destination: Dachau, with its extermination facilities. Thousands of the emaciated prisoners died along the way. But barely alive were the 160 prisoners who were killed in the hill above Neunberg. Rosa Hastreiter, then twenty-one years old, heard the gunshots as she lay abed. Eighty-one years old when she encountered Richissin, she said: *"It was those sounds that were so terrible, so awful, I could never forget."*

CHAPTER 20

Norton Scoop
on Mussolini

"The following dispatch by Mr. Norton was the first eyewitness veri-
fication of the death of Mussolini, and was cabled back to Europe by
the Associated Press."

So read the precede to one of the most sensational stories *The Baltimore Sun* published in World War II. To make sure the inattentive reader did not overlook the paper's biggest hard-news scoop of the global
conflict, two headlines just above that italic preamble proclaimed full
bragging rights:

HOWARD NORTON SEES BODY IN MUD AT MILAN;
OTHER FASCISTS KILLED

SUN CORRESPONDENT SAYS THOUSANDS FIGHT
WAY TO SPIT ON REMAINS—
FORMER DUCE'S MISTRESS WITH HIM

It was fitting, some would say typical, that Howard M. Norton
would be at the right spot at the right time to live every reporter's fan-
tasy. He had been *The Sun*'s utility infielder throughout the war: he
went to the South Pacific to report on the achievements of Johns Hopkins doctors in organizing that theater's medical efforts, an assignment reminiscent of Raymond Tompkins' reportage in World War
I. He covered the Pentagon, the homefront center of war news, after
Mark Watson took up his long European assignment. And he almost
got himself killed when a Japanese shell hit an American warship as
Norton covered the Saipan invasion. Finally, in the closing months of
the war, Norton flew to Italy for the last agonies of that bloody, ever-
controversial campaign. After the fighting ended, Norton went home

and won a Pulitzer Prize exposing an unemployment compensation scandal in Maryland. He was the kind of reporter who could handle any assignment—and handle it fast and professionally.

Born in Massachusetts and raised in Los Angeles and Miami, Norton graduated from the University of Florida in 1932 with a bachelor's degree in journalism. He then went to freelance in Asia, working in Osaka and Tokyo before becoming a Japan-based correspondent for *The Kansas City Star, The San Francisco Chronicle,* and *The Philadelphia Inquirer.* Returning to the States in 1940, he was hired by the Sunpapers. In 1942 he was appointed foreign editor of *The Sun.* The next year he got a coveted war assignment to the Pacific. Back in America, he worked for *The Sun* in Washington and, in 1957, opened the newspaper's Moscow Bureau. He left the Sunpapers in 1964 to join *U.S. News and World Report.* Norton, at age 82, died in Wilmington, North Carolina in 1994.

Harold A. Williams, author of the 1987 history of *The Sun,* told how Norton was resourceful enough and lucky enough to get his scoop: *"Norton and three other American correspondents were in a press camp in Verona, Italy, in the spring of 1945 when they heard a rumor that Partisans had captured the fleeing Italian dictator Benito Mussolini and his mistress Clara Petacci, sentenced them in a summary court martial, shot and killed them and were exhibiting their bodies in the mud of Milan's public square. The four rushed to Milan, saw the bodies, interviewed the Partisans, then drew straws to see in what order they would file leads with their exclusive news. Norton, drawing the longest straw, had to file last. The other three, including a* New York Times *man, first sent four-word flashes, 'Mussolini killed by Partisans.' Norton's lead was far longer and included pertinent detail. As soon as it was filed, sunspots (or should we say Baltimore Sunspots?) disrupted further communication with Europe. Later* The Sun *informed Norton that it was his dispatch that had been distributed by the Associated Press and other wire services, scoring a world beat."*

Norton wrote: *"With Italian Partisans in Milan, April 29 [By Radio]—The body of Benito Mussolini lies in the mud in the Piazza Loreto here this morning and thousands of Milanese are fighting their way through crushing crowds for an opportunity to spit upon it. The*

enormous shaved head and loose meaty jowls of the fallen Duce are
resting on the breast of his mistress, Clara Petacci, 25-year-old daugh-
ter of a Milan doctor, who, with Mussolini and about twelve other
high Fascists, was given a hasty trial and shot by Partisans near the
town of Dongo yesterday at 4:10 in the afternoon.

"Lying in grotesque positions, in a mass of blood and gore around
their leader, are other Fascists shot with him. They were all dumped
there without ceremony after dark yesterday by Partisans who
brought them to Milan in a moving van from the town where they
were tried and executed. This particular spot was chosen by the Par-
tisans to display the bodies for sentimental reasons. It was there that
fifteen innocent victims were executed by the Fascists and their bod-
ies left exposed for a full day. With seven other correspondents who
dashed in jeeps through 200 miles of Partisan territory yesterday in
the hopes of getting a chance to see and talk to Il Duce, I pushed
through the crowds this morning and saw the remains of Mussolini
and his cohorts."

All of the above was written in haste among frantic scenes of political upheaval. A week later [May 1, 1945] Norton returned to this
story for a column-and-a-half discourse on Mussolini's final hours, a
tale that historians and journalists have gnawed at ever since. Norton's source was one Ricardo Lombardi, the new prefect of Milan
province, who seized the chance to speak with nine American correspondents the day before U.S. forces arrived in his city. Lombardi said
the drama began four days earlier when Milan's transport workers
went on strike and German occupation troops barricaded themselves
in their barracks. Mussolini and Rudolfo Graziani, the minister of
war in the dictator's puppet government, sent a message to Partisan
leaders asking for peace terms. They got a predictable reply: unconditional surrender.

Mussolini then denounced his former Axis partners: *"They have*
treated us as servants, and harshly, for too many years. Now we've
had enough." Having issued this ploy, the Italian dictator fled north,
hoping to save his life in Switzerland. He was arrested near the border.
Norton quoted reports that *"Il Duce was traveling in an automobile*
by himself when arrested and was wearing the uniform of the Fascist

militia. His car was with a column of about 30 German vehicles. Mussolini was wearing a German overcoat in the hope he would not be noticed among the German troops. Il Duce was recognized, however. He was immediately placed under arrest and was taken to the vicinity of Dongo, near Milan, where he was killed."

In the decades since, historians have turned the details of Mussolini's arrest and execution into a cottage industry. His body, after all, was seen in the mud of a public square. Retribution was confirmed. The bombastic dictator who led his country into humiliation and disaster had gotten his reward. Nevertheless, if the Partisans had put him on trial rather than killing him, much more might be known of his long betrayal of his nation's interests. Instead, Italy was left to pick away at its ruins—its destroyed villages, houses, churches, bridges, and art works, all fought over by foreigners—Germans, British, Americans, and others.

After the war, GI veterans of the Italian campaign often complained bitterly that they risked life and limb in a "forgotten war." True, up to a point. In terms of American public attention, newspaper readers for months could follow Page One lead articles of hard fighting up the Italian peninsula. The war in Italy became an afterthought only after Allied armies landed on the beaches of Normandy on D-Day, June 6, 1945. Just one day earlier, June 5, 1945, Italy was the biggest story in the world as Rome fell to General Mark Clark's Fifth Army.

Clark was heard to complain that the *"bastards"* in Eisenhower's command had given him just one day of glory. And what about his troops? They had fought their bloody way up through Salerno, Naples, Cassino, and Anzio before their capture of Rome. They would have to keep fighting northward almost one year more, until the very last week of World War II, against a well-led German resistance. That eleven-month, ten-day stretch was the period when reports of their sacrifices on snow-covered mountains and swift-flowing west-east rivers were subordinated to the spectacular Allied drive to conquer Hitler's Germany.

"The 608-day campaign to liberate Italy would cost 312,000 Allied casualties, equivalent to 40 percent of Allied losses in the decisive campaign for northwest Europe that began in Normandy," wrote historian

Rick Atkinson, whose own best-seller, *Day of Battle*, took scant notice of the post-Rome struggles. "Among the three quarters of a million American troops to serve in Italy, total battle casualties would reach 120,000, including 23,501 killed."

Sun reporters Mark Watson, Lee McCardell, and Price Day successively covered the Italian campaign from its beginning on September 3, 1943, until the Allied invasion of southern France in August 1944. Day then went to the new front, leaving coverage of Italy to the wire services. Only in March 1945, as the Axis collapse neared, did *The Sun* send Norton to Italy to cover the final chaotic weeks of that ever-questioned campaign.

Norton, on his arrival, first described the outlook and atmosphere of Italy from Naples to Rome as one of despair, lethargy, and devastation [April 2, 1945]. Although thousands of Italian homes had been destroyed, he wrote, Italians had little incentive for reconstruction because few shovels, hammers, nails and mortar were available. *"There appears to be no ambition or initiative and little hope left in these people,"* he observed. The farther north he traveled, scenes of war's aftermath became steadily worse: *"Cassino itself is indescribable. In most of the villages there are some houses still standing which offer some possibility of rebuilding. In Cassino there are none. The highway still runs through the town, but everything else is gone and each faint breeze whips up a dense cloud of dust which makes the whole area as unpleasant physically as it is painful to the eye. The survivors of the town of Cassino, however, are in a way luckier than their fellow countrymen in the towns that suffered less. Because Cassino was so thoroughly obliterated, the Allied Military Government has provided new dwellings for the people. The new Cassino, built along the lines of temporary war housing development in the United States, is about a mile up the road and just around the mountain from it so the people do not have to look at the skeleton of their town."*

Beyond Cassino, Norton wrote *"the scenes of destruction diminish until the visitor enters a Rome not much different from what tourists saw before the war. Nevertheless, the average Italian is immobilized, a victim of German havoc of the nation's transportation system. Unemployment is severe and the impulse for leadership is gone, perhaps because the Fascists gathered all authority unto themselves. . . . Each section of the country has something the other sections need,"* he went on. *"For the average Italian it is hopeless to wish for anything that is not within walking distance or that he cannot carry on his back. The presence of so many Allied troops in Italy and the scarcity of so many civilian items have brought inflation to everything except Italian pay envelopes. And to a newcomer to this country, it is always puzzling how the average Italian keeps afloat.*

"There is one other reason why the Italians failed to snap out of their lethargy, according to an official of the Allied Commission, and he feels it is significant because we may run into the same thing to a lesser degree in Germany. 'It is simply this: These people have been under Fascism so long it has taken all the initiative out of them. They don't know what to do unless they are told, and the same holds true for the government. Even the leaders of the country have been taking orders for so long they have forgotten how to think for themselves.'"

Two days earlier, Norton filed an article in which he made the point that while the U.S. Army would be celebrating *"the happiest Easter of the war,"* its battle-seasoned veterans were tempering *"their optimism with the sobering reminder that there are still about 26 German divisions in Italy in first-class shape, well-supplied and apparently not in a mood to quit without fight, whatever happens in the Fatherland."* How right they were. Resistance to the American advance in the Po Valley north of Florence remained stiff until the end of the month, when the surrender of Nazi forces allowed Anglo-American troops, at last in joint contact, to race to the northern Alpine reaches of Italy. In a later article [April 6, 1945] Norton reported that German Colonel General Heinrich von Vietinghof was trying to keep his forces at maximum strength. All furloughs were canceled so his men could not be shanghaied for service on the Eastern and Western Fronts. This wily general thus was obeying Hitler's orders to keep fighting yet was also trying to safeguard his troops in the last weeks of conflict.

Attached to the Ninety-first Division of the Fifth Army on April 19, 1945, Norton offered this battlefront report: *"Only one more ridge lay between men of this division and the Po Valley tonight and advance elements were within seven miles of Bologna and looking forward to spending the weekend in the 'Sausage City.' Enemy opposition was only spotty as the troops moved up Highway 65, the main road from Florence to Bologna. The opposition had all the earmarks of a rear-guard action to cover a German withdrawal. This afternoon men were pushing through a valley so thoroughly cratered by our artillery that it looked as if the whole countryside had suffered a severe case of smallpox. There seemed never to be a space of more than 10 feet between the shell holes. This was a section where the Jerries had planted a thicker belt of mines than ever before seen in Italy, and our artillery had blanketed the area to give a safe footing for the troops. Once through this area and over the last ridge, the men in the front lines expect to be able to roll rapidly down the slope to Bologna, for when they get to that final ridge they will be in a position to make full use of tanks, which during the mountain phase of the Bologna drive had been used chiefly as mobile artillery.*

"*From a knoll just outside the hamlet of Zula, I watched while a company of infantry attempted to clear the Nazis from the last high point they hold above the road leading to Pianoro. The enemy position was obviously hopeless. They were surrounded and the 91st Artillery had been pounding them for hours. But every time our infantry men edged forward they got heavy fire from the hill positions. As small specks of khaki on the barren hillside neared a ruined stone farmhouse about 100 yards from the summit where the Nazis were holding out, our artillery support ceased in order to prevent injury to our men.*" He did not have to add that soldiers on both sides did not want to die in a battle quickly becoming meaningless.

When the Fifth Army finally took control of Bologna, an important city that had remained outside the Allied grip for so long, American soldiers may have expected cheering crowds and rapturous girls. They did not get them. Norton reported [April 22, 1945] that correspondents on the scene variously described the welcome as "*restrained*" or "*lukewarm*" or "*clearly sullen.*" "*It was a disappointing demonstration and does not in any way compare with the delirious welcome received in Naples and Rome. My jeep driver, Howard Miller, of Mount Airy, Md., who has been driving correspondents into newly liberated cities ever since Salerno, blamed the reticence of the civilians on their fear that the few Germans in the city might decide to shoot it out with us. There was no firing, however, and gradually more and more people came outdoors. By the time we had crossed the city, the streets were crowded. But there was very little shouting and I saw none of the hysterical hugging and kissing that had been reported from other 'liberated' cities. A few smiled as we passed and there was some handclapping but the majority just stood and stared. A few residents brought out bottles of wine and gave them to the troops, but a relative scarcity of liquid refreshments was a disappointment to the dust-covered troops, who invariably answered shouts of welcome with the cry of 'Vino, Vino, Vino!'*

"The happiest Italians I saw today were a small group dressed in blue denim with bundles on their backs, walking single file to Florence—70 miles away. They were singing snatches of Italian opera as they plodded along in the dust. All were well-dressed and appeared to be well-fed. For troops who had been fighting through towns completely leveled by six months of siege, the vista of undamaged buildings and relatively well-dressed people is so nice it is hard to take. It gives you a creepy feeling to ride with the vanguard into a city so recently occupied by the enemy, and every few minutes you get an overwhelming urge to turn and come back again tomorrow. Particularly when you happen to be riding down a deserted street between rows of tall houses where snipers might lurk. In the midst of one such moment of panic today, when this correspondent was on the point of telling the driver to turn back to the outskirts of the city, an American half-ton truck turned into the street and drove toward us. Across the radiator in large white letters was American Red Cross, and in the front seat were two wind-blown American girls in Red Cross uniforms covered with dust. 'Have a doughnut,' they shouted, and tossed us a couple. 'I guess it's safe up ahead,' the driver said. 'Let's go on.'"

In a delayed dispatch written April 28 but not published until May 1, Norton proclaimed *"the war's over in northwestern Italy and it was the Italian people who played the final scene."* Chasing eyewitnesses to this final scene, he wrote: *"In a fantastic 250-mile jeep ride from Verona through Mantova, Brescia and Como to the Swiss border, thence to Milan, I saw the shambles of the German army in the process of being taken over by Italian Partisans. Armed civilians lined every road and shouted themselves hoarse when they saw the four jeeps carrying eight American correspondents. We were the first Americans most of them had seen and they naturally thought we were the spearhead of the American army. The convoy passed columns of German troops who still had rifles and artillery but meekly obeyed orders of half a dozen Partisan guards and made no effort to use their arms against us. In town after town we saw truckloads of Nazis waiting to be told where they were going to be imprisoned. Many of them grinned and waved as we passed."*

What Norton did not know when he filed this article that awaiting him was one of the triumphs of his career: His world scoop on Mussolini's execution. What he learned later, especially after the sullen mood seen in Bologna, was the *"tumultuous welcome"* awaiting his group in Milan. The square before the Milan cathedral was *"so packed with screaming, waving people we couldn't get through. They swarmed over the jeeps, pounded us on the back, seized our hands, tore buttons off our jackets, hugged us, kissed us and insisted we make a triumphal parade through the city. 'When will your Army come?' they shouted. We promised again and again that the army would be here tomorrow. We had to explain over and over again that we were only correspondents."*

"Only correspondents," but Norton got himself another news beat when he and Grant Parr of NBC were the only members on hand as the last German units surrendered unconditionally in a U.S. Army trailer outside Milan. One Nazi general, Hans Schlemmer, would not sign because he had been pledged not to do so by Hitler—a pledge lifted when Hitler committed suicide. Earlier, Schlemmer had expressed relief to American reporters when told he and his men would not be turned over to the Russians for slave labor. Such a notion had been fed German troops by Nazi propagandists.

Norton's final story from Italy sounded a distressing note—one that would be heard again and again in all parts of Europe as the continent faced a hard, hungry winter after years of bloodbath. The people of

Milan, who had greeted American reporters so enthusiastically only a fortnight earlier, were now preoccupied by a severe food and fuel shortage—a condition produced by Allied bombing that effectively blockaded the city in the last days of war. Milan's fate, like Italy's fate, was that of a country fought over by foreign armies—enemies and allies alike. Mussolini deserved what he got. His people did not.

CHAPTER 21

April Advances into Germany

April 1945 was the last full month of the European struggle. During that month Roosevelt died of a massive stroke on April 12 at Warm Springs, Georgia; Mussolini was executed by Italian partisans on April 28 near Milan; and Hitler committed suicide on April 30 in his Berlin bunker. Churchill would lose power in a British election in early July. Thus four of the five leaders of the major belligerents in the greatest war in history would no longer be on the scene to shape the post-war world. Only Stalin remained and only Stalin was able to seize territory as one of the fruits of victory. The continent had been at war for ten of the last thirty-one years; there was scant confidence that it would or could avoid another of its periodic conflicts. Instead, Europe got Cold War, with half of Germany and most of Eastern Europe under Moscow's fist. Yet unexpectedly—and happily—the Cold War at least put an end to the hot wars between Europe's nation states that had caused death and destruction for centuries. In effect, the United States and the Soviet Union, with their nuclear duopoly, imposed peace on the Germans, French, British, Italians, and other Europeans. This was a great achievement for the Americans and the Russians. They initiated a period of non-belligerency that, as of this writing, has lasted sixty-four years—more than double the time from the beginning of World War I in 1914 to the end of World War II in 1945.

As the decisive April began, the anti-Hitler coalition was closing in on Germany from west and east. Allied forces on some days advanced as much as forty miles, in contrast to the mile-by-mile struggles that the Russians and the Anglo-Americans had waged earlier. Price Day, in a front-page article [April 1, 1945] said Germany was facing *"the most hopeless Easter of its history as six Allied armies, with parts of two more, plunged almost at will through German farmlands, across German rivers and down the white-flagged main streets of hundreds of German villages and towns."* He saw Allied forces advancing toward Kassel, Hersfeld, and Paderborn. *"This is not to suggest that we will make a sudden stab for any of these places, nor indeed, that if we did so, we could continue to advance at the pace of the last few days. There is as yet no indication, however, that the Germans are able to prevent our going almost anywhere we decide to go."* Traveling with speeding U.S. forces, he noted that the odometer on his jeep showed he was 140 miles east of the Rhine. *"Denied mobility that can even begin to match ours, the enemy is daily finding that a few more units, which might have been pulled back and organized for a defensive stand, are no longer available. For example, if the units holding the western bank of the Rhine from Bonn to Duisburg were to get out, they would have to walk 100 miles, and by the time they reached what is now the escape gap, no gap would be there."* Day's assessment accurately portrayed a German collapse that was to become more apparent and excruciating with every passing day.

In the next issue of *The Sun*, Day reported the historic encirclement of Nazi forces frantically trying to hold the Ruhr. Historians later estimated 325,000 German troops were eventually captured, a number even greater than Nazi losses at Stalingrad. He described the Ruhr as *"one of the world's great industrial areas completely lost to Germany. When the year 1945 opened, Germany had three important areas from which to draw the stuff with which to make war. Silesia fell to the Red Army. The Saar was taken by the United States Seventh Army. Now the Ruhr, too, is gone."*

Thomas M. O'Neill reported from *The Sun's* London Bureau that some military writers were tending to discount Berlin as a major objective of the Allied armies in the west. His report portended one of the most important and controversial decisions of the entire war. Against the impassioned advice of Prime Minister Churchill and his generals, President Roosevelt agreed at Yalta to change the U.S. objective from Berlin to southern Germany. He had the support of Dwight Eisenhower and George Marshall. This was a decision bitterly criticized in later years, not least in the United States, for setting up conditions that made Berlin a Cold War flash point until the Soviet Union collapsed in 1989. Millions of people in Eastern Europe had to endure forty-four years under Moscow's rule.

Another issue that was to spill over into the post-war period was a report by Lee McCardell [April 7, 1945] that Germany's hoard of gold bullion had been captured by the American Third Army. He estimated the treasure weighed 100 tons and was worth (in the dollars of that day) $100 million. The bullion was said to have been hidden in a salt mine near the village of Merkers. *"No one in the United States Army has yet seen the gold but Dr. Fritz Vick, adviser to the Reichsbank, said it was behind a steel door that had jammed and could not be immediately opened. According to Vick, the treasure had been removed from Berlin to the salt mines beginning last February 11. He reported that in addition to the bullion the hoard included $200 million in United States currency, $100 million in French francs, $110,000 in British paper currency, and smaller amounts in Norwegian crowns and in Turkish, Spanish, and Portuguese currency."*

This tantalizing evidence apparently spurred McCardell's newschasing instincts. He reported [April 9, 1945]: *"The gold is here. Bags and bags and bags of genuine gold bricks, believed to be the entire gold reserve of Hitler's German Reich. It is here in a salt mine, guarded by an American infantry force, commanded by Captain Clarence Dean, of Cambridge, Md.* (Note the home state angle.) *Boxed and crated in the same mine with the money are priceless art treasures from 15 German museums."*

Another Marylander, Lieutenant Colonel William Russell of Chevy Chase, was quoted as saying, *"It is unbelievable. It is utterly fantastic. It is as if the Germans had captured Fort Knox in Kentucky."* McCardell said the salt mine *"is one of the largest in the world. It covers an area more than half a mile square atop an underground maze of more than 150 miles of mine galleries."*

McCardell was with a group of correspondents who gained entry to the mine despite efforts to bar them. *"We went around to the mineshaft head. A German civilian mine employee rang the gong for the*

*elevator, a double-decker steel elevator designed to carry mine cars up
and down the pithead. We crowded in and started down through the
pitch darkness. A minute later, we had reached the treasure gallery
level, brightly illuminated by electric lights, and then we struck off
behind an officer to see Aladdin's cave. The mine galleries were warm
and dry, hazy with salt dust from the blast the engineers had set off to
blow open the vault. We passed the stack of 645 million Reichsmarks,
bagged in coarse sacks stenciled Reichsbank and wooden cases and
crates stenciled with the names of art treasures. In the treasure chamber, under a special guard, was bank adviser Vick, a lean, pinch-faced,
bespectacled man of 55 years. Vick said he had come from Berlin to
Merkers to remove the paper marks from the mine and take them
back to Berlin, where there was a shortage of paper currency. 'The
shortage,' he said, 'was due to the destruction of the paper money
printing presses in Berlin by an allied air raid last February 3.' Before
the money could be moved out of the mine and started back toward
Berlin by horse and wagon, the area had been overrun by American
troops."*

McCardell later revealed [April 16, 1945] that General Omar Bradley and his censors were *"deeply perturbed"* about the gold hoard
stories that appeared in the American press. Often a critic of censorship, McCardell said correspondents attached to the Third Army were
"unable to perceive wherein any breach of security" occurred in the
release of the story. He disclosed the situation in which army officials
who permitted coverage of the story ran into opposition higher up.
General Bradley ordered the story killed *"for consideration of highest policy,"* probably security problems in guarding the gold hoard.
Later this directive was rescinded and newspaper copy dealing with
the gold find was cleared by the censors.

Another treasure hunt was reported on April 12, 1945, by Holbrook
Bradley, who was then attached to the Ninth Army far to the north.
There was evidence that the Germans had set up a post-war storage
network for department store merchandise seized by the Nazis. The
material was crated and labeled by code to cite the city from which
it had been removed. The goods included English soap and Parisian
perfume, as well as bicycle parts, and had been stored in out-of-the-

way barns to escape aerial bombing. Near Bielefeld one army group found crates of toilet goods, ladies' underwear, towels, china, glassware, bolt cloth, rugs, shirts, and hundreds of other items.

This story appeared on the same day as McCardell was reporting the more gruesome discoveries of the Holocaust.

Another discovery by Bradley appeared in *The Sun* on April 14. He wrote that the former German chancellor Franz von Papen had been taken while walking along a country road, dressed in knickers, sport coat, and Tyrolean hat. Reluctant to talk about the war, the aged von Papen admitted only that *"he believed the German people realized the cause is lost and that the Nazis keep fighting only because they believe conditions will be so bad if they lose, they might as well keep on fighting."* On further questioning, he asked that politics be left out of the picture as further discussion could endanger his family.

Von Papen was chancellor from June to November 1932. He arranged Hitler's appointment as chancellor in January 1933, becoming vice-chancellor himself. *The Oxford Companion to WWII* has this quote from an obituary: "Franz von Papen will be remembered as the man who held his hands for Hitler to leap into the saddle."

In *The Sunday Sun* magazine of April 13, 1945, Mark Watson offered some ideas about how to treat the German people after the war ended. *"Even our anti-fraternizing rule, admirable though in purpose and generally sound in practice, must inevitably be relaxed. Even justice, if it has too severe aspects, is going to be difficult of enforcement at best. Yet genuine harshness will be much more difficult and inappropriate of enforcement against a whole people, and the well disposed Germans are unlikely to remain well disposed if it is they, rather than the evilly disposed, who receive harshness. The fact is that where we find German people well disposed, we should, for wholly practical reasons, encourage them in good behavior. No one with sense suggests that they should be fondled, which would be silly. But they must be treated with justice and dignity if we expect them to lead orderly, industrious lives. Order is almost the first need—the need not alone of the German people but of our administrators. We wish the Germans to grow the food they need, to make the clothes they need, to get the schooling they need, to do the very maximum of the routine work that alone permits orderly living. Only in that way is occupation a tolerable and thinkable thing. Even our fiercest anti-German does not wish the Germans to starve; nor does he think we should feed Germans indefinitely from our stores. Is there any alternative save to help the Germans to grow their own food? Extending this reasoning, is there any way to develop the sort of new Germany which we wish, save by our own effort and encouragement in that direction? The rebuilding of a sound Germany, wholly unlike Nazi Germany, may well be something to which the Allied world should give first attention. Our armies will soon finish Nazi Germany; our civilian concerns should be to make sure that our armies do not have to do that costly job over again."*

Watson thus anticipated what was to become the essence of U.S. post-war strategy. Fortunately rejected was a vindictive cry for retribution—for the reduction of Germany into an agricultural state lacking industrial capacity. By the early 1950s, with fervent U.S. support, the West German economic miracle was in full swing. The *Baltimore Sun* military expert, who had provided significant evidence to support an American arms buildup to check Axis aggression, now championed the rise of a peaceful West German ally—one that would join the United States in confronting Soviet aggressiveness. It was an exercise in nation-building rivaled only by America's support of a peaceful Japan. Watson, one can surmise, had seen enough of war. He had turned his ideas to the problems of occupation, seeking Germans capable of defending law and order in a structure lacking Nazi hate and dictatorial rule. His world was the post-war world even before the fighting stopped.

Lee McCardell was a correspondent who could not only see war in all its anguish but could seize instances of comic relief in human behavior under stress. One such instance appeared in *The Sun* [April 18, 1945] when he wrote about the allied capture of Bayreuth, the center of Wagnerian music—and the composer's family affiliation with Hitler. *"The park around the Richard Wagner Festspielhaus was honeycombed with underground air raid shelters. Some of their occupants had hung out white flags in anticipation of the arrival of the Eleventh Armored Division. Nobody came out at the time our party inspected the Festspielhaus, but as we walked back up the* Parsifalstrasse *we noticed a woman in a villa garden feeding rabbits in a hutch and a little girl who, an hour before was trembling at the sound of guns, now bouncing a rubber ball on the pavement."*

Ironically, in the shrine of Wagnerian mythology, these were not the only signs of the Nazi *Götterdämmerung.* McCardell went on: *"We saw hundreds of liberated Czech prisoners come pounding over a hill toward American forces. They had just been turned loose from a prison camp. They came shouting and dancing and waving white flags and handkerchiefs. Their gratitude was almost embarrassing. All looked miserably underfed. They wolfed K-rations which sympathetic tank crews shared with them. The Czechs all wore a prison garb of coarse blue cloth with yellow stripes around the right elbow and yellow stripes down the seam of each trouser leg. Their shoes were home-made wooden scuffs. They had a piece of an old map showing the border of their country only 30 miles away. They did not appear to be in any too good shape to hike even 30 miles. One was definitely weak from hunger, but they wanted to go home and were on their way. A couple of liberated Russians and an alarmingly hollow-eyed and emaciated Pole, a regular walking skeleton so ill and famished that he could barely totter, came along. They wanted food.*

"Then along came a young Polish girl with a suitcase and a sick baby in a baby carriage. She wanted to know if she could get out of town. 'Where was she going?' a soldier asked her. She said she did not know. She just wanted to get out of Bayreuth. An American officer told her she had better stay in town overnight. She said she had no place to stay. By this time, a half dozen Joes had gathered around the baby carriage and were making funny noises at the baby. When they heard the girl say she had no place to stay, they looked up in surprise, and one of them said: 'Hell, lady, we'll get you a house. Which one do you want?' She didn't understand, so they picked out the best looking, least damaged house in the block. Its German owners had vacated it. The Joes trundled the carriage to the front door, carried the baby upstairs into the best bedroom, found a baby's crib in another room, even dug up a collection of baby clothes. One Joe gave the mother a small can of evaporated milk. 'I feed it to mine,' he said. 'It's good for

the baby.' She explained that the baby was ill and had been put on a temporary diet of tea. Whereupon an American officer produced a packet of tea from his jeep. Somebody brought in a Coleman stove and began to boil water. 'But suppose the German people who own the house came back tonight,' the young mother asked nervously. They would put her out. Well, the Joes would attend to that. They penciled a sign, 'Polish mother and baby, Eingang Verboten,' and nailed it on the front door. They would like to see any Kraut put her out."

This anecdote kindled a memory in the author's mind of a day when he visited Bayreuth in the 1970s. The revived Wagnerian craze was in full flower. To attend a performance of *The Flying Dutchman*, one had to wear a white coat tuxedo and the women were adorned in elaborate gowns. But it was a miserably hot summer evening, and even before the curtain went up, the gentlemen had taken off their coats and allowed their suspenders to be viewed by all and sundry. At Wagner's old mansion, which had been turned into a place where visitors could reverently listen to Wagner's music round the clock, I visited a small museum. On a wall was a picture of an American GI sitting at the master's grand piano and probably tapping out a tune. What Teutonic outrage at such a desecration this must have caused.

Further evidence that the conflict was rapidly coming to an end was offered by Bradley in a story [April 20, 1945] describing the release of American prisoners of war from an internment camp maintained by the Nazis. It was *Stalag* 11B, 32 miles north of Hanover. One of the largest German prison camps, it could hold upward of 40,000 prisoners at any one time. Bradley wrote: *"It maintained the barest requisites of life, with small cramped quarters, in which two men were assigned to a bunk built for one, and where the men had no place for recreation or exercise. The barracks themselves are of flimsy wooden construction, with no lighting facilities, meager communal washing accommodations, and little if any toilet space. The mats serving each two men were rotten, stinking, and infested with vermin. Conditions in the camp had been the lowest possible. Each man received one-eighth of a loaf of black bread and a bowl of thin turnip soup per day. Medical treatment has been insufficient and the men have been supplied with only one blanket even in the coldest winter."*

Ever alert for items of hometown interest, Bradley included the names of fourteen Baltimoreans who were released from the camp. *"Directly across from Stalag 11B were a series of four-story modern buildings built recently by the German military for housing SS troops and training in that area. When the British reached the village, late on the night of April 16, most of the enemy already had left and the few remaining were captured. Dressed in parts of uniforms of almost all the Allied nations, with some even in civilian clothes, the first group of prisoners rushed to a Churchill tank at the main gate at dawn the next morning, too overcome to do more than shout briefly, and grasp the hands of the tank crews passing out their rations of cigarettes and chocolate."*

One reason why American military authorities were willing to forgo a drive for Berlin was a pervading obsession that Hitler and his paladins were intent on setting up a last-stand redoubt in the Bavarian Alps. There were suspicions that Hitler would leave Berlin to command such an operation. In a dispatch from Washington that appeared April 25, 1945, Watson said: *"General Eisenhower had shifted his right wing from east to south-east—into the crust of the enemy's mountain fortress. As a result of Eisenhower's shift of attack, General George S. Patton's Third Army, General Alexander M. Patch's Seventh, and the French First Army are now well within the western mountains of south Germany, and between them have locked off two separate pockets of German troops, who seemed to have no escape, save by seeking internment in Switzerland. It is too early to make any surmises about the intensity of ultimate German resistance in that mountain area. It may well prove to be as troublesome as advertised, but it is not too early to remark that whatever the intensity of German defense may be, the extent of the fortress area is not so great as we had anticipated.*

"The perilous Black Forest area already has been passed. This is an impressive fact. The Black Forest, lying just east of the Rhine, we thought a few months ago, would prove a tower of strength to Germany, and, indeed, it could have done so, for it is rugged as well as

wooded, and admirably adapted to defense—if enough men are used to defend it. The outer ramparts of that 'impregnable' position, one may say, already have been overcome, and at great speed, with resultant economy of our own manpower. How has this success been so unexpectedly gained? Why was the local German resistance so limited as to permit such swift advances by our troops? Chiefly, of course, it is a result of the heavy drains of German manpower in recent weeks. Eisenhower's forces have taken a million prisoners in April alone, which is almost as many as our whole bag from D-Day until April. Will the defense of the southern mountain fortress be as prolonged as the Nazis have been promising? That will depend on how many troops have actually been able to retire to it and how secure are the defense positions."

Watson's article, coming so late in the war, indicates how obsessive the Americans were about a German redoubt in the Alps, a specter that never materialized. This has long been a subject in which critics of General Eisenhower, especially British critics, have assailed the American decision to veer from Berlin to the south. Even on April 28, Watson wrote that General Eisenhower was continuing his steady drive toward the enemy's mountain redoubt, a redoubt that existed only in the unfounded speculations of the American military. Meanwhile, the Russians were closing in on Berlin.

For Lee McCardell, what must have been one of the most joyful days in his long, long war assignment occurred on April 26, when he rushed to the Elbe River town of Torgau for the first meeting between American and Russian soldiers. A day earlier, three separate U.S. patrols had encountered the Russians and eagerly informed their officers. Similar news was conveyed to the Russian brass across the river. A formal, official meeting was set up next day for the American press and the folks back home.

This was the first time the veteran *Sun* reporter ever saw any Russian soldiers in battle dress. *"They were slim, youthful, smiling, artless and talkative. In American uniforms they would have passed unnoticed for average American soldiers. Their uniforms were gray-green belted smocks and flaring riding breeches. Most of them were armed with submachine guns slung like carbines behind their shoulders. Their uniforms were of lighter, coarser wool than those of our soldiers. They were no dirtier, no cleaner. I shall remember that though I spoke no Russian, and few of the Russians whom I met today spoke any English, there were never any periods of strained silence, never any lack of understanding between us. They were plain people who liked us. We were plain people who liked them. We filled our glasses and smiled at each other and drank to each other's health and good luck. In my own memories it will be a day when I came among strangers who took me in and shook my hand and smiled as if they meant it. It was a day of sunshine on the Elbe River when an old unhappy war receded into the distance."*

The foregoing is an example of how McCardell's copy had become looser, more personal, increasingly laced with his thoughts and feelings. No wire service "objectivity" inhibited him. The meeting of forces was one of the great historic scenes of the war, destined to be inscribed in future chronicles, he commented, *"But to those of us whose job it is to report it, and who sat on a plot of grass bordered by pansies in front of a German barracks this afternoon, waiting for the generals to arrive, it does not seem to matter much whether we describe the event or not. Like everyone else in the war, we are tired. The end of the war is much closer. And I think all of us correspondents would have been much happier if we could have just sat there on the grass until the sun went down—instead of running back to army headquarters to file dispatches like this one."*

With the hindsight that comes from having seen Soviet-American rivalry grow to world-threatening proportions, McCardell's report might sound a bit naïve. But is it more naïve than George W. Bush's assertion six decades later that he had found "soul" in the eyes of Vladimir V. Putin? After all the blood and misery and ruin McCardell had experienced, there can be no grudging his exultation. And despite the celebrations, he reported ominous signs of the future: German civilians, German soldiers, even some Soviet soldiers scrambling westward to escape Stalin's baleful regime. They were the lucky ones. Stalin sent not only Germans into his gulag, but also Russian soldiers he considered contaminated by what they had seen of the democratic west.

CHAPTER 22

Surrender at Rheims

Victory in Europe seemed tantalizingly close on May Day 1945, the first day of the month that was to bring the unconditional surrender of Hitler's Germany. Dispatches by *Sun* reporters Price Day and Lee McCardell confirmed the capture of city after city as Allied armies advanced virtually unchecked. *"Germany tonight is on the verge of utter military annihilation,"* Day wrote from Supreme Headquarters Allied Expeditionary Force (SHAEF) headquarters, noting that even Hitler's Austrian birthplace, Brunau, had fallen. At the same time he put to rest a vital U.S. military miscalculation, one that had sent Allied armies southward to the German-Austrian Alps while leaving Berlin exclusively to the Soviets: *"There is every indication tonight that the much-discussed 'redoubt'—a name given to the region by German propagandists—is without even a shell of protection."*

McCardell concentrated on the welcome liberation of a large prisoner-of-war camp (capacity: 20,000) in the town of Moosburg north of Munich. Among the officers freed was Colonel P. R. Goode, who had been commander of the 175th Regiment of the Maryland-Virginia Blue-Gray Twenty-ninth Division during the D-Day Normandy landings. He had been captured several days later. In contrast to the deplorable conditions McCardell had seen farther north in Nazi POW camps—near starvation, rampant disease, miserable quarters—he found Moosburg prisoners in fairly good health and well-supplied with Red Cross parcels. But *"'cleanliness was impossible,'"* one freed POW told McCardell. *"'You'll notice we all speak through our noses because we are suffering from head colds or sinus infection. The barracks are badly over-crowded and we've had no heat in them since I've been here.'"*

Probably typical of the pace of war then prevailing was the Nazi loss of Moosburg. As McCardell described it: *"When the 14th Armored Division approached, the German commander sent out an International Red Cross representative to meet and ask that Moosburg be declared a neutral zone so the Germans could evacuate their prisoners further back. The suggestion was turned down flat and the Red Cross man was sent back with an ultimatum to the Germans to surrender immediately. German SS troops began taking up defensive positions along the road into the town from the north and opened fire on the Americans. The 47th Tank Battalion then moved forward. Within an hour and a half every SS man along the road and in the adjacent fields had been killed or captured and the tanks were roaring into town.*

"The prisoners of war, frantic with jubilation, rushed forward to meet their rescuers as the tanks crashed through double ten-foot barbed wire fences of the first prison camp they reached. Then they stopped dead, while cheering, overjoyed Allied soldiers, tears streaming down their faces, swarmed over them. 'You damned bloody Yanks—I love you,' screamed a six-foot Aussie, throwing his arms around an American jeep driver. A dirty, bearded American paratrooper, weeping like a child, leaped on one tank and kissed its commander. An American Air Corps lieutenant tried to embrace the tank itself, kissed its dusty armor plate and shouted, 'God damn! I do love the ground forces.'"

Mark Watson in the same May 1 issue assessed problems Americans were destined to have with the French and their imperious Charles de Gaulle. The specific issue was the French seizure of Stuttgart, a city Americans had sought to control as an important administrative center. The French rejected General Eisenhower's request that they leave. *"This was decidedly awkward,"* Watson wrote. *"Frenchmen still think of their country in terms of the past. They seem not only unwilling but unable to accept the humiliating realities of the past five years and refuse to accept placidly any secondary place in world affairs. They writhe under the condition of having the 'Big Three' dispose of world affairs without inclusion of France and in particular are furious at having no full and equal role in conferences which discuss such military matters as the area of Germany which France will occupy. We will do ourselves no good by thinking of these 'discourtesies' as de*

Gaulle's exclusively. The basic cause of them all is a proud and asser-
tive French nationalism which is common to almost all Frenchmen.
It must be recognized as a reality which argument will not overcome.
We will do better to adjust ourselves to it."

As panicky Germans fled wherever Allied troops had not yet
advanced, Day reported that fighter-bomber pilots were calling it a
"reverse Dunquerque" (note use of the French spelling). It was an
apt barb because many of the fleeing Germans were getting across the
North Sea to Norway, where an uncertain welcome awaited them.
Vidkun Quisling, the Nazi Norwegian who had given his name to
the language, had already been arrested. He was destined to be tried
and executed. After citing various pockets of German holdouts soon
to be overrun, Day wrote a memorable dismissal of Nazi militarism:
"The greatest war complex ever seen on the globe was going down
to the greatest and one of the shabbiest defeats in history. Even if full
surrender should come tomorrow, Germany's complete bankruptcy
of reason has been thoroughly displayed before the world. Caught
in their false logic that had no place for failure, the German leaders
had no resources except blind and hysterical resistance with which to
meet the defeat that has for so long been inevitable."

On May 9, 1945, Price Day wrote one of the major *Sun* achievements of the war. The headline, six columns wide, read:

PRICE DAY'S EYEWITNESS REPORT
OF GERMAN SURRENDER

An italic precede described his scoop:

Price Day was the only staff correspondent of an individual
newspaper to witness the surrender of Germany at Rheims. He was
offered a last minute opportunity to cover the historic surrender for
EXCHANGE TELEGRAPH, a British news agency, which enabled
him to be present.

"Rheims, France, May 7—At 2:45 o'clock on this warm spring
morning, Col. Gen. Gustav Jodl signed his name for the fourth time
and carefully put down his pen. Europe's long war was over. Jodl
stood up. His back was rigid, his heels in their black boots were close
together. He rested the tips of his fingers on the wide, battered oak
table that filled a good part of what, until tonight, was the most secret

of all the secret chambers of Europe—SHAEF's War Room. General Jodl said in German: 'With this signature the German people and German armed forces are for better or worse delivered into the victor's hands.' Lt. Gen. Walter Bedell Smith, Chief of Staff to Gen. Eisenhower, watched him impassively. So did four other Americans, three Russians, one French, and three British officers seated at the table. On Jodl's left a German admiral, on his right a German major stared straight ahead. Still speaking of the civilians and soldiers of his beaten nation, Jodl said: 'In this war, which has lasted for more than five years, they both have achieved and suffered more than perhaps any people in the world. In this hour I can only express the hope that the victors will treat them with generosity.' He sat down and then at once stood up again. The admiral and major stood up with him. There was no answer. There were no salutes. His face gray with strain, but his step steady, Jodl turned and walked from the room. He was followed by the others, the major carrying Jodl's cap with its German high command insignia. Seventeen Allied war correspondents shifted aside to let them pass.

"With their going, the solemn tableau of the surrender broke up. The Allied officers spoke a few words to each other, rose from their chairs, chatted quietly for another moment, and strolled from the room. Everybody was very tired. That was how it was. That was it—the victory of all the Allies over all the German forces on land, sea and air. This was not an armistice, it was surrender, total and complete.

"More than 45 hours must still go by before the peace effected tonight at General Eisenhower's headquarters in Rheims' barracks-like, pinkish brick Ecole professionale would settle over the battle-field. But of these battlefields, only a few were still the scenes of battle. Every man around the table knew that this ceremony was in large part simply the recognition of the accomplished fact of the defeat of Germany. The signing of the surrender document by Smith, Jodl, Major-General of Artillery Ivan Susloparov of the Red Army, and General Sevez of France, came at the waning of a long night, in the course of which it had begun to seem certain that the great event would have to wait at least until the dawn of another day. For five and a half

hours, the German representatives had been conferring alone in a billet in a house on Rue Godinot near the great cathedral of Rheims. The Americans, British, Russians and French had no word from this conference throughout the evening. Then, deciding that the acceptance seemed unlikely tonight, they all left headquarters. Many went to bed. As midnight came and went, a hush fell over Rheims, except in one corner of the G-4 or supply sector, of the main building of SHAEF's command post, where the correspondents waited.

"Military police guarded every corridor and gate as, indeed, they do on all nights. Perhaps tonight they watched even more carefully, and stood a bit straighter at their posts. Out in the darkness of the wide, graveled courtyard, enclosed by low utilitarian brick buildings, rested jeeps, trucks and dozens of high-echelon staff cars with their red-plaqued fronts and rears studded with a milky way of stars. A faint, warm breeze came through the open windows. Here and there an electric light shone out on the pale green foliage of the trees that ringed the courtyard. Everything was still and suspended, waiting.

"At 1:58 o'clock this Monday morning, Brig. Gen. Frank A. Allen, public relations director of SHAEF, called the correspondents together in one small room. 'I think something is going to happen shortly,' he said. And then when the scuffling of feet ceased, he said, 'Gentlemen, I think this is it. All the staff officers have been recalled.'

"We filed through the wide barren hallways, with their checked floors of grey and black tile, up a flight of concrete steps and into Room 119. Before this room lies a short entrance way cluttered tonight with photographers' gear. On the other side of the entrance way a door opens into the room, which is in shape a fat L that for the past months has been the brain center of the Allied armies in the west. It is a room of maps. Its walls are papered entirely from floor to ceiling with maps—that bugaboo, the national redoubt, the regions of China, Burma, and the Philippines, of the air operations, a minesweepers' chart of the North Sea, maps of the pockets on the Atlantic coast, of the army's railway system, and of the airfields of the world. Over the widest wall stretches the battle map, showing in heavy crayon the battle order of the triumphant Allied armies. Tonight, even if the German Chief of Staff cared to examine these maps—in fact, he

will not so much as glance at them—or to read the tabulations of casualties on the side wall, it wouldn't matter. At last, it wouldn't matter.

"*The conference table, 20 feet long and 8 wide, is directly in front of the battle map. Its top is painted black and its edges are nicked and scarred. Its perimeter is crowded with plain pine chairs, except on the long side away from the map, where there are only three chairs, precisely centered. Each chair but one has before it a thick block of ruled white paper, with a new yellow pencil, with eraser, laid neatly on its top. Most of the places are marked with names printed on narrow strips of paper. There are six unusually small white porcelain and two unusually large green brass ashtrays. There is a small microphone and the stand holding two pens. The paper, pencils and ashtrays were not used. Nor were these particular pens.*

"*At the moment the room looks more like a movie set than either a war center or a place for a great conference. From all angles and elevations, batteries of cameras are aimed at the most important table on earth while the photographers are making their last minute adjustments and scurry and climb about like monkeys. The room blazes with a stark white light. Air Marshal Sir J. M. Robb, Chief of Air Staff, who walked into this light at 2:29 a.m., was the first of the conference group to enter the room, though he was preceded by one minute by Capt. Harry C. Butcher, Naval Aide to General Dwight D. Eisenhower. Butcher carried two pens of brown composition material with gold tops which, never used, had been carried by Eisenhower since the end of the African campaign. Another pen, a plain brown, turned up later. Nobody knew where it came from. Robb was followed by General Carl A. Spaatz, Admiral Sir Harold Burrough, and General Smith, looking tired, but as always extraordinarily self-contained and precise.*

"*Along the short right end of the table the chair closest to Robb was marked for Maj. Gen. H. E. Bull, Assistant Chief of Staff of G-3 of SHAEF, who at this moment was arranging on the table two cream-colored cardboard folders. The documents contained in the folders were three—the instrument of surrender to be signed in quadruplicate by Smith, Jodl, Susloparov, and Sevez, the naval term for the signature of Burrough.*

"The most important things in the room at 2:38 o'clock were the three vacant chairs in the center of the table facing the battle map. Admiral Burrough leaned forward and tested his pencil on the pad of paper before him—the only mark made on any of the pads. General Smith glanced quickly around then nodded toward the door. At 2:39, Jodl, the new German Chief of Staff, and Admiral Georg von Friedeburg, the new Commander-in-Chief of the German navy, walked into Room 119, followed by Jodl's aide. They went straight to their chairs and all the men around the table sat down at once. If there was any bowing, it was extremely slight. Jodl sat in the center with Friedeburg on his left and his aide on his right. Friedeburg, who wore a blue uniform, held his cap in his lap; Jodl put his, with his gloves inside, top down on the table by his right arm. The aide placed his cap on the floor beside him. Jodl's grey-green uniform was new and a good fit, its flared trousers showing a wide red stripe down the outer seams. The scarlet and gold of his epaulets were no less brilliant than that of the British staff officers across the table.

"At 2:40 began a flurry of silent signing of names. Seventeen minutes later it was all over. The Germans by then would have walked from Room 119 to meet the escort to take them upstairs to General Eisenhower's simple and comfortable suite to spend two minutes with the supreme commander. Leaving him, they would stand for a while in a narrow hall talking among themselves before leaving the scene of the final act of Germany's greatest defeat. The signing of the paper that symbolized the defeat grew directly from the earlier surrender of the German troops in the north to Field Marshal Montgomery. After that agreement of capitulation had, on May 3, become history, the Germans made it known that they wished to discuss the question of the surrender of the whole of German armed forces. Eisenhower agreed. He named Rheims, already rich in history, as the place of discussion, and he named May 5 as the date."

Price Day wrote a separate story the same day describing the meeting in General Eisenhower's office:

"The outer room boiled with people, most of them moving around and all of them talking. Correspondents jammed thickly toward Eisenhower's G-2, Maj. Gen. K.W. D. Strong, to check with him the

exact wording of General Jodl's short speech at the surrender formalities just ended downstairs in the war room. Officers from full generals on down went in and out. They looked happy and tired. For the most part they talked briefly to each other. Little needed to be said at this moment. There was no shouting, though the sum total of noise was considerable. The general hum was punctuated by the pitifully grateful cries of correspondents as pretty 2nd Lt. Kay Summersby, personal secretary to Eisenhower, distributed packs of cigarettes.

"It was just after 3 o'clock on this wonderful morning. A few minutes earlier Jodl, Friedeburg and another German officer had stopped at attention before Eisenhower and his great deputy, Air Chief Marshal Arthur Tedder, as the Supreme Commander asked: 'Do you understand the terms of this unconditional surrender and are you ready to comply with them?' After General Strong had interpreted the question, Jodl clicked his heels and nodded and the interview was over. At this moment, Germans were outside in the narrow corridor talking together as heavy traffic jostled them as it crowded by. After this, Eisenhower had posed for pictures, insisting as always that Tedder stand close by him and balking for a moment at the photographers' suggestion that he hold two of the three of the surrender pens in a V for victory although he finally did so.

"Now the picture taking was over and the crowd had moved from the tiny inner room to the outer room to join the larger crowd already there. As the many sided conversations centered around Strong continued, I glanced back through the wide doorway. The Supreme Commander was alone, sitting back in a chair behind his small plain desk, one leg crossed over the other. From the fingers of one of his big hands cigarette smoke curled upward in the motionless air. Deliberately he raised the cigarette and took a long drag. His amazingly mobile face with its wide mouth and forehead was relaxed. He appeared tired, but content and thoughtful. The only things to look at in the room are six photographs, one of Eisenhower, one of Eisenhower's wife, one of his son, two large photographs and a small snapshot of his mother, and one each of Roosevelt and Churchill.

"Right now he wasn't looking at these, he was looking at nothing in particular, staring into space. Certainly no one could guess what

the leader of armies who had just achieved victory in the most terrible of wars was thinking at this moment, but he knew that in a few minutes he would have to say something for the newsreels.

"The chances are he was thinking about that, forming phrases in his mind—'Just a few minutes ago Germany surrendered all its forces,' and then of his feelings for the men of the Allied armies, navies and air forces—'To them I owe a debt of gratitude that can never be repaid.'

"I turned for a minute to catch something Strong was saying. When I looked again, Eisenhower had pulled his chair up to the table, picked up a pen, and was writing on a small white piece of paper."

On the same front page publishing Price Day's eyewitness report, McCardell filed a story of the reaction to the surrender among soldiers in the Third Army deep into Germany:

"The end of the war is an anticlimax. The shooting ceased at 8 o'clock yesterday morning. Unofficially it ended days ago. It ended at different times for different soldiers. It ended when the Germans in front of them gave up. Here with the Third Army, on the last of the fighting fronts, we've watched the war peter out. The end was not less welcome when it did come, but we were expecting it, waiting for it. Now that it's here, most of the soldiers accept it quietly. There has been no sign of wild rejoicing. There has been no sudden letdown, no sharp cessation of strain and tension. There has been no sudden silence after a steady and continuous roar of guns. The sound of gunfire died away gradually days ago.

"I am writing this at 9 o'clock on the morning of Tuesday, May 8. The war ended more than 24 hours ago. But I have been told that I will not be permitted to file this dispatch until midnight tonight; that is the hour at which the official announcement of the end of the war will be made—the artificial and anticipated end. So this, I suppose, is sort of the last day of the war in Europe. Down here in Bavaria it's a gorgeous day. After a long spell of cold rainy weather, the sky is solid blue. The sun is bright and the air is warm. The window at which I write looks out on the street of a German town, a narrow street leading into an old cathedral square. Opposite my window are the bombed shattered windows of a German drug store. They are still

boarded up. And there is no traffic in the street except for the occasional American Army vehicles.

"German civilians and a German policeman walk up and down the sidewalks. The women carry market bags and the men carry briefcases. There is no change in their manner or their attitude since yesterday. At this particular hour—or rather at 9 o'clock this morning Baltimore time—I imagine the people of Baltimore will be walking through Mulberry Street, past Baltimore's cathedral in much the same manner these people walk past theirs—except that the shop windows of Mulberry Street will be whole, and the people of Baltimore will not be a defeated people. When I awoke this morning at 6:30, the first morning I awakened to know that the war was actually over, I was conscious of a great relief, but it took me a moment to realize why. And my next thought, naturally enough, as were the thoughts of many others, was—'At last—Thank God. I am still alive and I can go home.' And I thought of Maryland, with summer moving across it gently, and of the letter that arrived last night from home, a letter in which someone I love very much had written: 'I leaned out of our front window this morning. The rose bushes are filled with buds. Do you really think you will be home in time to smell them?'

"Sunshine streamed through my window, and I was keenly conscious of the fact that I was one of the lucky ones who could think about going home. There were others not so lucky, who would never go back. They were the dead whose graves belonged to the sandy wastes of North Africa, the olive groves of Italy, the hedgerows of Normandy, and the hills of the Ardennes. Men who, in some higher mathematical calculations of the infinite, were killed in battle in order that we, the lucky ones, might survive."

Baltimore Sun coverage of the European war during that decisive month of May came to a fitting conclusion with a visit by Price Day to the battlefields of Normandy. His first story took him to the town of St. Lo, where American troops broke out of the hedgerows of Normandy into open country leading to Paris and eventually the German border. The breakout came only after seven weeks of harsh, mile-by-mile fighting against a German army that repeatedly showed its expertise in defensive warfare.

"*From the absence of the smell of death and, from the fact that the wild flowers pushing through the ruins are not covered with white dust, you can tell that this is last year's destruction.*" So Day began his description of St. Lo. "*There are few other ways of telling. Essentially, the town must look today as it looked when the 29th Division entered it last summer. The streets that were bulldozed through the rubble have, it is true, been packed hard by months of traffic, but they are still properly speaking not streets at all but wide rough paths through a ruined city. This is not a dead city. The parts of it that were not razed are full of people. Even on top of the ruins a few rough wooden shops have been erected and are doing business. Actually a good deal of cleaning up has been done and the streets have been cleared many times but as each building, or what remains of each building, is slowly taken apart, pieces of plaster, stone, wood, furniture and clothing are thrown into the street. It is partly this that makes the place look so newly bombed.*

"*The truth is that in three seasons that are passed since the war drove beyond it, St. Lo has not come back. Neither has Caen, nor Vire, nor have dozens of grey little Norman villages that were so unfortunate as to lie along the axis of the Allied advance. The slowness of Caen, St. Lo, and Vire in returning to life is due in part to lack of machinery—all work is done by hand—and in part to the fact that only now is sufficient labor beginning to drift back. To many liberated prisoners of war and forced labor, freshly painted signs welcoming them back to their shattered towns must seem a bit ironic. To what extent these larger Norman towns will eventually be rebuilt is hard to say. Certainly such structures as the two abbey churches that William the Conqueror and his wife Matilda built in Caen will be repaired in time. A town, however, and especially a European town, is not built. It grows. Only a sudden era of intense prosperity, in fact a boom, could possibly provide wealth with which to rebuild. Normandy is rich, but it is a slow, solid, pleasant sort of richness—the kind that builds good towns over 1,000 years, not in 10 or 20 or 50.*

"*What lies ahead for all the battered towns and villages of Normandy is grim. None of these places, it should be remembered, is totally destroyed. There is no Cassino among them. They are no more*

*badly hurt than dozens of German towns of similar sizes and econom-
ic patterns. The general atmosphere is one of at least moderate gloom.
Rich as Normandy is in food, rationing has hit the restaurants."*

The next day *The Sun* correspondent went to Omaha Beach, a lasting
place of reverence for American visitors. Here's how Price Day described
it [May 29, 1945] as the first anniversary of D-Day drew near:

*"A wide expanse of shining sand stretches out toward the surf
through which almost a year ago the first American troops came
ashore in northern Europe. Many signs remain of the invasion of last
June 6. Where the ground begins to rise behind the beach, there is a
giant junk pile of landing craft and twisted steel, some of it still protected by grey paint, and some rusted a deep orange red. Beyond the
surf rises the immobile silhouette of the warship Black Prince and of
other vessels—aged freighters and squared off concrete ships—sunk
to form a makeshift harbor. A few scattered landing vessels still sit on
the sand itself, but except for these the beach is level and clean. Far to
the left in front of Vierville, the initial objective of the 116th Infantry
of the 29th Division, a single dark figure strolls on the sand. Except
for a flock of white shore birds, he is the only living thing in sight.
You can look out on this bleak and utterly peaceful scene from the
ridge in front of St. Laurent-sur-Mer, and you can look out because
the hedgerow that once obscured the view has been removed by the
Graves Registration Detachment that cares for St. Laurent.*

*"As military cemeteries go, this is not a large one. It is not so large,
for example, as the 29th Division cemetery at La Cambe, back toward
Isigny. But this was the first cemetery in northern Europe. It is here
that the men of the 29th and Ist Divisions, killed in the early hours
of D-Day, are buried. They lie parallel to the beach, the crosses and
stars of David that mark their graves facing west. A dog tag is nailed
to each one of them, but some of these have no names impressed on
them, and some of the markers are stenciled 'Unknown.' A third of
the crosses nearest the sea are not marked at all. Set apart from the
rest by a wide graveled walk are the graves of the Germans killed on
D-Day. This is about all there is to this little piece of land officially
known as United States Cemetery Number 1—neat walks parting as
you approach to circle the white flag pole.*

"As if to suggest only a small bit of what D-Day must have been like on Omaha beach, a tremendous black cloud rises from beyond Vierville, followed after a long interval by the noise of an explosion. Engineers there have set off a big pile of land mines. The cloud diffuses and quiet descends again over the beach.

"Beyond the ridge overlooking the sea, Normandy is what the guidebooks say it is, a varied landscape of hedgerows, orchards, fields and pastures. But the hedgerows today make you think of how hard it must have been to see a man behind them, and the orchards and fields still have that grim look. They are covered with rank grass of the new season and blanketed with daisies and poppies, but it will be long before they lose the scars of the heavy vehicles and artillery. Of those not so scarred, many are still heavily mined. A few are filled with rusted impedimenta of war, knocked out tanks, jeeps twisted by mines, and shattered trucks. Sleek, placid cattle now graze among the ruins. Like other grey little towns along this northern coast, Vierville shows marks of actions that swirled around and through it. It was here on the night on June 6 that the troops of the 29th received their first counterattack. Little of the damage of that day and night has been repaired. In another year many of the remaining signs of the conflict will have disappeared. In still another year, many more. Even now you realize that this is not war you are looking at. It is history."

On the precise first anniversary of D-Day [June 6, 1945] Bradley followed Day's footsteps to Omaha Beach. He had personally witnessed the fighting there from the first day after the landing when he was attached to the Twenty-ninth Division. Now he was back.

"On the Normandy coast, French children now build castles in the sand that twelve months ago was red with the blood of boys of the 116th and 115th Regiments—boys who fought to make their slim foothold secure while German battalions on the chalk cliffs above poured a hail of lead and steel into Yanks scrambling to gain cover behind walls and even of the bodies of their own comrades-in-arms. Many those who died lie in solemn rows covered with grass, each marked with a simple wooden cross. Nearby at La Cambe, taken by the 175th push at Isigny, are others—men of the division who fell at Vierville-sur-Mer, St. Jean de Daye, Le Carrefour, Lison and Mon

Surielle (one can almost hear Bradley reciting place names he feared would be forgotten). *The 29th fight from Normandy to the heart of Germany is worthy of comparison with any military in this or any past age. . . . Rough, tough boys before St. Lo, when our losses in the hedgerows ran 200 to 300 daily, when recruits were moved to the front and often killed or wounded on the first day. The regiments fought their way, yard by yard, through Moyen, Beaucoudray, Landalles and Compigny to Vire, which fell on August 6.*

"*The 29th Division then moved out to the Brittany peninsula to take the job of reduction of the fortress of Brest. From the St. Renan jump-off line through the battles of Plouzane, Le Conquet, Trinte and Recouvrance, there was some of the toughest fighting the division had gone through. October 1 I saw the Blue and Gray come to grips with the enemy near Kerkrade, Holland. It was a few days later that the 115th's Company K was captured or killed almost to a man, gaining ground to Germany with its own blood.*

"*The road to the Roer River ran through Alsdorf, Soersdorf, Aldenhoven and the bloody battles of Bourheim and Julich and on to Munchen Gladbach, which fell without a shot. When the 9th Army relieved a division from combat in the Rhine crossing that followed, priority went to the veteran 29th but, even so, the outfit was slated to see more action. The 116th Regiment was called in for mopping up the Ruhr and the 175th was assigned to clear the Klotze Forest. Today the men of the 29th, veterans and new members alike pay tribute to the near 5,000 officers and men—infantrymen, artillery men, engineers, medics, chaplains, tankers and those attached—who gave the greatest sacrifice so the division could achieve the outstanding record in the fight to bring Germany to its knees.*"

Bradley was on the scene at Le Havre when many veterans of the Twenty-ninth sailed for the United States [June 17, 1945]. He listed the names of 54 Marylanders, thirty of them from Baltimore. "*There was little about the departure to remind the seasoned doughboys of the September morning in 1942, when the Blue and Gray Division first headed overseas for the long tour of training duty in England and then almost a year's fighting on the Continent. Gone was the secrecy that veiled the wartime movement. The entire port knew the time of departure, route and destination. On the Army's latest transport, the* Admiral Mayo *doughboys lining the rails cheered and whistled in relief at being on their way at last."*

One of the outstanding articles of the post-surrender period came in Price Day's account [July 5, 1945] of his first visit to battered, defeated Berlin. *"The American troops billeted tonight in Berlin were not prepared for the scene of devastation that was to confront them in the center of the city. They had heard that Berlin was virtually destroyed, which approximates the truth. They had heard it was 'leveled'—which is certainly not true. Berlin is not flat. It still has a skyline. From a mile away, block after block of its great government and commercial buildings appear almost intact. But the skyline is squashed, its sharp angles are rounded as if they had been beaten by a giant mallet, or as if they had been eroded and cracked and crumbled by a thousand years of rain and blowing sand. Whole blocks are gutted ruins, roofless, windowless, chipped and split on the outside and a mass of tangled wood, steel and brick on the inside. Along the entire length of* Kurfurstendam, *once lined with fashionable shops, only one ground-floor café and one small motion-picture house are in operation.*

"Faded yellowish streetcars, riddled by small arms fire or chewed by shell and bomb fragments stand where they stopped. On Budapesterstrasse *the aquarium has not been fit for fish for a long time and this street is now a home of no animals but rats. It is the wooded Tiergarten, where Berliners once strolled on Sundays, that tells best how fierce was the battle for Berlin. Littered insanely along its fringes with rusted wrecks, the Tiergarten is a wasteland of earthen defenses and splintered trees. It looked like pictures of the trench warfare battlefield of the First World War. A walk through Brandenburg Gate* (into the Soviet Zone) *does not draw gunfire or for that matter any comment from two Russian guards at the gate.*

"People move and live in the littered streets that lead through piles of waste. Like their surroundings they are drab and gray people. They walk among the ruins, carrying a string bag or a worn suitcase or a faded knapsack, a thoroughly beaten people. Not even these wispy people walk along the Wilhemstrasse. Here the silence is almost com-

plete. Off to the left is the long side of the new Reichchancellery, the pride of all Hitler's efforts to build a '1,000-year Reich.' The street is blocked off but the Russian guards wave you through. Except that the bodies of many who must have died here—probably including Adolf Hitler and Eva Braun—have been removed, nothing has been cleaned up.

Around the corner lies the main door of the Chancellery. The gateway into the courtyard is blocked by three crudely placed planks. Three young Russian soldiers, armed with tommy guns and wearing faded uniforms stand guard. It is a temptation to say that the building tells the story of Berlin, but there are few buildings that don't. It is not merely part of Berlin that is dead. It is the whole city."

Considering that twenty-first-century Berlin is one of the greatest, liveliest, and architecturally exciting cities in the world, it is hard for today's reader to imagine the devastation. However, this author visited West Berlin four years later in the summer of 1949, still a sorry place for a population dependent for food and coal on an American airlift while surrounded with hostile Soviet forces. Berlin awaited the "German miracle" of the 1950s.

CHAPTER 23

Europe's First Days
of Peace

In the frantic days of May 7 to 9, 1945, peace came to Europe not with the drama of an earthquake but as rumbling, stuttering, and fervently welcomed aftershocks. The capitulation of the German generals witnessed by Price Day on May 7 might have been V-E Day in American eyes. But at Stalin's insistence the formal Big Three announcement came in Soviet-occupied Berlin on May 9, the official V-E Day ever since.

Three days later, Day reported the unanticipated: The first motor truck to be built in defeated Germany had come off the assembly line in Cologne [May 3, 1945]. *"Painfully Europe wakes from its long nightmare,"* he wrote. But there was plenty of downside to offset the encouraging news from Cologne. France had just been told it faced four or five years of food rationing. (A far too gloomy prognostication.) Shiploads of food were going to *"famished Holland."* Norway's problems had yet to be ascertained. Italy could *"raise its despised and ridiculed head"* because some of its people finally rose against fascism. *"At the center of all Europe's problems lies Germany,"* then under undefined and competitive four-power control. Food was the biggest problem. *"Germany itself must help as much as possible in the handling of its own food as well as its production,"* Day commented. *"Allied help of all kinds will go first to the countries oppressed by Germany. The truth is that urban and industrial Germany has been almost smashed out of existence. Few of its cities are leveled. Many houses stand undamaged. Some factories are untouched. But a city, above all an industrial city, is an intricate structure, and, as organisms, Germany's cities are gone."*

McCardell offered readers a glimpse of General Patton, *"tall and sharp and smart and straight"* as he concluded his last wartime briefing for correspondents covering the Third Army. *" 'Gentlemen,' said Patton, 'the war is over.' He shut his mouth tightly on that, sucking in his cheeks, a typical Patton gesture when he is pleased. This was the last time we would ever be in the old man's war room. We looked for the last time at his great map of the Western front. How far we had come, from that little neck of land, the Cherbourg peninsula away over to the left, to the mountains of Bavaria and the eastern valleys of Austria, away over in the right-hand corner. How far it had seemed last June from our little battlefront in Normandy, across the face of central Europe to the Russians' long front, miles east of Berlin. Now those two fronts met in the very center of Germany and all but a few of the little red numbered rectangles representing German troops—all but a few still posted in Austria—had been squeezed off the old man's position map.*

"Well, it hadn't happened overnight. There on the map, where the army's password was posted, from day to day, was the war's calendar. It read: 'Today is D-Day plus 336.' There was the statistic chart of casualties and prisoners and tank losses. The Third Army casualty figures, which we cannot quote, were only a fraction of the Germans. But to us, they were the starkest on the chart. They represented the men who would never go home, the men who had paid for the victory with their lives. He asked us to note casualty figures, even though we couldn't print them, and comparative tank losses of American and German armies. But the best things he said, as is often the case with Patton, were off the record. He answered all our questions. He thanked us for what we had done as correspondents. Then we filed past him and shook hands and said goodbye. And for us, the war was over."

The Baltimore Sun's front pages right after the advent of peace in Europe provided dramatic evidence that American attention had shifted largely to the Pacific war, where the nation faced the ominous task of invading the Japanese home islands. In large black headlines, the newspaper blared *"400 B-29's RAID JAPAN"* on May 10 and *"B-29's BOMB JAP PLANE PLANT"* on May 11. But Mark Watson, Lee McCardell, Holbrook Bradley, and Price Day had work to do before finishing up their long assignments in Europe.

Watson tapped his experiences after World War I to offer suggestions on how the Germans should be handled after World War II. He focused on the publicity given to *"de-Nazification"* programs, warning that too much emphasis on Hitler's enforcers and ideologues would leave *"the German military machine"* off the hook. *"When the Kaiser abdicated (in 1919), we were prepared to believe that German militarism was dead. We were rewarded by a second world war, and the tragic fact is that we appear likely to repeat that error. Our public pronouncements excoriate only the 'Nazis,' which have inevitably influenced the Allied public's thinking. We think that Nazism alone brought on the war and that having destroyed the nation's leaders and many of its rank and file we already are beginning to think that the war's cause is exterminated. The fact is that Nazism was used by militarism, rather than vice versa, and that German militarism at this moment is preparing to profit from Nazism's fall."* He described the German military machine as a *"perpetuating group which is simply the German nation in uniform."* In hindsight, it is obvious Watson's fears were exaggerated. Germany emerged from its direst chapter as a nation with an extraordinary aversion to militarism as well as Nazism. But his hindsight on World War I was on target. The militarists in that era blamed their defeat on a stab in the back by their political leaders, a charge the Nazis exploited to the hilt in their rise to power.

Watson's early assessments of Europe's post-war plight repeatedly focused on a food shortage that was to plague the continent in the 1945–1946 winter [May 15, 1945]. *"Of all the problems troubling our armies of occupation, this is the most troubling. The certainty of a food shortage is so complete that most German civilians already are being put on rations equaling 1,150 calories daily. Men doing heavy work are given materially more, as are pregnant women and a few other special categories, but fully four-fifths of the German population will get only that limited allowance, as compared with the 2,000-calorie diet assigned to their late 'slaves,' who are still awaiting shipment home, and as compared with the 3,000-calorie rations for American soldiers on active duty."*

Food shortages also figured in a dispatch from Howard Norton in Milan [May 14, 1945]. *"Most of the people here haven't had a really good square meal in nearly two years. It has gotten so bad that even the black market has little to offer in edibles. The trouble was caused by Allied bombing, which so completely smashed the railways between Milan and the food centers at Brescia and Bologna, that it mounted to an almost complete blockade of this city. And now that the bombing is over the Milanese feel very strongly that the Allies should do everything to help them reopen the lines and lift the blockade."*

In a dispatch [May 13, 1945] Mark Watson gave his attention to *"displaced persons,"* a term for the millions of people—slave laborers, concentration camp survivors, freed prisoners-of-war, and whole populations on the move—whose survival depended on the help of the victorious powers. They confronted Allied occupation armies with tasks that outstripped their resources. In one DP camp, six Americans were put in charge of 30,000 people. In another, a single WAC lieutenant had to use administrative talent in dealing with 2,000. *"The problem,"* Watson wrote, *"is to assemble, feed and house them and give them medicine and such few comforts as we have available.*

"It is urgent work, and difficult, and there are not many persons really available to do it. It is believed that Germany brought in from captive nations 8 million workers, some as plain slaves, some on a more or less voluntary basis. We already have at organized camps about 1.5 million and a like number have been reported on their way into camps. There may prove to be a good many more for us to take care of. So many people provide a considerable addition to the Army's already heavy tasks. They call for food, which is not too plentiful, and for transport and responsible personnel, which the Army combat units could not well spare under any condition during the days of combat, and are reluctant to reassign even now. The relief work was something which had to be done without delay for the sake of those wretched newly freed slaves, and often for the sake of their late masters, upon whom the slaves had turned with savagery."

What Watson was describing was a situation that would not go away swiftly. Even four years later, in 1949, as a neophyte reporter, the author of this book encountered hundreds of DPs living in bleak temporary facilities in Germany and Austria while they tried and tried to obtain resettlement in foreign countries. Those heading for America had to have proof of a sponsoring family, good health, and a means of livelihood. As for the German people, who at least found themselves in a country they could call home, post-war life was lean.

A sure sign of the end of combat came with the deployment of the battle-scarred Twenty-ninth Division to Bremen and Bremerhaven, ports much needed for supplying the beleaguered continent. Howard Norton reported [May 27, 1945] that the division's three famous regiments, the 115th, 116th, and 175th, all of whom fought from Normandy to Germany, were given military governance duties. Three days later he wrote that the division had suffered *"about the largest divisional casualty total of the war in Europe—20,668, or about 130 percent of the average total strength of the division throughout the war."* Of this number, 4,839 officers and men died in action, 15,146 won Purple Hearts, 329 were still missing in action, and 354 had been prisoners-of-war.

Mark Watson, Lee McCardell, Price Day, Holbrook Bradley, and Thomas O'Neill remained in Europe covering the aftermath of the German surrender. O'Neill wrote [June 1, 1945] of the closing of the world's greatest *"hotel,"* the London subway system that had provided bomb-proof underground shelters for tens of thousands during the Blitz and the rain of German rockets. Day devoted many articles to such post-war subjects as the shifting of Allied and Soviet armies to conform to the Yalta directives of Roosevelt, Stalin, and Churchill. He also reported Austria's rejection of its ties to Germany, and the failure of U.S. Army efforts to enforce non-fraternization between its troops and the German people. Bradley continued to follow the Twenty-ninth Division. McCardell remained in Europe for several months, seeking information on missing Marylanders. Watson headed to Asia to look into China's clouded future. So ended the war in Europe.

CHAPTER 24

To the Pacific

On the morning of May 7, 1945, when *The Evening Sun* was first with the welcome headline, *SURRENDER,* the Baltimore newspapers executed an abrupt switch of emphasis in war reporting. The focus was no longer Nazi Germany but a Japan fanatically girding for defense of its home islands. Forewarned by the increasing bloodletting in island-hopping battles culminating at Iwo Jima and Okinawa, Americans faced the dread prospect of casualties in the hundreds of thousands. They had no way of knowing two atomic bombs would soon explode over Hiroshima and Nagasaki, at last bringing an end to World War II.

Back in Baltimore, before the nuclear age began, *Sun* editors braced for more warfare—a lot more. They had learned during the European campaign that a regional newspaper could acquire prestige and influence and the gratitude of local readers by sending its own top reporters into the field. *The Sun* had come a long way since its boastful blurb on September 3, 1939, that it had *"a mighty news staff"*—meaning Associated Press reports available to all newspapers—to cover the global conflict. Half a decade later, it was ready to proclaim that thirteen of its own men were engaged in war coverage from Europe to the Pacific.

"As millions of fighting men move toward the Pacific battle zones, and problems of occupation and reconstruction multiply in Europe, the Sunpapers' corps of staff correspondents is being redeployed," the paper announced [July 15, 1945]. *"Four Sunpapers men are in the Far East or on the way, and others are to follow. Two new staff correspondents are going abroad to report the rebuilding of Europe and the role*

of both the liberated and the defeated nations in world affairs. Other veterans of overseas assignments are moving to new scenes."

An eight-column headline and the pictures of thirteen correspondents appeared on an inside page—probably the inspiration of Neil H. Swanson, the newspaper's flamboyant executive editor. *"He directed his far-flung staff with the verve of a field marshal, moving colored pins back and forth on his wall map to locate his correspondents, when he knew where they were,"* wrote Harold Williams in his 1987 newspaper history. A visionary journalist, Swanson was a key figure in *The Sun*'s ascendancy, promoting the clustering of related news subjects, frequent use of photographs and bigger headlines to avoid the gray look of the past. During his reign, 1941–1954, *The Sun* won more Pulitzer Prizes than any other newspaper except *The New York Times.*

In covering World War II, *The Sun* pursued the same "Germany First" policy that had been adopted by the Churchill government in London and the Roosevelt administration in Washington. Reporters Mark Watson, Lee McCardell, Price Day, Holbrook Bradley, and Thomas O'Neill had fulfilled long, long assignments in Europe, covering the Nazi Blitz on Britain and the Allied campaigns in Sicily, Italy, France, the Low Countries, Austria, and Germany.

Meanwhile, in the vastness of the Pacific, only two reporters were available for periodic assignments. Gifted and daring, Howard Norton and Philip Heisler almost lost their lives in the process. But continuous coverage of the kind seen from Normandy to the Elbe was not provided for the Japanese war. Only after Germany went down to defeat did *The Sun* enlarge its staff coverage of the Pacific conflict. By the time the Japanese surrendered, no less than three *Sun* reporters were present on the deck of the *USS Missouri*. Also on the paper's docket was coverage of the MacArthur occupation of Japan, the liberation of the Philippines, and the civil war in China. Korea, in September 1950, Vietnam, in March 1965, Afghanistan in 2002, and Iraq in 2003 would come later. *Sun* war correspondents would be on hand from the outset of each war.

Howard M. Norton became the first *Sun* reporter to witness the invasion of an enemy-held Pacific island, in this case Saipan. He called it *"the biggest battle of the Pacific war to date and probably the toughest."* The amphibious landing at Saipan on June 15, 1944 came nine days after D-Day in the English Channel. *"The stench of death already hung over the beach as we waded ashore,"* Norton wrote in a story delayed by censors to June 20. *"Bodies of Marines, who established the beachhead, lay where they had fallen along the water's edge, covered with ponchos or shelter halves from their own packs. The invaders of Saipan had been too busy to spare men for burial squads.*

"Swollen bodies of dead Japs lay farther inland among the trees and along the embankment of a narrow-gauge sugar cane railway, which they died defending. In the stockade near the shore the Marines had concentrated several hundred women and children. The mothers were already busy with family washing, taking turns at empty gasoline drums provided by the Marines. Din and dust on the beachhead is terrific. At this moment a battery of heavy guns a few hundred yards away is laying a barrage on Jap positions in the hills beyond the town."

Earlier in this story, Norton reported the Japanese were doing *"a masterful job"* in their retreat from Americans who were now firmly established ashore. He warned readers the consensus of newsmen on the island was that American troops had not yet come against the main Japanese force on the island. *"All are convinced that they're watching a battle which will take a place in history beside Guadalcanal as one of the war's turning points."*

Long before Pearl Harbor and the paper's tentative reach westward, *The Sun*'s military expert, Mark Watson, had his eye on the Pacific. Citing *"the new sort of war which 1940 has disclosed,"* one in which air power would be needed to augment sea power in defending the nation, Watson delivered a wakeup warning [May 22, 1940]: *"The bald fact is that all our defense plans by air as well as by sea have been based on the traditional assumption that we would have the support, whether active or passive, of the British navy, and that with its support our own Navy could hold off all enemies. That assumption, it is becoming grimly apparent, is no longer one that can be relied upon indefinitely, anymore than can the fundamental fact of the British navy's continuing existence."*

Within days after the Japanese attack on Pearl Harbor, Watson had assessed [Dec. 10, 1941] the devastating losses to the nation's Pacific fleet: Citing *"new calculations and new weapons,"* Watson calculated Japan had gutted the American battleship fleet at Pearl Harbor but, in a vital piece of luck, U.S. carrier forces were at sea. They proved to be the key to America's eventual victory and changed naval doctrine forever. Aircraft carriers replaced huge dreadnaughts in effectiveness. As B-29s bombed Japanese cities at will, highly improved submarines almost strangled Japan.

Watson's almost daily commentary became *Sun* examples of distinguished war coverage. As German subs prowled the Atlantic in an effort to break Britain, he declared [July 23, 1942] that if anti-submarine warfare was not more successful *"the war is going to be in a very bad way before autumn."* Losses of merchant ships were *"the heaviest in history,"* outstripping replacements. Although encouraged by turning-point battles at Coral Sea, Midway, and the Aleutians, Watson warned against exaggerating U.S. accomplishments. *"These were essentially defense actions against an advancing foe. Not yet have we recovered one foothold previously lost to Japan in the whole vast length of the Pacific. In no case have we taken a clear offensive of the sort that is the necessary part of a true victory."* [Sept. 8, 1942]

It took another year before *The Sun* sent Norton to the Pacific. His initial stories, from Australia, dealt with Maryland medical personnel taking care of wounded servicemen. Whether intended or not, this was in the tradition established by Raymond Tompkins in World War I. Including fifty names and twenty-four pictures of doctors and nurses, Norton's dispatch described an immaculate convent-turned-hospital atop a high hill: *"a scene of natural beauty that was a tonic to the mud-splattered wounded from the jungles."* One soldier told Norton: *"'This ain't no GI outfit. They treat you like a paying guest.'"*

"One of the Baltimore physicians, Captain Theodore A. Schwartz, a specialist at the University of Maryland School of Medicine, had attracted the attention of the medical world through his "sensational success in removing shell fragments imbedded in eyes and ears," Norton reported to home folks. He also asserted [Sept. 24, 1943]

that Maryland doctors had a big share in the war's *"secret medical weapon."* Was it penicillin? The reporter didn't say.

By December 1943, Norton had moved to first-hand war coverage in the battle for New Britain. *"Skimming the jungle treetops in a Mitchell medium bomber you get a glimpse of the world's worst battleground, which makes it easy to understand why a year and a half of fighting has failed to drive the Japanese from New Guinea. It is a battleground without ground. Everywhere water glistens darkly through the dense blanket of trees. In the clearings it flows sluggishly around the roots of the razor-edged Kunai grass, which will cut a man's clothing to ribbons. You rush across broad rivers which snake their way seaward, cutting aimless channels through the trees and with no apparent banks to prevent their spreading out. Nowhere is any ground visible—wet or dry. It seems impossible that any human being could force a way through the thick morass, even without a well-armed enemy to oppose him. But it has to be done, and the enemy has been driven hundreds of miles northward."*

In a story on December 17, 1943, Norton gave this eyewitness account: *"From a Liberator bomber piloted by First Lt. William R. Dean, Jr. of 2804 St. Paul Street, this correspondent today saw American forces invade New Britain and saw Japanese positions hit by one of the heaviest bomb loads ever dumped on western defenses of that strategic enemy-occupied island. Dean called it a gravy run—no ack ack, no machine guns, no interruption. The target was a bald and apparently barren hill which photo reconnaissance showed was honey-combed with coastal defense guns and machine gun nests. Every bomber passed squarely over it and every bomb appeared to land in the target area. As we neared the coast of New Britain ships of the American invasion fleet came into sight. Smoke puffs showed where the destroyers were pounding Japanese shore defenses. In rifts through the clouds we could see the invasion barges scurrying among the ships. At the signal bombs away, while kneeling on the floor peering out of the open bomb bay doors, I was thrown flat as the Liberator lurched upward when thousands of pounds of steel and T.N.T. fell away. Far below there was a brilliant flash and a burst of smoke and dust and then a rush of air which again tossed the huge bomber*

upward. Then it was all over and the formation headed homeward."
Again, four days later [Dec. 12, 1943] Norton described the American takeover of Cape Gloucester after the Japanese made no attempt to stop a U.S. invasion even though the Japanese knew what was coming except the exact date and time of assault. "*The most amazing fact was that with all advance information and thousands of tons of invasion equipment stacked under their very noses the Japanese did not make a single attempt to interfere.*

"*Night after night lights blazed along miles of New Guinea beach where the Marines were bivouacked less than an hour's flying time from Japanese territory. For days a vast invasion fleet stood boldly off shore. At night the whole beach was lighted like a summer resort. Yet in the face of this the Japanese did not drop a single bomb in the staging area during the days this correspondent spent there. There have been no reports of bombing before or since.*"

Norton reported [Jan. 1, 1944] how three socially prominent Baltimore Marine officers played a key role in the capture of Tarawa. It was their assignment to accompany Marine troops landing on the island, observe enemy strong points, and direct Marine air attacks on the Japanese targets. The officers involved were Captain James McHenry, Major John E. Semmes, and Captain Stuart S. Janney Jr.

"*It works like this,*" Janney told Norton after having gone ashore in a rubber boat onto one of Tarawa's hottest beaches. "*The commander tells me his men are having trouble with a pillbox and asks if the air arm can help. If planes happen to be waiting overhead for call, I contact them and the pillbox is usually reduced within ten minutes.*

"*If no planes are available in the immediate vicinity, I call the aircraft carrier and get an estimate of the time required to bring air support into action. Perhaps the answer is 'one hour.' I contact the ground commander and he orders the men to draw back from the area to be bombed. Within an hour, enemy positions are reduced and we move ahead.*"

McHenry told Norton the battle of Tarawa had "*demonstrated that ground forces can advance with minimum losses if properly supported from the air.*" Major Semmes, a Marine battalion executive officer, had remained in touch with Janney and McHenry during the battle.

While the battle for the Marshall Islands raged [Feb. 1, 1944], Norton wrote an article from Pearl Harbor emphasizing how *"the gigantic American carrier task force offensives against the enemy's mid-Pacific"* islands showed how far the *"fleet air arm"* had come in the past two years of war. That it was *"almost certain disaster for carrier-based planes to operate against land craft. For carrier-based planes to attack island air bases now has become the rule. Navy carrier pilots maintain an average of better than five enemy planes shot down for each American plane lost. Navy airmen had less difficulty today with Japanese land-based fighters than with craft from Japanese carriers. Why? The Japanese carrier pilot is the cream of the crop. His plane is not better than the dry-land Zero, but he can do a lot more with it."*

Moreover, Norton reported, the American Hellcat was proving to be a faster, more heavily armed and armored plane than the Zero, that, admittedly, was better at making sharp turns in combat. Norton looked forward to the replacement of the U.S. Dauntless dive bombers with new Helldivers. As or more important were the superior training and manpower numbers of U.S. pilots which neither the Germans nor the Japanese could match.

Watson's companion page one piece welcomed the advantages of combining carrier-based and land-based aircraft in assaulting the Japanese mid-Pacific islands with *"the greatest naval task force in history. One by one are the links of Japan's defensive chain in the South Pacific being weakened, and as each loses its strength the chain itself weakens, and our enemy is compelled to place his reliance upon a shorter chain, somewhat nearer Japan itself. Because the war is moving along into its third year, our forward movement sometimes seems very slow. At the outset it was not an advance at all but a retreat. Only when our naval victory of the Coral Sea stopped Japanese progress and the far greater victory at Midway reversed it did our forward movement begin at all.* [Feb. 17, 1944]

"Our successes have been made possible by the possession of new weapons in very large quantity. The victory in the Marshalls furnishes the best example to date of the enormous superiority which our task forces possess over any conceivable opposition near the target. Our

first really modern sea-air task force included carriers and battleships in such number that the fleet was itself almost invulnerable."

Watson's burst of confidence contrasted with his gloom both before and immediately after Pearl Harbor. His high regard for carrier task forces stands the test of time. But what he could not foresee was the Japanese resort to kamikaze suicide attacks later in the war. They proved very effective in sinking U.S. ships and killing GIs.

On July 21, 1944, as U.S. forces stormed into Guam, a once and future U.S. possession, Norton had a very close brush with death while aboard a Navy subchaser. His story, probably delayed by censors, did not appear in *The Sun* until July 30. Excerpts: *"Jap shore batteries did not do much firing today, but one of them did enough to convince this correspondent that his aim was excellent. The subchaser from which I watched the first wave land this morning was one of the few craft to receive a direct hit. And there is no doubt that the Jap gunner did it on purpose. It happened shortly after 8:30 this morning, while we were idling off shore, guiding the second wave to the beach.*

"Suddenly, and without warning, a shell burst in the water off the starboard side, throwing up a geyser. As the lieutenant who skippers this craft ran to the speaking tube to give the order to get underway, there was another violent burst close to the starboard side and several pieces of shrapnel tore through the wooden cabin. 'Duck,' somebody yelled. 'They've got us bracketed.' Observers and officers sitting on the deck scrambled for cover. I ran back to the rear door of the main cabin from the exposed forward deck where I had been talking to the gunners. I was unable to get through the door because two men were crouching in front of it. I crouched down between them. On the forward deck, a Philadelphia gunner's mate continued his attempts to get the overheated 40-mm back into action, and a Negro steward's mate, a yeoman, and one seaman kept on hoisting ammunition from the magazine.

"I hardly hit the deck when a third shell burst with a terrific roar smack on the forward guns' ammunition cases, about ten feet from where the three of us were crouching. The three men handling the ammunition were killed instantly. The steward's mate, beheaded and dismembered, lay beneath a gun. The yeoman and the seaman, both

badly mangled, were thrown against the rail. A pharmacist, the only man aboard qualified to give expert first aid, was severely wounded in the chest and unable to move. A seaman, struck in the groin, appeared to have little chance of surviving. Men crouching on the other side of me were badly hit and bleeding. The right arm of the man nearest the rail dangled from a thread of flesh. The man on the inside was wounded on the hip and shoulder by shrapnel which passed through the cabin wall. A couple of yards away a 20-year-old coxswain from Havre de Grace, Md., looked dazedly at the deep dent in his helmet. 'I wouldn't take a million dollars for this little old tin hat,' he said.

"This correspondent echoed that sentiment with a hearty 'Amen' for on surveying my own personal damage I found the metal visor of my helmet had deflected a bit of shrapnel and that another small piece had passed the jutting forepart of the pith lining. So much blood was spilled over me from my injured shipmates that I had difficulty convincing the skipper I was not injured, and he refused to be satisfied until he, personally, looked me over and found nary a scratch. By a freak of chance the gunner's mate, who was standing on the forward deck more than six feet from where the shell burst, was barely scratched. Twelve other crewmen were variously injured.

"In spite of the disaster, this plucky little subchaser continued the business of guiding the invasion traffic. The cabin was riddled with shrapnel; the magazine flooded; the radio knocked out; bits of human flesh mingled with the kapok filling of life preservers were spattered over the forward deck. The slippery film made footing uncertain. Four of the most seriously wounded were taken off by a landing craft returning from the beach, while the uninjured crewmen gathered up the remains of the dead, scrubbed the decks and plugged the shrapnel holes. Fortunately, the craft was not seriously holed beneath the waterline. Late this afternoon this subchaser and its tight-lipped skipper were still on the job. And the crewmen who escaped injury were cheerfully doubling for their wounded shipmates and murmuring reverent thanks to Providence that they were still alive."

So ended an account of one intimate instant among all the thousands that occurred that day. It is fair to say Norton's underlying message was the vast cost to individuals unlucky enough to be in the wrong place at the wrong time. But for his reporting, the ordeal of the subchaser, which lost more than half its crew, would have gone unrecorded in the avalanche of news reports and histories about the invasion. Mind-numbing numbers, victories and defeats of clashing forces, the strategic consequences of hard-fought American successes —all would overwhelm later memories.

When Norton returned home from the Pacific, his arm in a sling due to a wrenched back, he wrote a bitter article [Aug. 22, 1944] complaining about the greater prominence the American press was giving to the war in Europe rather than the struggle in the Pacific. (This, after all, was the summer of D-Day in Normandy and the liberation of Paris.) But old-Asia hand Norton was not mollified. *"Perhaps it is natural for a correspondent just back from the Pacific to feel that the 'Jap war' is the biggest, toughest, most important and least appreciated of all the wars with which this world has been scourged. In geographical magnitude, physical and climatic difficulty and fanatical fighting zeal of the enemy, there is no war in history to equal it.*

"In the matter of casualties and numbers of men involved in actual fighting on both sides it is already almost on a par with the European war, and probably will far surpass it before the Pacific becomes truly pacific. Our successes in the Pacific certainly are comparable to the successes in Europe, but the fighting Americans who won these successes with their blood in steaming jungles and on blistering atolls feel that the people back home have relegated them to the minor league. They are bitter about it. And repeatedly they have asked me to tell you these facts.

"On Saipan our forces found more guns per mile than on the invasion coast of Europe. Three divisions took part in the 24-day battle for Saipan and casualties mounted to more than one full peacetime division. The assault on Europe offers no battle to compare with this. When recent dispatches announced that 200,000 Japs had been cut off and left to starve or die of disease in the South Pacific jungles, Americans at home did not seem to comprehend the significance of the news. In the two years since Stalingrad the world has been amazed by the Russian army's advance of more than 900 miles. Yet in the last nine months alone our forces in the Central Pacific advanced 3,000

miles and in the Southwest Pacific nearly 1,000 with comparably little fanfare. We have recaptured more than 8,000,000 square miles—most of it in the last year. This represents an area more than twice the size of the whole of Europe, including Russia and as far east as the Urals. Yet with all this vast area behind us we are only now getting to bases that will permit us to begin the main assault on the enemy. The United States Navy alone is holding a Pacific front line nearly 6,000 miles long. Launching an assault on Saipan was like launching an assault on Berlin from a base in New York harbor. At Saipan our forces were more than 3,000 miles from their nearest big supply base and over 5,000 miles from the American Pacific coast.

"The Japs are tough because they have been schooled to fight to the death, and they do just that. They are tough because they are scattered over millions of square miles and will have to be hunted out. We will have to go into some of the world's most rugged areas to smoke them out. The Japs still hold everything they seized of economic value. We hold the initiative now but the invasion of Japan's stolen empire is only about to begin."

CHAPTER 25

Heisler at Iwo Jima and Okinawa

For reasons that no one could have predicted except those privy to the Manhattan atomic bomb project, Philip Heisler returned to Baltimore from his Pacific assignment with a forecast [May 29, 1945] that World War II would end in three months or three years. At the lower end of that bracket, he was right on the nose. The long struggle came to a close on August 14, precisely two months and eleven days later. For a guy who liked to bet on the horses at Pimlico, that was a pretty good prediction. Those with the advantage of hindsight could argue that the higher end of Heisler's timeline might have been more accurate but for The Bomb. For in May 1945, the United States still faced a probable need to invade the Japanese homeland. Heisler had witnessed the bloody struggles of Iwo Jima, where he went in with the sixth wave of Marines, and of Okinawa, where a tropical illness limited him to aerial observation of that island under U.S. attack. From both vantage points he proved to be a masterful narrator of very complicated battles. In the course of his assignment he traveled 100,000 miles with U.S. forces—from Pearl Harbor to the Philippines, Saipan, Guam, and the skies over Japan aboard Flying Fortresses.

After the war, Heisler became a fast-rising star in Baltimore. At the age of only thirty-three, he was appointed managing editor of *The Evening Sun,* a post he held for a record thirty years. A boss whose door was open to members of his staff, he made changes later adopted by most executives in the newspaper business: an emphasis on local news, women's news, sports news, and financial news. When he retired in 1979, he tacked up a letter in the news room. *"I avoided the goodbyes because I was afraid I might tarnish the tradition that all managing editors are tough, hard-hearted and unsentimental war-lords. I hope I will run into each of you at some nearby bar, race track or drug store. Perhaps then I will be able to express my heart-felt appreciation for a most happy time."*

Heisler was born in Dallastown, Pennsylvania, in 1915, went to Penn State, worked for a time for the McKeesport (PA) *Daily News* and came to the Sunpapers in 1939. He soon was covering the Pentagon and later the Pacific war before returning to Baltimore for a series of executive jobs. He died in 1988 at the age of seventy-three.

Rarely did he talk about the war. However, already in print was his celebrated yarn of being aboard an escort carrier during a Pacific typhoon. Let him tell the story [Feb. 18, 1945]:

"She was just a jeep carrier, one of those emergency jobs with a flight and hangar deck built atop a Liberty ship hull. You could almost see her blush when in company of the big battle-line carriers. On this trip she was taking a load of replacement planes and pilots from a forward navy base to the fast carrier fleet. 'It looks like a typhoon,' the ship's weather officer told me. 'The wind is hitting 50 knots and getting worse every minute.' By this time, walking on the ship was impossible. To get from one spot to another, the men had to crawl or pull themselves along the safety lines. Everyone not otherwise engaged was lashing down anything that could move. Over the ship's loudspeaker came the warning for all hands to don lifejackets. The flimsy lifebelt seemed a pathetic safeguard against the seas crashing into the ship. In the ready room, the pilots were huddled around the radio speaker. As the ship rolled to the starboard the heavy cabinet, chairs and tables slid across the steel deck, crashing into the men and pinning them to the bulkhead. No one could move until the ship rolled to port.

"If the groaning ship tried bucking the waves head-on she was almost certain to break in two. If she stayed in the trough of the waves, there was a chance of capsizing. The captain decided to chance the latter. Claws of wind tore at the planes lashed to the flight deck as though they were made of paper. Suddenly one plane tore loose. It thrashed into three other planes until all four crashed over the side of the ship. Other planes began tearing lose. One was lifted several feet

*in the air, turned over on its back and landed at a side smokestack.
'Fire! Fire! Fire! on the flight deck,' came the call on the squawk box.
The burning plane blazed furiously for several seconds. Then the ship
went into another violent roll that sent a huge wave crashing on the
burning plane and carried it out to sea.*

*"Below decks there was little anyone could do but hold on to
something solid, wait, hope and pray. Each roll tipped the ship more
on its side. Men huddled in clinging groups kept up a steady stream of
wisecracks but the laughter was hollow and the grins were frozen.*

*"Suddenly the ship's loudspeaker squawked. 'All hands not engaged
in necessary work lay over to the port side.' When you are down to
using ship's personnel for ballast there is not much more that can be
done. It was about this time that the ship sent out its SOS and a cruiser and a destroyer were sent to stand by in the event that we capsized.
For two hours I wedged myself in a passageway straddling the expan-
sion joint amidships. Somebody told me the ship was built in less than
a month by women war workers. It was not a comforting thought.
Most of the planes on the flight deck had been blown over the sides
by now but a torpedo plane was thrown back on deck and crashed
through an open elevator pit, landing on top of a fighter plane. From
then on, after seven hours of being buffeted, things got better. The
next morning the sea was calm as Druid Hill Park Lake."*

Heisler's first action reports from Iwo Jima were datelined February 19 and 20, 1945, D-Day and D-Day Plus One. Both appeared in
The Sun on February 21. The Marines found it comparatively easy to
seize a beachhead, only to be raked by fire from well-dug-in Japanese
forces farther and higher inland. This was a strategy concocted by
Lieutenant General Kuribayshi Tadamichi at Peleliu. It was repeated at Iwo and Okinawa, at great cost to American troops gathered
densely on the beaches. A purely defensive strategy, like kamikaze
suicide attacks at sea, it was designed to goad the Allies into accepting
a negotiated peace rather than insisting on unconditional surrender.
Here are excerpts from Heisler's reports:

D-Day—*"The battle for Iwo Jima was already three days old when
United States Marines battered their way ashore at zero hour today.
Battlewagons and cruiser work horses have been lying off the rugged*

island, trading punches with Jap shore batteries in the most concentrated bombardment of the Pacific war. Some 50 warships made up the fleet that approached Iwo through the dawn mists of February 16. Iwo Jima is 7.79 square miles in area. United States warships poured more than 4,000 tons into that small target. Added were almost hourly carrier air-strikes. All this came to a climax this morning when for five screaming minutes thousands of rockets completely obscured the island in a flash of fire just before the troops landed. After a quick trade of punches the Japs apparently decided to capitalize on the safety of poor visibility than to try to hit back. The Japs were not given a single moment's rest, day or night, in the last three days."

D-Day Plus One—*"The battered 4th Marines inched into protected high ground on the Jap airfield at dawn today, after being pinned to a narrow 200-yard wide beachhead raked by Jap mortar fire for seventeen hellish hours. Charging onto the bare sloping beach forming one sector of the landing area, the 4th Division units advanced swiftly for the first fifteen minutes of the attack until they ran into a wall of sunken pillboxes surrounding the Japanese airfield above them. At the same time, hidden Jap mortars opened up a barrage against our pinned-down troops in their cramped beachhead foxholes scooped in the black volcanic sand. This was the only protection the stalled Marines had throughout the daylight on D-Day, but under cover at night demolition squads knocked out enemy defense points, paving the way for an advance today. The 5th Marines, landing on another portion of the beachhead, encountered relatively light opposition and within a few hours had reached the airfield.*

"With the close support of 90 carrier-based planes and a continuing rolling barrage from naval guns, both Marine divisions prepared for a general advance. The Japs are still holding catacombed Suribachi volcano and apparently the only way to dislodge them is to dig and burn them out. The Japs are also reorganizing their lines across the wide northern portion of the island. From the rugged gorge and cave terrain there, they are expected to put up a stubborn, costly resistance to the end, but the outcome of the battle is now certain.

"The beach where the Marines landed reaches to a ridge which forms the perimeter of the airfield, some 500 yards inland. Black sand

churned by constant shelling formed a black fog that covered the entire area and obscured the sun, so that one did not know when daylight ended and night began. Although the sun was shining brightly above the clouds of dust and smoke, frontline positions could be determined only by a line of twinkling flashes from enemy fire, or by occasional sheets of flame when Marines succeeded in crawling up to a pillbox and frying the enemy position. When one Marine division was tenaciously holding an almost untenable position, another, landing on the left bank, rapidly advanced inland to drive a wedge directly across the narrow neck of the southern tip of the island—thereby severing the towering Suribachi volcano from the main body of the island. Reaching the opposite side of the island, these Marines fanned out, the left column forming a line about the base of Suribachi and the right column swinging up onto high ground behind the airfield and threatening the rear of the Jap positions that were punishing the division.

"At the same time, landing craft gunboats just a few feet offshore poured rockets into Jap mortar positions, while battleships and cruisers farther out lobbed heavy shells into the remaining Jap artillery positions. By nightfall Jap fire on the beach noticeably lessened but still pinned down the troops into a narrow corridor. As the sun came out behind Suribachi this morning, the Marines were moving forward again. During the night a demolition squad had knocked out half a dozen concrete pillboxes on the lip of a ridge before them. Medical corpsmen this morning were able to gather up a number of men who had been wounded early yesterday but had been isolated in foxholes under fire day and night."

Next day's story [Feb. 23, 1945] found Heisler aboard a troopship a couple of hundred yards off Iwo's shore. There he witnessed a Navy emergency hospital as it received wounded men from the battlefront. *"The wounds, like the fighting, are dirty on Iwo Jima,"* his dispatch began. *"Bloodstained tags giving the names of wounded men and the types of their wounds dangle from stretchers as they are carried below. The casualties are stretched out on long rows of metal mess tables. The more serious are treated there until they can be taken into the ship's operating room. A half a dozen doctors, stripped to the waist, but still wearing lifebelts, and scores of weary hospital corps-*

men roam up and down the rows on a mass-production system of treatment.

"One man cuts the clothes from the wounded. Another writes out a report. A third administers morphine or stimulants. Most of the wounds are caused by shrapnel and most of the wounded are suffering from loss of blood. Jugs of blood plasma hang above each table. Seldom is a man brought aboard who doesn't need blood. The physicians are using gallons of cold blood which is being flown into the seabase here directly from the States. Most of the wounds are dirty. All of Iwo Jima is covered with a coarse black volcanic sand that gets into the wounds and every grain must be picked out singly to insure prompt healing.

"The physicians have been working day and night with naps for a few minutes whenever they can catch them. Lieut. Walter Revell, formerly of the University of Maryland, worked for fourteen straight hours, then caught three hours of sleep on a stretcher under a dressing table and now is back on duty."

On a front page carrying the most famous photograph of the war, the picture of Marines hoisting the Stars and Strips atop Mount Suribachi, Heisler described [Feb. 25, 1945] how American troops fought their way up the volcano. *"They can talk about the flea-eye accuracy of Navy gunfire and pinpoint bombing, but there is nothing so accurate as a stick of dynamite placed next to the enemy you want to get. There is also nothing so dangerous to the guy who is doing it. Naval gunfire and planes have knocked out just about all the Japanese defense positions. Fighting on the front line is now almost too close to risk fire from anything less accurate than a rifle or a machine gun.*

"Throughout yesterday I watched Marine demolition squads blast pillbox after pillbox along a high ridge across the north-center sector of the island. Marine demolition men make sure of a direct hit by squirming up on the topside of a pillbox, burying the charge of dynamite there and then blowing the pillbox and all the Japs to Kingdom Come. While riflemen pepper a pillbox to attract its fire, the demolition men in camouflaged uniforms circle around the flanks of the pillbox until they come to the extreme side of the defense position. Sometimes they come under the fire of a supporting Jap pillbox. Often

they are stopped by Jap mortar fire, since the Japs think nothing of throwing mortar fire down on their own underground defenses.

"Sometimes the demolition men trail a thin line of wire behind them for setting off the charge. At other times they dash up as close to the pillbox as possible and toss the lighted charge into it by hand. While demolition men and flamethrowers are cleaning out the Jap positions immediately in front of the slow-moving United States line, naval gunfire and planes are hitting the enemy rear on the northern tip of the island. The discovery of hundreds of Japanese defensive structures not previously known is driving home the military lesson that despite the excellence of aerial photographs, eye reconnaissance reports from foot soldiers actually on the site are best for an accurate appraisal of the situation."

Ever on the lookout for home state men, Heisler filed the following report from Iwo Jima [Feb. 28, 1945]: *"The battle still raging on the scarred hills of Iwo Jima is the roughest yet fought in the Pacific war, according to Corporal Edward Rutherford, 4510 Weitzel Avenue, Baltimore, a veteran Marine fighter who has seen his share of the Pacific invasions. Rutherford was a Marine paratrooper in the Bougainville campaign and fought through the Solomons.*

"He hit the bleak beaches of Iwo with the first waves of D-Day and has been living in foxholes ever since. Sitting in a sandbagged shell hole to escape the Jap shells still falling with disconcerting regularity on the rear beaches, Corporal Rutherford told me the story of how he played hide-and-seek with a Jap sniper the entire first day of the invasion.

"'I hit the first shell hole about 200 yards up the beach. I was trying to get my breath back to start another dash when a sniper started throwing slugs my way. I didn't get out of that foxhole all day, and the Jap mortars kept me in it all night. The next morning as soon as it was light enough, the Jap sniper started shooting at me again, but during the night I had dug deeper. I couldn't see the sniper so there was nothing I could do about it. Then a Marine sharpshooter in a foxhole next to mine told me to make the sniper shoot at me again. I used the old gag of putting my helmet on the end of my gun and raising it above the edge of the hole. Sure enough the Jap let fly at it. The Marine told me to do it once more. The Jap sniper shot again and a

split second later the Marine let go with a burst. That was the end of the Jap sniper. I got awfully attached to that foxhole all that time but I was glad to leave it.'

"*Col. Frederick Dowset, of Annapolis, is an officer with the 5th Marine Division on Iwo, and he agreed with Corporal Rutherford on the fierceness of the Iwo campaign. 'I don't think there's ever been a battle fought on such a small area,' Colonel Dowset said. Lieut. Walter Brooks, of 5821 Royal Oak Avenue, Baltimore, was one of the first Marines ashore with the company that later reached the Suribachi volcano.*" Sun editors back in Baltimore added a short biographical sketch of each man.

Next came a story [March 2, 1945] from Heisler that signaled the approaching end of the Iwo Jima battle: "*Advance Marine patrols probing on this forsaken island today reported finding the bodies of Japanese women who had apparently committed suicide when the Jap troops were forced to retreat or face annihilation. The Marine who had infiltrated into the village during the night could not say if the women had committed suicide or had been murdered by the Japs before they pulled out. The women were dressed in ceremonial kimonos, with fatal knife wounds in their bodies.*

"*Other patrols cleaning out pillboxes and caves reported finding an increasing number of Jap officers who had apparently committed hari-kiri in the face of almost certain defeat. The officers' bodies were found in clean fancy uniforms with full gold braid and wearing ceremonial swords and decorations. There appeared a possibility that the Iwo campaign may end with the same mass suicide that marked the close of the Saipan campaign when hundred of Japs threw themselves over the cliffs into the sea.*

"*The Marines today continued advancing steadily but slowly against fanatical resistance. Scattered Jap artillery fire was still falling around Marine assault bases and enemy mortar fire was still coming from the caves. United States planes were circling the island like buzzards during the day, strafing, rocketing and bombing the two-mile area held by the Japs where their defensive positions were still strongest. The Japs no longer are able to put up any effective anti-aircraft fire against circling planes. Marine casualties are now mainly from small arms fire but are still heavy. However, the certainty of victory in the Iwo campaign was typified today by the arrival on the scarred beach of a landing craft loaded with shining band instruments and bundles of brooms.*"

Yet four days later [March 6, 1945], *The Sun* published a much different Heisler story, this one filed from Advanced Fleet Headquarters, Guam: "*Costly Iwo Jima, still being bought with the blood of thousands of Marines, paid its first dividends as a United States base when a B-29 Superfortress, returning from bombing Tokyo, made an emergency landing on the tiny volcanic island. The sky giant, piloted by Lieut. Raymond Malo, of Danville, Illinois, ran into trouble over Tokyo when its bomb-bay doors wouldn't close after going over the target. On the way back to the Tinian base the crew discovered the gas in the reserve tanks couldn't be transferred to the regular tanks, and it appeared certain that the Superfortress couldn't make it back. The crew had been alerted to ditch the plane when someone remembered Iwo Jima. A message was radioed to the Marines on Iwo and the air-field was cleared by fighting men still dodging Jap mortar shells.*

"*There were three unsuccessful attempts to land on the meager captured strip before the plane hit the landing field and skidded down 3,000 feet of runway before coming to a halt. The plane was surrounded by Marines who smothered the crew with questions regarding the Tokyo raids. 'One Marine colonel told us that if we remained overnight they'd have another thousand feet of runway built for us to take off the next morning,' a Superfort gunner reported. When the Superfort took off four hours later it did so on 2,500 feet of runway. The crew returned safely to its base and claimed a special citation for its navigator for his ability to find tiny Iwo. The feat points up the value of the tiny little island and foreshadows increased aerial activity over Tokyo when the island is secure.*"

According to the *Oxford Companion to World War II*, capturing Iwo Jima had been expected to take 14 days. It took 36, by which time over a third of the Marine force—5,931 killed, 17,372 wounded—had become casualties.

Philip Heisler filed a gem of a war feature story [March 10, 1945] looking back on his days at Iwo Jima: "*Ask almost anyone in the*

Pacific who has the roughest, toughest, fightingest job of the war, and they'll tell you it's the hard-slugging assault Marines. But ask the same question of any Marine and he'll tell you the honors go to the 'Elsies.' Elsies are fighting men and officers who take amphibious and landing craft—the LCIs, LCTs, LCMs, LCPs—through hell and high water into the invasion beaches. It's the Elsies who hit the beach with the first wave and then hit it again and again to supply, reinforce and evacuate assault troops.

"Nowhere in the Pacific to date did the Elsies do a more superlative job than on the black, sandy beaches of Iwo Jima—the bloodiest beach of all. Death came to meet the landing craft 100 yards off shore and rode into the beach with them. It came closest at the lapping water's edge where they had to discharge their cargo and then—despite a constant hail of mortars falling around them—wait patiently while they loaded up with wounded men and took them back to hospital ships. There's no protective reef surrounding Iwo Jima and the seas throughout most of the landing period were rough. Officers and men of the bouncing landing craft performed miracles of seamanship to keep a chain of supplies and reinforcements pouring onto the beaches.

"On D-Day Plus Two I saw an LCT wallowing in the surf just a few feet off the beach and obviously ready to sink at any minute. From the sides of the sinking craft, Elsies were throwing cans of food to Marines on the water's edge. Elsies swarmed over the rough waters both day and night. Through the pitch blackness and air raids, the exposed Elsies kept on the job, their young skippers and coxswains literally feeling their way among the maze of moving ships that threatened to crush them at any second. Since the beach conditions could change from minute to minute the young skippers of the LCTs—usually ensigns—were on their own and made decisions that could make or break the success of the invasion.

"On the evening of the fourth day, I was sitting in a smashed Jap pillbox serving as a battalion command post above the beach. One of our ammunition dumps had just gone up after a Jap hit, sending huge plumes of black sand, fire and wreckage into the air. But through the glasses we could see 5th Marine units working their way up the rugged base of Suribachi. 'We've got them now,' a battalion commander said. 'If the Elsies can just keep coming through with the stuff we need.' The Elsies came through. Seaman Philip J. Sgrol of Baltimore was a crew member on the first landing craft to hit the beach. Thirty men started for the beach in the late afternoon on D-day but only eleven got ashore.

"The Elsie I'll remember the longest was a little LCVP that drew alongside a battle ship during a Jap air raid. The battleship blazed away with all guns at a plane moving across a dark sky while the LCVP fired with its only machine gun still in working order. Suddenly the Jap plane burst into flames and plunged into the sea a mile away. Then came a shout from the LCVP to the bridge of the battleship. 'Ahoy, bridge. We would like to claim a probable.' Then a few seconds later the voice of the LCVP coxswain came through the darkness: 'We'd also like to report that we are a probable ourselves. We got full of shrapnel shells on the beach and don't know how much longer we can stay afloat.' "

The next, last, and toughest objective captured by Allied forces before the Japanese surrender was Okinawa. Heisler called it [April 2, 1945] "a prize strategically unequaled," its successful completion promising "a complete air-sea blockade of the Japanese mainland." It took until June 22 before the large island was declared secure. Because of his illness, the *Sun* correspondent could not cover ground fighting but he flew over Okinawa on D-Day and after. His lucid reporting of the complex naval operation preparing for the first assault gave Baltimore readers a feel for its massive yet intricate nature:

"As the time for the landing grew nearer, mine sweepers moved into the close waters around Okinawa and swept clear the sea lane. All this time hundreds of ships were loading up with men and supplies at a dozen different ports thousands of miles apart. They sailed at closely timed intervals until they converged into the fleet of more than 1,400 ships that moved as one giant flotilla against the objective on D-Day."

Heisler wrote that "the capture of Okinawa will place United States forces directly astride the Japanese maritime empire, squarely across her water route to the Indies and Formosa and threatens to sever her completely from her forces and resources in China and Korea. Since

Okinawa is of such immense strategic importance, military leaders grimly expect Japan to resist the current invasion with unequaled fanaticism and tenacity." This held true for both land and sea forces as the long battle continued. Marines and Army infantry lost 7,613 killed and 4,824 wounded, according to the *Oxford Companion*. More than 4,900 seamen were killed as the Japanese relied more and more heavily on suicidal kamikaze planes and motor boats.

CHAPTER 26

The Atom Bomb

Centuries hence, when World War II can be considered through the haze of time, one event will be remembered above all others. On August 6, 1945, at 8:15 a.m., Pacific time, the first atomic bomb exploded over Hiroshima, instantly destroying the city, subjecting thousands of Japanese citizens to radioactive death, and altering history forever. Even the horrors and heroism of global war could not match the fateful implications of the nuclear era. As a new century began fifty-five years after Hiroshima, the threat of vastly more powerful hydrogen bombs and the promise of a fusion energy source to replace fossil fuels cross-hatched the human consciousness.

The Bomb, developed secretly in the United States in a race with Germany, could be described only in superlatives as Hiroshima and Nagasaki vaporized. That it quickly ended the war set off well-justified celebrations among the Allies. But its human miseries could not be hidden.

In a dispatch [Sept. 1, 1945] *Baltimore Sun* reporter Philip Potter was unsparing in the details. Quoting a Japanese newspaperman, who had talked with survivors, he described the death of a man *"who complained that his insides were burning. An autopsy showed his internal organs had been destroyed."* A woman from Hiroshima *"first felt a small swelling in her wrist but thought nothing of it until a few days later the swelling spread over most of her body and her hair began to fall out. She died within a week."*

Such grim tales would become commonplace as the full story of the Japanese catastrophe was unveiled over the years. But at the moment of Hiroshima, Americans were relieved that hundreds of thousands of U.S. servicemen would be spared the awful prospect of invading the Japanese home islands. Mark Watson described the post-Hiroshima situation with his usual caution. *"Greatly heightened is the prospect of early victory, thanks to Russian entry into the war, along with American employment of the mightiest weapon yet developed. There is no visible lessening of the American military effort. Nor is there likelihood of any. With our foe distracted, this is not the time for us to relax, but rather to double our blows by air and sea and, when possible, by land. The stake is large; it is the lives of our men who are yet to be employed in invasion. The more that Japan can now be weakened, and the sooner, the fewer will be our losses. The hope, of course, is that there will be a swift weakening of the enemy's will to fight."* His analysis appeared on the same front page announcing the use of a second atomic bomb over Nagasaki.

Watson's assignment of priority to the Russian declaration of war rather than to The Bomb may seem misguided to later generations. But when he wrote, in real time, the extent of nuclear devastation was not fully perceived. Leading militarists in Japan were all for fighting to the death on their mainland. For Americans concerned about the bloody prospect of invasion, the lessons of Iwo Jima and Okinawa were real and frightening. With the Cold War still in the future, Americans had good reason during the era of good-fellowship to welcome the Russian invasion of Manchuria. Watson cautioned against any *"tapering off"* of the U.S. war effort *"so that when peace comes it would find our last shell and bomb and cartridge just expended."* He explicitly mentioned how *"we had hopes of early victory in Germany but many months were spent in their fulfillment."* And, no doubt, he remembered how unprepared America had been when World War II began. In only five more years, with a vastly depleted military establishment, the United States would be again at war—this time in Korea.

The dropping of the atomic bombs on Japan was the culmination of a period of massive redeployment of U.S. forces to the Pacific. *The Sun* followed the shift, assigning veteran journalists Philip Potter, Thomas O'Donnell, and Robert Cochrane to the Japanese war.

Tom O'Donnell, a reporter steeped in Baltimore politics (and later a press aide to Mayor Thomas D'Alesandro Jr., the father of future

House Speaker Nancy Pelosi) sailed with the new carrier *Antietam* on her shake-down cruise. [July 1, 1945]

O'Donnell was intrigued by the exacting job of signal officers, men who had to wave incoming planes onto the landing deck at hair-raising, two-minute intervals. *"In the few seconds at his disposal the signal officer must determine the type of plane coming, take account of its landing speed and altitude, all of which helps him to determine just when to give the cut signal. Perfect coordination by the deck team and absolute obedience from the oncoming pilot mean the difference between a safe landing and a disaster,"* O'Donnell wrote. He then described a near-disaster: *"A jittery pilot cut his turn toward the stern of the carrier a little too fine and one wing dipped ominously. Swiftly the signal officer waved for leveling and the pilot, now almost over the fantail, over-corrected the fault, dropping the other wing within inches of the flight deck. Without hesitation, the signal officer gave the pilot a wave-off. Down the deck the plane thundered, one wing high in the air, the other low enough to catch in the hook cables had they not been quickly lowered to deck level. Motor groaning mightily under the strain, the plane fought its way back up, foot by foot, leveled off and then turned into a wide climbing circle."*

Bob Cochrane, a future top executive at a *Sun*-owned television station in Baltimore, rode aboard a troopship carrying veterans of European battles into their new theater of operations [July 15, 1945]. Few were combat soldiers. They were specialists *"in building bridges, reconstructing blasted tunnels, relocating railway tracks, reconstituting harbor facilities. These are the men who will build the bases from which American sea, air and land forces will spring their great trap on the Japanese empire. These men are good and they know it. Though most disappointed at not being redeployed through the United States and though they are by no means anxious to experience enemy action, they want to get it over with and get home."* Such was the mood at that moment.

Another *Sun* newcomer on the Asian scene was that old European hand, the enduring Mark Watson. After a home leave when he picked up his Pulitzer Prize, he went to China. There two struggles were gestating—Japan's defeat after years of ravaging its huge neighbor and the incipient civil war between the Communists and Nationalists. U.S. aid had been and would continue to be sent to Generalissimo Chiang Kai-shek's forces, a losing cause as time would tell. When Watson was in Kunming he took heart by the ability of Nationalist forces to drive the Japanese back from a winter offensive that had denied China vital airfields [July 17, 1945]. But in discussing the internal division that would eventually result in Mao Tse-tung's victory, he found little to cheer about. The Communists had resisted U.S. efforts for reconciliation and were firmly entrenched in provinces to the north. In an interview with the Generalissimo—a leader Watson called "Gimo" in parts of his dispatch [July 13, 1945]—he wrote that Chiang *"stood like a rock, smooth, polished, a very firm rock"* who resisted any compulsion that would force his party into a coalition with the Communists.

"He is a monument of realism and shrewdness, clothed with such urbanity and graciousness as might deceive the casual visitor into thinking him easily swayed. One could hardly make a poorer guess. He states a distasteful fact with an unchanging smile, a gentle voice and twinkling eyes. All the pressure which can be applied to alter his views ended with the Generalissimo's eyes still twinkling."

Phil Potter, a future Washington Bureau chief who would dedicate much of his career to Asia, followed Watson to China. He did so by flying over the "Hump" from India. On his arrival, he found himself marveling at China's high rate of inflation, telling Baltimore readers it cost 1,500 yuan for a pound of sugar and 2,000 yuan for a bar of soap. He also got an overnight loan of 10,000 yuan—the equivalent of four dollars—from a public relations officer. Potter described how inflation made it almost impossible to set up adequate medical services in China, much less adequate diets. In an interview [July 31, 1945] with Major General Claire L. Chennault, organizer of America's "Flying Tigers" volunteers in China, Potter found this visionary officer contemplating a large U.S.-backed aviation industry in post-war China. *"We ought to step in before another country does,"* Chennault said. Though he was ready to offer his services, Chennault was actually on the way out of China, having feuded with General Joseph Stillwell, head of U.S. forces in the China-India-Burma Theater.

Meanwhile, in that same issue of *The Sun*, Watson filed a revealing story from Manila, which had been recaptured by General Douglas MacArthur's forces five months earlier at the cost of 1,000 American, 16,000 Japanese, and 100,000 Filipino lives. Military historians were to ask later why MacArthur had not bypassed rather than batter Manila. Before journeying to Asia in the closing weeks of the war, Watson had seen the harbors of Naples, Cherbourg, and Le Havre, all strewn with wreckage caused by retreating Germans seeking to obstruct Allied shipping. Now, he reported, the mess in Manila presented more wreck-salvage work than all three European ports combined. *"Practically all* (wrecked ships) *were sunk by our aerial bombers,"* he related. They had been carrying Japanese seeking to flee. His source was Commander William A. Sullivan, *"the Navy's chief miracle man"* in clearing harbors. Long before the Japanese snipers had been driven off the waterfront, Sullivan arrived only to encounter an American guard asking to see written orders allowing him to enter such a dangerous zone. *"Sullivan beamed on him,"* Watson wrote. *"'I am a chaplain. In fact I am a rabbi' and he breezed on toward the waterfront."*

The next day [July 25, 1945] Watson, Cochrane, and O'Donnell were all on the front page. The latter two reported massive American air attacks not only on Japan itself but on territories from Korea to the Celebes. A record 350-plane attack on Shanghai sank at least three ships, perhaps ten more. *"The lack of even anti-aircraft fire is the most surprising aspect since the Kiangwan airdrome is the largest Jap base in China,"* wrote Cochrane. From Guam, O'Donnell quoted Japanese radio to confirm that 2,000 U.S. planes had attacked Japan with B-29s and P-51s flying from bases in the Marianas. They had done so, Japanese propagandists asserted, in order to send a message to the Potsdam Conference that 10,000-plane raids were in prospect. This was described by the Japanese radio as a government *"change in tactics"* from carrier-based raids that *"requires very close watching,"* O'Donnell reported.

Watson, for his part, asserted that the Pacific war had assumed *"increasing similarity to the pattern used in the conquest of Germany,"* meaning the massing of large land forces as well as air and sea. *"Our military leaders have gained the very threshold of Japan where enemy strength must be expected—Okinawa was a sample,"* Watson wrote. *"We are fortunate that at the very time when we will clearly need all the strength we can assemble against Japan, we are approaching the point when we can apply that need."*

Actually, at *"that very time,"* in deepest secrecy, American scientists were evaluating the successful initial atomic test explosion at Alamogordo, New Mexico, on July 16, 1945. The first atomic bombs soon were crossing the Pacific on their way to Japan, to victory and to history.

CHAPTER 27

Surrender
on the *Missouri*

"*W*orld War II ended today on the deck of the U.S.S. Missouri."
With these unadorned words, *Sun* correspondent Robert Cochrane
reported Japan's official surrender [Sept. 2, 1945] six years and one
day after German forces had rolled into hapless Poland. He and colleagues Thomas O'Donnell and Philip Potter were witnesses to this
unforgettable event. A huge battleship in Tokyo Bay. Its crew lining
the decks in Navy whites. Fifty generals and fifty naval officers in
attendance. Representatives from all the Allies. The tableau unfolded
with top-hatted Japanese envoys signing away their defeat before the
Allied Supreme Commander, General Douglas MacArthur, who was
destined to rule and change their country beyond all expectations.

Despite Pearl Harbor, despite the Bataan death march, despite the
cruelty of POW camps, MacArthur brought peace rather than the
retribution the Japanese had feared. Under his no-nonsense guidance,
the population repudiated the military clique that had led them to
disaster, adopted democracy, and worked hard to become a major
economic power. The spectacle on the *Missouri* was as triumphal a
moment as any in American military history. Two atomic bombs and
the massing of conventional weaponry in strangulation proportions
led to unconditional surrender without a blood-soaked amphibious
invasion. The United States had become an undoubted world super-
power.

Cochrane filed a short deadline dispatch that appeared that memorable Sunday, then followed up next day with vivid details as part of a
three-man reporting team. "Sun *Correspondents Describe Jap Surrender Aboard Missouri From Various Points,*" the newspaper headlined

on its front page. Cochrane, Potter, and O'Donnell in subsequent days were among the first to get ashore on the Japanese mainland. They rushed to Tokyo in a manner that recalled the race of Mark Watson and Lee McCardell to Paris. They even got a forbidden glimpse of Emperor Hirohito.

The days between Hirohito's submission and the actual American entry into Japan were nervous ones. They entailed a very complicated military operation and Japanese cooperation that was by no means assured. Philip Heisler, who had served in the Pacific (Iwo Jima and Okinawa) and was now assigned to the Pentagon, raised searching questions [Aug.16, 1945]: *"Will the Japanese troops completely obey the Emperor's 'cease fire' order? Can the United States trust to send a small token force into Japan to occupy the country while Japan has a strong organized army there? Or must the United States send a full, battle-ready 'invasion' force there? How are the thousands of Japanese troops on by-passed islands going to be told—and convinced— that the Emperor has surrendered? What will be the status of the millions of Japanese soldiers on the Japanese mainland when American occupation troops take over there? Will they be prisoners of war and thus dependent on the United States armed forces for food and shelter? Unlike the final surrender of Germany and the occupation of that country, American military leaders do not have a great deal of information as to just what conditions are like inside Japan."*

As it happened, the occupation of Japan proved far less dire than Heisler's questions suggested. But at the time this was unknown. O'Donnell reported [Aug. 5, 1945] that hundreds of thousands of leaflets had been dropped on Japan warning inhabitants to leave twelve cities due to be hit by fire bombs—hardly a message reassuring to the Japanese. Then came Hiroshima and a day later *The Sun* published another O'Donnell story, this one quoting Colonel Paul W. Tibbets, pilot of the fateful flight to Hiroshima:

"'There was no disturbing influence, no flak or fighters when we made our bomb run. We dropped our bomb visually. Immediately after releasing it I knew we had to get out of there in a hurry. We made a sharp turn and left the target area. My immediate reaction was that it was kind of hard to believe. Below us there was rising rapidly a huge

cloud of smoke of such proportions that the city was obscured and the only way you could tell where you were was by the surrounding countryside. We stayed in the target area or near it about two minutes trying to see the damage and then started for home. The explosion came so fast that we couldn't even see what happened.'" Debate on the necessity of this action would come later. Some historians held a tightening blockade would have caused Japan's collapse; but others cited attempts—even after the atomic bombs—by Japan's military leaders to overcome the Emperor's capitulation and keep fighting. As for the common people's reaction, after all their suffering, nothing was known.

Cochrane reported [Aug. 17, 1945] a suspicion that the Tokyo government was *"stalling"* on MacArthur's order that it issue an immediate cease-fire. Japan pleaded that it would take some days to notify its forces, some in remote locations. *"Meanwhile,"* wrote Cochrane, *"Pacific harbors are packed with ships loading around the clock for their northern migration (to Japan). Air transport eastward across the Pacific has been frozen as all available aircraft are being concentrated in this theater. Vast and complex problems attach to this movement."*

In a highly significant policy decision, MacArthur refused to issue the kind of non-fraternization order promulgated by General Eisenhower in Germany. These two generals rarely agreed. Philip Potter wrote [Aug. 27, 1945] that MacArthur had free rein to follow his own desires. *"On the basis of past performance, he is not expected to impose for long a military control over civilian affairs. In the Philippines he is discontinuing (U.S.) participation in the civil administration. It is considered likely, too, that Japanese mediums of information soon will be reestablished under Japanese management. It appears to be the policy of MacArthur to deal with the Japanese people through the existing government, if it continues to act in good faith—which will be in contrast with the situation in Germany, where a military government was organized from the ground up. MacArthur wishes to bring about amicable relations between the Japanese and the occupying forces."* Potter's scenario was to prove remarkably accurate.

In that same issue of *The Sun*, Cochrane reported that two separate U.S. military entries into Japan were planned, one under Navy direction, the second with the supreme general at the head of the first airborne wave on August 30. *"Powerful American and British forces are now prowling the Honshu coast to support the landings. The advance party of Americans who are to land at Atsugi Airport (August 27) is poised at Okinawa for take-off. The fact that the signing* (of the surrender document) *is set for the third day after the landing indicates the official feeling is that no trouble is expected."* Clearly, momentous events were unfolding.

In the August 30, 1945, edition of *The Sun*, O'Donnell reported from Yokosuka Naval Base that *"United States Marines of the famed 4th Regiment swarmed ashore on Japanese soil today under a canopy of American and British planes. A few miles offshore the mighty fleet itself moved back and forth ready at a second's notice to cover the landing forces with a hail of fire, if necessary. To the men of the 4th Regiment, veterans of Makin, Guadalcanal, Tulagi, New Georgia, Bougainville, Guam and Okinawa, today is simply a dress parade by comparison with the furious assaults they had earlier made on other islands in the Pacific. Today they simply stepped ashore."*

In an adjoining article, Cochrane wrote that *"thousands of the 101st Airborne Division troops landed from transport planes at Atsugi today to begin the formal occupation of Japan."* MacArthur would soon arrive in his silver plane *Bataan* and begin *"the final chapter of the grim story that began with the bombing of Pearl Harbor. It was an exciting and history-making scene. The skies were filled with planes— squadrons of long-range fighters which had accompanied MacArthur on the long flight from Okinawa during the early morning hours and now were spread across the heavens in a tremendous swarm."*

O'Donnell, for his part, described the following scene: *"The Marines, and the three destroyers which escorted them, had rendezvoused with the fleet during the night as planned. For as far as the eye, even aided by binoculars, could see, the ocean seemed filled with ships of all descriptions—row after row of destroyers and destroyer escorts, even some of the old four-stack destroyers given to Britain before we were attacked, battleships, aircraft carriers, light and heavy cruisers, oil tankers and ammunition ships. As the Marines became aware of the presence of the mighty armada in the pink light of early dawn, cheer after cheer rent the air and the men pounded each other on the back. 'Look,' yelled a husky, sun-bronzed Marine, 'Halsey is waving to us.' More and more ships came into view and by 7 a.m. a rapid count noted 91 ships outlined against the horizon. Gone was the anxiety that some Japanese submarine or plane might get a whack at the transports. Any die-hard Jap certainly would have been court- ing suicide if he had attempted to tangle with this collection of Ameri- can and British warships."*

For the first time a Tokyo dateline—or more specifically an *"Outside Tokyo"* dateline—appeared in *The Sun* on August 31, 1945. Written by Cochrane, it told of Americans landing in force in Japan on a busy little airfield, finding *"no signs of resentment or lack of cooperation."* However, the Baltimore reporter was himself a passenger on a plane that was fired on by ack-ack while crossing the island of Miyake. One of a very few displays of Japanese opposition, the incident caused no damage.

The next day [Sept. 1, 1945] two Tokyo datelines appeared, one by Cochrane, the other by Potter. *"The road to Tokyo runs through scenes of almost incredible destruction,"* Cochrane wrote. *"The dam- age is not measured by acres or blocks but by miles. For a half hour at a time one can drive without seeing a block of buildings intact; then may come an area of modern close-built factories with high chimneys still smoking; then the ruin begins again. I have talked to half a dozen people who lived in Tokyo through the war. They maintain that only 20 to 30 per cent of the city is still standing. While Tokyo itself is technically out of bounds, roaming knots of uniformed Americans, mainly correspondents, explored portions of the business district, vis- ited the Imperial Hotel for lunch or went exploring on its suburban trains. The passengers seemed cheerful and several of them struck up conversations. Two weeks ago in Manila, MacArthur's top authority on the Japanese people said they must be in terrible turmoil through the sudden change in information they've been fed.*

"Today I ran into almost the same words from a long-time resident of Tokyo who said the people went around dazed. They had been told Japan was winning the war until the moment of the Emperor's announcement. They were told that the final battle to defend the

homeland would destroy the Allies. The fact that the Emperor positively wills the compliance of the people to the demands of the Allies makes the occupation of Japan simple, these residents say. It is difficult for a westerner to appreciate the complete obedience he commands. It is uncanny but it is a fact."

Well, not quite a fact. Potter wrote in the same issue of the paper that "*many* (Japanese) *army and navy people opposed the surrender.*" One pamphlet dropped over Tokyo by the military clique said, " '*We cannot believe that our Tenno (Emperor) should have surrendered to our enemy. No doubt these surrender terms were accepted by cunning high persons surrounding the Emperor. We of the air corps and the navy will act independently.*' *One executive of one of the largest newspapers in Japan said they* (the rebellious militarists) *got no public backing and the Emperor's Government was able to deal quickly with what he described as a 'very riotous atmosphere'* (among some elements of the armed forces). *The Army, one newspaperman said, had wanted to go on fighting, expecting to make any invasion so costly that the Allies would settle for less than unconditional surrender.*"

The dramatic, choreographed signing spectacle aboard the *Missouri* on the morning of September 2 occurred less than four months after the hastily assembled, middle-of-the-night German surrender at Rheims on May 7. And *The Sun* was the only newspaper in the world whose own correspondents witnessed both surrenders. (See Chapter 21.) What a contrast they provided. General Eisenhower left it to his subordinates to conduct the signing at SHAEF headquarters. The European ceremony took place around a scuffed table in a crowded workaday conference room. Later, in his private office, Eisenhower required German General Alfred Jodl to acknowledge that he understood the unconditional surrender terms. Then he dismissed him. Wire service reporters plus *The Sun's* Price Day rushed to their typewriters.

This low-key approach did not accord with the style and public relations instincts of General MacArthur. He put on a blockbuster show that would have been a credit to a Hollywood producer. The event provided plenty of copy for Cochrane, Potter and O'Donnell. Here is Bob Cochrane's story:

"*Japan's dream of conquest died under the frowning guns of the mighty battleship* Missouri *when Foreign Minister Mamoru Shigemitzu and Gen.Yoshiji Umezu affixed their names to the instrument of surrender which placed Japan unconditionally in the hands of the Allies. It was a ceremony that followed fixed military procedure, but was as stately regal as a religious procession.* MacArthur, *conducting the ceremony in plain uniform, spoke through a battery of microphones in firm, full terms and loudspeakers which carried the emphatic conviction of his voice echoing along the decks and across the waters to where the battleships* Iowa *and* South Dakota *were anchored.* 'I announce it as my firm purpose, in the tradition of the countries I represent, to proceed in the discharge of my responsibilities with justice and tolerance'—*his voice rising slightly in volume*—'while taking all necessary dispositions to insure that the terms of surrender are fully, promptly and faithfully complied with. Let us pray that peace be now restored to the world and that God will preserve it always. These proceedings are closed.' The ceremony was scheduled early and concluded early.*

"*It was a gray day for Japan, and the squat little men who boarded the ship to make peace seemed grotesquely puny to have caused so much sorrow and worry in a nation which could produce weapons like this floating fortress.*" Then in four short words Cochrane expressed a joy fulfilled: "*So the war ended.*"

Tom O'Donnell put in a good word for the Navy in his dispatch. "*The United States Navy, which fought the Pacific war virtually single-handed for so long, rightly was given the lion's share of honors today. Although it was General MacArthur, who as supreme Allied commander acted as ringleader during the ceremony and was the first to sign after the Japanese, the Navy provided the location of the ceremony and put on a dazzling display of the carrier-based strength which smashed the Japanese fleet and paved the way to final victory.*" Fleet Admiral Chester Nimitz signed the surrender document on behalf of the United States.

Phil Potter wrote of the solemnity of the occasion, then added a detail sure to resonate with Americans of a later generation: "*What little levity there was came from Vice Admiral John S. McCain, whose loud guffaw was heard repeatedly as the high brass of the Army and Navy gathered on the promenade deck. He was the most animated person aboard and he went from group to group greeting acquaintances and frequently his hearty laugh rang out."* His grandson, another John McCain, was the best-known American hero of the Vietnam War, spending five brutal years as a prisoner of war. He survived to become a U.S. senator and Republican nominee for the presidency in 2008.

On that long-awaited September day of 1945, it was time for relief and remembrance, time to mourn the millions who had died and suffered in history's greatest struggle, time for families and sweethearts to reunite, time to pray for peace on earth. As in the aftermath of World War I, it was not to be. The Cold War came quickly, aligning Communist nations against democratic allies of the United States. There was only a five-year respite before Americans were at war again in Korea, years in which hundreds of thousands of demobilized doughboys returned home to the American Dream. They went to college under the GI Bill of Rights. They got government assistance to invest in housing. They found a nation in which millions of poor African-Americans and poor whites from Appalachia had migrated to find defense jobs alongside women—Rosie the Riveters—who otherwise would have remained at home. America had changed in ways more profound than at any time in its history. And as it changed, so too did the world. The Cold War; hydrogen bombs threatening world destruction; Western Europe rebuilding under the Marshall Plan; British, French, Dutch, Belgian, and Portuguese empires unwinding; China emerging; Muslims advancing; nuclear, space, and electronic science exploding. American boys and their generals and their political leaders emerged from war as "the Greatest Generation."

In assessing *The Baltimore Sun's* war record it is important to note its limitations as well as its achievements. The paper had been slow to find its war-reporting niche, missing Guadalcanal and most of North Africa. But after this its correspondents followed American troops to Iceland, Britain, Sicily, Italy, France, Belgium, Holland, Luxembourg, Germany, Australia, New Guinea, Saipan, Iwo Jima, the Philippines, and Japan. The paper made little effort to cover battles or campaigns in which American forces were not directly involved. The mighty struggle between Nazi Germany and the Soviet Union was left to the wire services, as were Britain's efforts in many parts of its shrinking empire.

As an East Coast newspaper, *The Sun* was far more focused on Western Europe than on the Pacific war—a situation that lasted from the American landings in Sicily, Italy, and France, until the defeat of Germany. Then the culminating battles to defeat Japan took pride of place.

The Sun made its mark, and it was a big mark, in the quality of its reporting wherever its correspondents were on the scene. This was very much a reflection of the paper's culture. Reporters were free to follow not only the obvious stories, the ones stressed in official communiqués, but the human side of the greatest war in history. They were free to express their personal feelings and opinions with total disregard for wire-service "objectivity" or for the editorial stands of their own newspaper. They were free to pursue scoops and features, even disappearing for days at a time, with a confidence born of their professional competence.

From beginning to end, *The Sun* never forgot who its readers were. The Maryland-Virginia Twenty-ninth Division, the Blue and Gray heroes of D-Day, always received special attention. Families of Maryland boys overseas were often pleased to find the names of their loved ones in the news columns. It happened 6,000 times. On Sundays the paper printed summaries of "News from Home" that could be clipped out and sent by mail to service men and women. Probably these "Service Editions" went out by the tens of thousands. Almost always, there were pictures of pretty girls, barracks jokes, sports news, local chatter, police blotter happenings—even the weather. On September 12, 1943, the Service Edition described jubilation in Little Italy over the surrender of the Mussolini government—a joy that was not to last. The August 5, 1945, edition focused on 64,598,166 tons of rain that fell on Baltimore in July. *"The water that drenched the city would have floated—with a little to spare—twelve times the number of combat ships that the Navy reported as of June 1944."*

Having learned so much in its coverage of the war, *The Sun* was ready to augment its reputation for international and national coverage in the years ahead. In post-war years it sent dozens of correspondents abroad—some to crisis hot spots, some to maintain bureaus in important capitals, others into global boondocks to find out how very different populations lived. Most of the men who served as World War II correspondents remained with the Sunpapers, often in positions of top leadership. They had been seasoned by seeing death and danger up close. Let's call the roll one last time: Mark Watson, Lee McCardell, Price Day, Holbrook Bradley, Thomas O'Neill, Howard Norton, Philip Heisler, Robert Cochrane, Thomas O'Donnell, and Philip Potter. And so, aboard the battleship named after Harry Truman's home state, with three *Baltimore Sun* reporters as witnesses, World War II at last came to an end.

Selected Bibliography

The following books were consulted frequently to place in context the daily newspaper reports of *Baltimore Sun* combat correspondents in World War II:

The Oxford Companion to World War II, edited by I. C. B. Dear (New York: Oxford University Press, 1995) was by far the most useful reference book available. It provided accurate, well-written summaries of the battles, strategies, and top officials in all phases of the war.

Day-by-day almanacs were very useful in finding out what was going on in the global conflict on the same days *The Baltimore Sun* was printing dispatches of its correspondents. The following were especially helpful:

Davidson, Edward, and Dale Manning. *Chronology of World War Two.* London: Cassel & Co., 1999.

Davison, John. *The Pacific War.* St. Paul, MN: Zenith Press, 2004.

Dickson, Keith D. *World War Almanac.* New York: Facts on File, 2008.

Goralski, Robert. *World War II Almanac, 1931–1945.* New York: Bonanza Books, 1984.

Wagner, Margaret E., Linda Barrett Osburne, Susan Reyburn, eds. *Library of Congress World War II Companion.* New York: Simon & Schuster, 2007.

There have been many broad brush histories of the war in its totality. Herewith are the books used for general background:

Hart, B. H. Liddell. *History of the Second World War.* Old Saybrook, CT: Konecky and Konecky, 1970.

Keegan, John. *The Second World War.* New York: Viking Penguin, 1989.

Natkiel, Richard, and Robin L. Sommer. *Atlas of World War II*. North Dighton, MA: JG Press, 2005.

Weinberg, Gerhard L. *A World at Arms*. New York: Cambridge University Press, 2005.

Baltimore Source Books:

Balkoski, Joseph. *Beyond the Beachhead: The 29th Infantry Division*. Mechanicsburg, PA: Stackpole Books, 1999.

Bradley, Holbrook. *War Correspondent: From D-Day to the Elbe*. Lincoln, NE: iUniverse Inc., 2007.

Fitzpatrick, Vincent. *Gerald W. Johnson*. Baton Rouge: Louisiana State University Press, 2002.

Harrison, S. L. *The Editorial Art of Edmund Duffy*. Cranbury, NJ: Associated University Presses, 1998.

Johnson, Gerald W., Frank R. Kent, H. L. Mencken, Hamilton Owens. *The Sunpapers of Baltimore*. New York: Knopf, 1937.

Rodgers, Marion Elizabeth. *Mencken*. New York: Oxford University Press, 2005.

Teachout, Terry. *The Skeptic: A Life of H. L. Mencken*. New York: Harper Collins, 2002.

Williams, Harold A. *The Baltimore Sun, 1837–1987*. Baltimore: Johns Hopkins University Press, 1987.

Rick Atkinson's prize-winning works were especially helpful on the North African and Italian campaigns:

Atkinson, Rick. *An Army at Dawn*. New York: Henry Holt, 2002.

———. *The Day of Battle*. New York: Henry Holt, 2007.

Other helpful war books included:

Ambrose, Stephen E. *Eisenhower, 1890–1952*. New York: Simon and Schuster, 1983.

Bradley, James. *Flags of our Fathers*. New York: Bantam Books, 2006.

Bradley, Omar Nelson. *A Soldier's Story*. New York: Henry Holt, 1951.

Burns, James MacGregor. *Roosevelt: The Soldier of Freedom, 1940–1945*. New York: History Book Club, 2006.

Hastings, Max. *Armageddon: The Battle for Germany, 1944–1945*. New York: Knopf, 2004.

————. *Overlord: D-Day and the Battle for Normandy*. New York: Vintage Books, 2006.

————. *Retribution: The Battle for Japan*. New York: Knopf, 2008.

Miller, Nathan. *The War at Sea*. New York: Scribner, 1995.

Sebag-Montefiore, Hugh. *Dunkirk*. Cambridge, MA: Harvard University Press, 2006.

Stafford, David. *Endgame, 1945*. New York: Little Brown, 2007.

Thomas, Evan. *Sea of Thunder*. New York: Simon and Schuster, 2006.

Toland, John. *The Battle of the Bulge*. Chatham, U.K.: Wordsworth Editions Limited, 1998.

Weigley, Russell F. *Eisenhower's Lieutenants*. Bloomington, IN: Indiana University Press, 1981.

Acknowledgments

Without the friendship, encouragement, hard work, and expertise in publications of ANNE GARSIDE, director of communications at the Maryland Historical Society, the preparation of this book might have been a pursuit without an end. My gratitude is boundless.

Sincere thanks go to many people who helped me along the way. In rough chronological order, the importance of their assistance is manifest:

• JEFF KORMAN, manager of the Maryland Department of the Enoch Pratt Free Library in Baltimore, gave me access to long-ago *Baltimore Sun* index cards citing articles, and their dates, of war correspondents whose work appears in this book.

• TOM BECK, chief curator of Special Collections at the Albin O. Kuhn Library at the University of Maryland Baltimore County, allowed me countless afternoons to read parts of UMBC's one-of-a-kind collection of actual, ink-on-paper copies of *The Sun* since its beginning. His special assistant, SHANNON BUTCHECK, trundled heavy volumes, dated month by month, from 1939 to 1945, to my reading desk.

• VINCENT FITZPATRICK, curator of the H. L. Mencken Collection at the Pratt Library, provided World War I scrapbooks of Mencken's columns in *The Sun*. Librarians at the Periodical Room at the Pratt assisted in printing microfilm copies of *Sun* correspondent Raymond S. Tompkins' reporting from France in World War I.

• PAUL McCARDELL, *Baltimore Sun* librarian, sent me scores of the newspaper's pages containing selected articles from the World War II era, thus providing essential help during the days of actual writing. (Paul is not related to Lee McCardell.)

- BARRY RASCOVAR, ERNEST B. (PAT) FURGURSON, JAMES H. BREADY, and FRED RASMUSSEN—old colleagues from newspaper days—read rough drafts of the manuscript and offered many helpful suggestions and corrections.

- MICHAEL YAGGY, a neighbor and a retired Marine officer who served in Vietnam, also read the manuscript and provided insights from his knowledge of military history.

- HOLBROOK BRADLEY, the only *Sun* World War II reporter still alive at the time of going to press and author of a memoir, *War Correspondent from D-Day to the Elbe*, was generous in discussing what it was like to cover the European campaign.

- Special Collections curators at the Milton S. Eisenhower Library of Johns Hopkins University provided copies of cartoons by *Sun* cartoonist Edmund Duffy from the World War II era.

- J. MONTGOMERY COOK, editor and senior vice president of *The Baltimore Sun,* offered his support for this project.

- PATRICIA DOCKMAN ANDERSON, editor-in-chief at the Maryland Historical Society, expertly guided the manuscript through the production process. Thanks also to the Maryland Historical Society's Publications Committee, H. THOMAS HOWELL, chair, for accepting the manuscript.

- DONNA SHEAR, copy editor and indexer, was meticulous in editing the manuscript.

- PAM JEFFRIES, designer at the Maryland Historical Society, contributed the striking cover design, and JULIE BURRIS the attractive page design and layout.

- The superb marketing team of the Johns Hopkins University Press has been enthusiastic in promoting the book.

- MARIAN and HARRY RANDALL, my housemates in Sparks, Maryland, gave me love and support throughout and made no complaints about stacks of books and piles of manuscripts littering the family room.

Index